MW00799736

PRAISE FOR *WHISTLE-STOP POLITICS*

"In fifty-two years of journalism, I never knew what it was like to travel on a campaign train or bus—until *Whistle-Stop Politics*. Reading it, I now feel as if I had had those experiences—the history, the drama, the proximity, the uncertainty, the photos, even the old cartoons. A great job by Edward Segal."

—Bob Woodward, associate editor of the *Washington Post* and author of fifteen No. 1 *New York Times* bestselling books

"*Whistle-Stop Politics* is a great read! Especially for anyone who loves history and old-fashioned politics. Author Edward Segal takes us back to what pure politics and campaigning used to be."

—Jeff Pegues, chief national affairs and justice correspondent for CBS News and host of the podcast *America: Changed Forever*

"*Whistle-Stop Politics* is a one-of-a-kind book about politicians and train travel. It reflects the author's love for a mostly bygone era, and it succeeds because of the many anecdotes he has collected from the politicians themselves and the journalists who covered them. White House reporter Merriman Smith once toppled from a train, straining to judge the size of a crowd for Truman. Columnist Mary McGrory claimed Nixon's secretary Rose Mary Woods tried to pour a glass of Scotch down her back for failing to rise sufficiently high to greet her boss. 'The Yellow Rose of Texas' meant LBJ would soon start speaking, and when Robert F. Kennedy started quoting George Bernard Shaw, it meant he was wrapping up. *Whistle-Stop Politics* is a refreshing look at politics as it once was and a trip down memory lane, when trains stopped in small towns and time seemed to move more slowly."

—Eleanor Clift, political reporter at the *Daily Beast* and coauthor of *Selecting a President*

"*Whistle-Stop Politics* is a great collection of stories and anecdotes that show why presidents and candidates love to campaign by train. Edward Segal gives us plenty of reasons for the popularity of whistle-stop campaign trains with the public, politicians, and their staff. There is really no better or more effective way for candidates and office holders to see America and connect with voters. Whistle-stop trains are fun, but more importantly, they provide those who want to lead us with a view of the country they can't get any other way. That's another reason why it would be better if politicians campaigned more by train than by plane."

—Mike McCurry, press secretary to President Bill Clinton, 1995–1998

"For all my adult life, I have had a love of trains, politics, and history. With *Whistle-Stop Politics*, Edward Segal has combined all three into a must-read for every politician, political pundit, and political science major in the country."

—Douglas MacKinnon, former White House and Pentagon official, national columnist, and bestselling author

"*Whistle-Stop Politics* rolls through two centuries of campaigning from the back of trains. In his entertaining account, Edward Segal presents a wealth of information about the candidates who benefited from whistle-stop trips and the reporters who endured them."

—Donald A. Ritchie, historian emeritus of the US Senate and author of *Electing FDR: The New Deal Campaign of 1932*

"Edward Segal takes readers on an entertaining journey across nearly two centuries of American politics. His book is chock-full of illuminating anecdotes about candidates who rode the rails in search of votes and the journalists who followed along in pursuit of stories. *Whistle-Stop*

Politics is a worthy addition to the bookshelf of anyone who loves presidential history."

—Bob Riel, author of *Quest for the Presidency: The Storied and Surprising History of Presidential Campaigns in America*

"Edward Segal has pulled together a fascinating narrative that provides unique insights into one of the most overlooked aspects of railroad and political history: how and why candidates campaigned by train. Segal takes us on a deep dive into the whistle-stop campaigns of well-known train-loving politicians. His extensive research resulted in intriguing and unexpected anecdotes and stories that show how ingrained railroads are in our political and American cultures."

—Todd DeFeo, publisher and editor of Railfanning.org

"Edward Segal's *Whistle-Stop Politics* is a flavorful compendium of great anecdotes from an age when our campaigns were more fun—and our candidates more spontaneous and less packaged. An absolute pleasure to read."

—Richard North Patterson, *New York Times* bestselling author of *Trial*

WHISTLE-STOP POLITICS

WHISTLE-STOP POLITICS

Campaign Trains and the Reporters Who Covered Them

Foreword by Jules Witcover, author of *85 Days: The Last Campaign of Robert Kennedy*

EDWARD SEGAL

Rock
Creek
Media

Published by Rock Creek Media, Washington, DC
WhistleStopPolitics.com

Edited and designed by Girl Friday Productions
www.girlfridayproductions.com

Cover design: Emily Weigel
Interior design: Rachel Marek
Project management: Kristin Duran
Editorial production: Laura Dailey
Cover image courtesy of the Lawrence Public Library, Lawrence, Massachusetts

ISBN (hardcover): 979-8-9886450-0-9
ISBN (paperback): 979-8-9886450-1-6
ISBN (ebook): 979-8-9886450-2-3

Library of Congress Control Number: 2023920153

First edition

*To William Jennings Bryan, Theodore Roosevelt,
Harry S. Truman, and the hundreds of other politicians who
followed their whistle-stopping examples; and reporters
Mary McGrory, Merriman Smith, Richard L. Strout, and their
colleagues who covered candidates on the campaign trail.*

CONTENTS

FOREWORD

Edward Segal's massive history of the whistle-stop campaign in politics is an exhaustive account of this particularly American phenomenon.

It effectively demonstrates the role played by working journalists in bringing to the public the views of the presidents and other politicians when the press had extraordinary access to them as daily traveling companions on the campaign trail.

The author has devoted a huge period of time to recording this vivid history from William Henry Harrison through Joe Biden, enriching the public with knowledge for all to read.

Segal's impressive narrative reflects a comprehension of the role of the whistle-stop trains and buses in educating American voters about the process of presidential elections.

Never before has the whistle-stop campaign been explained by a scholar of the world's greatest enduring democratic process.

Jules Witcover
Veteran Washington, DC, correspondent; award-winning reporter;
former political columnist for the *Baltimore Sun*; and author of
85 Days: The Last Campaign of Robert Kennedy

INTRODUCTION

> You may not believe this, Lyndon, but there are still a hell of a lot of people in this country who don't know where the airport is. But they damn sure know where the depot is. And if you let 'em know you're coming, they'll be down and listen to you.[1]
>
> —President Harry S. Truman's advice to Lyndon Johnson

> We . . . noticed in one of Amtrak's old publicity brochures that they said when presidential candidates wanted to get somewhere quickly they would take an aeroplane, [but] when they want to make a statement they would take a train.[2]
>
> —Ryan Cooper, executive producer, CNN International

AN AMERICAN INVENTION

The role whistle-stop campaign trains have played in our elections evolved along with how Americans travel and communicate. The 1930s, '40s, and '50s are regarded by some as the golden age of campaign trains.

In fact, my research (see Keeping Track on page 217) shows that more politicians campaigned by train in the 1960s, '70s, '80s, and '90s than in those earlier decades. At least nineteen politicians are known to have campaigned by train between 2000 and 2022.

The earlier train trips could last for weeks at a time and cover thousands of miles. The more recent railroad tours were usually conducted over several days or hours—or a few hundred miles.

In the 1950s, candidates seeking national office began to rely more on planes than trains. The introduction of more efficient ways to reach and communicate with people eventually forced cross-country campaign train tours to take a back seat to television, jet planes, and social media as major ways to help connect with voters. Many candidates credited their victories to their train trips, while some journalists saw the tactic as a factor in their election.

Before embarking on his underdog presidential campaign train tour in 1948, President Harry Truman told two members of Congress, "I'm going to make it a rip-snorting, back-platform campaign to what [Ohio Republican senator Robert] Taft calls all the whistle stops, but I call them the heart of America. When they count the whistle stops' votes, Taft may be in for a big surprise. I think the whistle stops will make the difference between victory and defeat."[3]

"My one-man crusade took effect," Truman recalled later. "The people responded with increasing enthusiasm as the day of election neared. I never doubted that they would vote for me."[4]

In a letter reflecting on the experience, George McGovern, although he failed in his 1972 race for the White House, said his train trips helped win two states—California and Nebraska.

"I can tell you that I carried both of those states in '72 against stiff competition—Hubert Humphrey—and I think the train ride had a lot to do with it," he wrote later. "In my opinion, it is the most enjoyable of all forms of presidential campaigning."[5]

A Herblock Cartoon, © The Herb Block Foundation, used under license.

Franklin Roosevelt had fond memories of whistle-stopping across the country in 1920 as James Cox's vice-presidential running mate, according to presidential historian Doris Kearns Goodwin.

"Traveling by train to nearly forty states, he worked eighteen hours a day," she wrote. "'We really had trouble holding Franklin down on that trip,' [FDR political advisor] Louis Howe recalled. 'His enthusiasm was so great that we were after him constantly to keep him from wearing himself down to his bones.'"

But Roosevelt would not heed their advice, Goodwin wrote. He spoke wherever the train stopped. Why? Because, as he told Howe, if he was ever elected, the people he was talking to now would be his "bosses," and "they've got a right to know what they're hiring."[6]

Campaign trains could bring politicians into much closer contact with people, as United Press (UP) reporter Merriman Smith noted.

"Tipped off by his locomotive engineer, FDR once had a [long] campaign train stopped late at night at a Montana grade crossing to greet four people."[7]

Senator Robert F. Kennedy campaigned for president aboard a whistle-stop train tour of Nebraska on April 17, 1968. "A Kennedy speechwriter later said the tour was the most successful day of the senator's 82-day campaign—cut short by his assassination in June after he won the California primary—because he began to believe he could win," the *Omaha World-Herald* reported.[8]

CBS reporter George Herman thought that Lyndon Baines Johnson's 1960 whistle-stop tour as John Kennedy's running mate "helped the ticket, because there was old Johnson standing from the back of the train in every small town through most of the southern states to reassure them that they still had this good old boy in Washington, and everything would be all right.

"I think the South would have been tempted to bolt [from John] Kennedy otherwise."[9]

Richard Nixon, who campaigned by train several times during his political career, preferred that method of connecting with voters, according to his staff.

"It was easier to campaign by train than by plane," Nixon aide Murray Chotiner told *Trains* magazine in 1971. Nixon "found it better to talk with the party brass. It gave him a chance to talk with his staff people."

Chotiner apparently preferred trains himself.

"I still like a good train campaign. There's still nothing better to build campaign morale and momentum than a campaign train. And it's infectious. A train was really very effective."

According to the magazine, "In Chotiner's view, the novelty of the train itself will draw many people who otherwise wouldn't pay any attention to a candidate, much less go to an auditorium to hear him."[10]

Gerald Ford was inspired to campaign by train in 1976 after seeing pictures of Dwight D. Eisenhower's whistle-stopping train tour, which made a stop at Ford's hometown of Grand Rapids, Michigan.[11]

Ford credited his train tour for helping to beat Ronald Reagan in the Republican primary by a two-to-one margin.

In 1976, the Democratic National Committee sponsored Jimmy Carter's eighteen-car campaign train tour through several states.

"We expect this train will do the one thing Jimmy Carter likes to do better than anything else: campaign at the grassroots where the people are," DNC chairman Robert Strauss said.[12]

ABC News correspondent Jim Wooten, who covered Carter's 1976 whistle-stop train tour, recalled that "late in the evening, in the dusk of a long hard day, [author] Teddy White and I were returning to our seats after a stop in Johnstown (I think).

"As the train moved out into the more sparsely populated reaches of the community and eventually into the rural countryside, Carter's voice could be heard echoing against the empty landscape. 'I hope ya'll [sic] can help me, now,' he was saying over and over, hoping somehow that if he said it one more time, it would make the difference between winning and losing."[13]

Mike McCurry, White House spokesperson in the Clinton administration, called Bill Clinton's 1996 train tour during his reelection campaign "one of the more fun presidential campaign journeys I was able to take over the course of a half-dozen presidential campaign cycles." McCurry said, "It was all small-town Americana. President Clinton would sit on the back of the 'president's car' which was a refurbished train car that I believe had been used in previous presidential whistle-stops. [It was] antique and beautiful.

"He had a sound system and would call out to citizens who lined the train route. 'Love your dog!' was one of his favorites, to the point that the press adopted it as a favorite meme to evoke a giggle."

Clinton "waved to everyone, even those with anti-Clinton or Dole '96 banners, sometimes with the slightest of scowls," McCurry said.

He remembered, "I rode mostly with other senior staff and in the press car, which was equipped as a mini-filing center, although these were days without Twitter and Wi-Fi, so filing [stories] usually involved telephone calls for the reporters.

"I think we helicoptered from Michigan City [Indiana] to Soldier Field in Chicago, where we were arriving for the Democratic National Convention. The juxtaposition of the train ride with a helicopter flight across Lake Michigan brought us back to twentieth-century campaign politics from the quaint revival of a more nineteenth-century style of campaigning. I wish we had been able to do much more of the latter."[14]

Alfred J. Tuchfarber, director of the University of Cincinnati's Institute for Policy Research, said, "There were two main political purposes for [Clinton's train] trip. One was to create some excitement and some media attention leading up to his arrival at the convention, partly because they probably knew that their convention wasn't going to be all that exciting. . . . The other was to win over voters in key states."[15]

Contrary to conventional wisdom, whistle-stop trains are alive and well on some campaign trails.

A case in point was presidential candidate Joe Biden, who in September 2020 conducted a whistle-stop campaign train tour of Ohio and Pennsylvania.

The *Washington Post* reported, "This train tour will help Biden drive home the 'Scranton vs. Park Avenue' contrast that he's been trying to draw to highlight his humble roots and Trump's privileged upbringing. During the tour, Biden is set to meet with workers, including union members, to hear 'how they have struggled to get ahead in Trump's economy,' according to his campaign."[16]

Barack Obama was no stranger to whistle-stop trains either. He rode one in Pennsylvania during his run for the White House in September 2008 and again on the way to his inauguration the following January.

On the Sunday before Election Day 2022, Democratic congressman Peter Welch, seeking to replace retiring senator Patrick Leahy, embarked on a sixty-seven-mile whistle-stop campaign trip from Burlington to Rutland, Vermont. Welch's "Railroad to Victory" tour held special significance, echoing the train tour he took when he first ran for Congress in 2006.

Sixteen years later, Welch won his race for the Senate.[17]

The Biden, Obama, and Welch campaign train tours are the latest examples of a colorful way politicians can connect with the public—a strategy that has served as the setting for drama, intrigue, tragedy, deception, humor, death, and triumph for more than 185 years.

Biden, Obama, and Welch are certainly in good company. Other well-known whistle-stopping politicians include Ronald Reagan,[18] George W. Bush,[19] and George H. W. Bush.[20]

Mary McGrory, then a columnist for the *Washington Star*, was on Adlai Stevenson's 1956 whistle-stop train, and remembered the trip with fondness.

"It was the poetry of campaigning," McGrory said. "It was beautiful as we went through the Midwest, and the scenery was gorgeous. The trains were also fun. You could roam up and down the aisle in some sort of comfort, have a snack, and look out the window."

The trains had "a more informal atmosphere [with] less barriers between staff and candidate. It was an easier way to campaign with more space," she said. Compared to airplanes, there was an extra benefit to train travel: there were no takeoffs and landings, which McGrory noted "are always the subject of suspense."[21]

The trains were so familiar to Americans that they were featured

- in newsreels that were shown in movie theaters across the country;[22]
- as the backdrop of a popular book about a murder mystery;[23]
- as the theme for a highly publicized satirical cross-country train tour by one of the most famous comedians of the day;[24] and

- in editorial cartoons and political drawings in magazines and newspapers around the country (some of them are featured throughout this book).

The trains could be fodder for jokes by late-night comedians. Over the course of hosting *The Tonight Show,* Jay Leno told 4,607 jokes about Bill Clinton—more than he did about any other politician or public affairs–related topic.[25]

One of those jokes, about Clinton's four-day 1996 campaign train trip to Chicago, referred to Hillary Clinton's decision to shut down the White House travel office.

Leno said, "The whole trip takes *four* days! That's what happens when your wife fires the White House travel office. You have to make your own arrangements."[26]

Memories of the pivotal role whistle-stop campaign trains have played in national, state, and local elections fade a bit more with the passing of each generation of voters.

"There was a time, not too many years ago, when you could see, hear, and even talk to the President of the United States. You could shake his hand, too," the *Los Angeles Times* observed in 1968.

"All you had to do was walk down to the train station and wait for the President's train to roll in. This was back in the days of the great whistle-stop campaigns when, for more than eight decades, the President or his opponents, or sometimes both, climbed aboard their campaign trains and, with secretaries, aides, speechwriters, party politicians, and assorted hangers-on, took for the hinterlands in search of votes.

"They didn't dodge the dangers, the challenges. They met them head-on. And the tossed eggs, the overripe fruit, the

"Oh, Hello, Tom—I Thought It Was The Secret Service"
TRUMAN
WESTERN
TRIP
DEWEY
WESTERN
TRIP
HERBLOCK

heartbreak, the failure, they were a part of it, just as much as the bands, the bunting, the torchlight parades, the great speeches, the wonderful victories."[27]

Ironically, given the importance of visuals and pictures to television and other forms of communication, whistle-stop trains continue to be of strategic value to politicians, but for a different reason: as backdrops for photo ops that attract the attention of the media and the public. In their new role as "eye candy," campaign trains still fulfill their original purpose: helping politicians reach and communicate with as many people as possible.

SOME ASSEMBLY REQUIRED

After studying dozens of local, regional, and national railroad campaign tours, I've compiled a composite picture of what a typical whistle-stop train was like.

The car carrying the candidate was always last on the train and featured a platform from which they would speak to crowds at rail depots.

The car behind that was reserved for security personnel, representatives of the railroad company, the press relations staff, and other campaign aides.

The next two or three coaches served as the quarters for the rest of the candidate's staff, including speechwriters, secretaries, political advisors, medical staff, mimeograph operators, and assorted VIPs.

A lounge car followed, for use by the staff and press, after which was a working car for the traveling reporters with typewriters, tables, and a Western Union rep who made arrangements to send their stories back to their home offices.

Completing the configuration were three or four Pullman cars, a luggage car, and a locomotive.

"If the President were aboard, he had a special car fitted with the best living accommodations on rails and all of the latest electronic equipment with which to keep in constant touch with the White House—and through it the world—on all the internal and external affairs of government," according to Associated Press reporter Jack Bell, author of *The Splendid Misery: The Story of the Presidency and Power Politics at Close Range.*[28]

Then, as now, planning and organizing a campaign train tour took time, money, and attention to detail. But the payoff could be worth all the trouble.

"There is nothing in politics—or out of it—that has the lure and fascination of a presidential candidate's special train," recalled James Farley, author of *Behind the Ballots,* who helped engineer several election triumphs for FDR. "Getting the train fitted out properly is a job for experts, and the tiny details which have to be worked out in the most thorough fashion almost defy description.

"The right kind of living quarters must be provided for the candidate himself, members of his family who may be going along, and the staff of secretaries and assistants who help in preparing speeches, handling the press, and greeting visiting politicians," Farley noted.

"In addition, space must be found for dozens of newspaper correspondents, news photographers, movie cameramen, representatives of telegraph companies, and radio announcers. An invitation to go along is considered a high honor, and the person delegated to make up the list of guests must be as snooty as a society hostess in issuing invitations for a swank party.

"The trip usually develops into a 'family party' with everybody becoming fast friends before it is over," Farley concluded.[29]

In addition to preparing guest lists, selecting the best-qualified people to staff the trains and accompany the politicians could be an important element in ensuring that the trips were as comfortable and well run as possible.

President Franklin Roosevelt, for example, had favorites among the traveling railroad officials. "The Boss was always partial to Dan Moorman [of the Baltimore & Ohio railroad], as were other members of the Presidential party," Grace Tully, Roosevelt's private secretary, wrote in her book, *F. D. R.: My Boss*. "We knew it would be a 'happy train' with Dan aboard. He paid special attention to the cuisine on the diner, stocking it with special foods he knew the Boss liked, and ordering special treats when a Presidential trip coincided with an anniversary of some sort or other."[30] Tully recalled:

> For the non-operating personnel [on FDR's campaign trains] such as porters, waiters, etc., the same ones were called on through the years and gradually established a seniority system among themselves for this particular assignment.
>
> Quite naturally, these employees became accustomed to the manner of life on a Presidential train and to the varying needs and desires of those who made most of the trips, the service was maintained on a high level of smoothness and efficiency.
>
> For all of this special thanks were due to Harry Lucas, the porter in the President's own car, A. Dickson, the porter in the adjoining car, Samuel C. Mitchell, who began as a porter in the press car and was later promoted to the President's car, and the other porters, Fred Fair, J. M. Thompson, Eugene

> Lapura, Albert Sandal, Bill Reid, J. H. Daniels and Ike Hammond—all of whom have their own modest but important place in the Roosevelt story for services performed.[31]

THE STOPS AHEAD

This book seeks to set the record straight about the history of campaign trains in American politics and the journalists who covered them—and shine a new spotlight on that history. It represents the culmination of decades of research, including interviews and stories about the politicians, candidates, their staff, journalists, Secret Service agents, and workers behind the scenes, and hours spent online and at libraries across the country. I combed through thousands of books, magazine articles, newsreels, websites, and other sources for hidden, ignored, or long-forgotten stories, photographs, or other nuggets.

In the course of my research, I came across first-person accounts of some of the politicians who campaigned by train, the people who organized the trips, and the reporters who covered them. As appropriate, I've included their experiences and recollections in their own words.

My extensive research has yielded a wealth of political anecdotes that open a new window into the personalities and campaigns that have shaped our history.

They include

- how the whistle-stop train of a candidate's wife helped change the role of women on the campaign trail (page 19);
- the Soviet leader who, during a highly

publicized visit to the United States, made an American-style whistle-stop appearance at a train depot in California (page 209);

- the president who traveled the railroads so much that Congress questioned whether any work he did outside of the nation's capital was legal (page 10);
- the two presidents who rode a whistle-stop campaign in two countries—the United States and Egypt (page 210);
- why politicians occasionally had other people impersonate them on train trips (page 68);
- an innovative way that pickpockets profited from the rear-platform speeches of one candidate (page 124);
- the mischief and embarrassing situations caused by protesters and pranksters (page 114);
- why a reporter was glad that he fell off the train and that bystanders assumed he was dead (page 150);
- how a politician's aide showed her displeasure with a traveling journalist (page 168);
- why one heckler hoped that the campaign train of a presidential candidate would not stop in their town (page 128);
- the VIP guest on two presidential campaign train trips who later became president (page 75); and
- the interesting and unusual gifts presented to candidates at train depots (page 82).

I became interested in campaign trains when, in 1984, as the press secretary for Congressman Mickey Edwards, Republican of Oklahoma, I was looking for ways to generate publicity about his reelection campaign. It turned out that there was a set of abandoned Amtrak tracks running through his congressional district and across the state. We wound up conducting an old-fashioned whistle-stop train tour on those tracks.[32]

After confirming that the tracks were still usable, the congressman's campaign manager found that they could rent a train from Santa Fe Railway. The configuration included two locomotives, a passenger car, and a rear-platform car once used by Dwight Eisenhower.

Ironically, one of the last people to campaign by train in the state was President Truman. Our 102-mile trip mimicked his, with public rallies at four depot stations, brief rear-platform speeches by the candidate, a band, decorations, and a traveling group of reporters.

Edwards, who worked with other members of the state's congressional delegation to restore train service to Oklahoma, told depot rallies that "if you send me back to Washington, I'm going to keep trying until trains run over these tracks on a regular basis."[33]

As I helped organize the congressman's train trip and depot rallies, I searched in vain for a substantial body of information about the history of whistle-stop trains.

In the aftermath of the congressman's successful train trip and reelection, collecting anecdotes, recollections, and stories about whistle-stopping politicians and the reporters who covered them became my hobby, sometimes my obsession—and eventually this book.

CHAPTER 1

A Sentimental Journey

> You get a real feeling of this country and the people in it when you're on a train, speaking from the back of a train, and the further you get away from that, the worse off you are, the worse off the country is.[34]
>
> —Harry S. Truman

> It's embarrassing that we have reached the stage that no one knows what a whistle-stop train is anymore.[35]
>
> —Arthur Edson, Associated Press

Whistle-stop trains were often regarded as special and memorable events in the lives of those who came to see them. Train visits by candidates running for the White House or the governor's mansion were front-page news, a matter of community pride, and became an important part of local history.

Schools and businesses would close for the occasion. The population of entire communities would show up, blocking streets and surrounding the railroad depot, to see and hear a famous politician. These were once-in-a-lifetime events for residents of small-town America—a bit of "I remember when" history to pass on to their children and grandchildren.

Herb Thompson, who saw President Dwight Eisenhower's train tour in North Carolina in 1952, said, "I dare say the presidential candidates of today wish they could move around the country with the ease and comfort which 'whistle-stopping campaigning' provided."

The train gave them privacy but also a room "where they would relax and rest," he noted. "Then, too, there was an air of enthusiasm and adventure for the thousands of people who always greeted them at the scheduled stops."[36]

More than 150 years after President Lincoln stopped briefly to say a few words at the rail depot in Peekskill, New York, while on his way to his inauguration in Washington, the local paper noted that "Lincoln's whistle-stop appearance was a shining moment for the Hudson Valley burg, an event that instantly became a permanent part of its lore."[37]

Decades after he saw President Harry S. Truman speak briefly at the train depot in Albany, New York, Edward Gill still remembered the encounter.

"When the President first appeared on the platform, someone in the crowd hollered, 'Up and at 'em, Harry!' Truman laughed and said, 'I'm up and I'll get right at 'em!'" Gill wrote.

"I recall he talked about the high price of pork chops, among other trivia, and in conclusion said, 'Would you like to meet the real boss of the White House?' and to scattered applause, Bess Truman came out to join her husband and made small talk.

"Truman and his wife waved good-bye and thanked us for coming out, and the train departed for his next stop."[38]

Forty years after the campaign train of Democratic presidential candidate Robert F. Kennedy stopped in their community, residents of Lodi, in central California, still recalled the visit by the charismatic politician.

"It was very exciting," said Peggy Hamilton, who remembered being "a fairly politically active 10-year-old" when she saw Kennedy's stop in Lodi. "I remember that more than anything much he said. I was very excited to be able to see him in person. I was a very, very passionate supporter of Bobby Kennedy. It was more the romance of the name than understanding policy beyond the Vietnam War, which I did understand."[39]

Bill Maxwell, then a sixteen-year-old sophomore at a local high school, still remembered the details from that day and why he went to see the anti-war candidate.

"Those were kind of my [hippie] days. It was hot. I was barefoot and my feet were covered with railroad track grease. It was a pretty good-sized crowd, considering Lodi was pretty conservative. I went because it was something to do in Lodi. The war was omnipresent and I was looking two years down the road and being eligible for the draft."[40]

Five decades after he reported on the brief 1964 visit of Democratic vice-presidential nominee Hubert H. Humphrey at the train station in Tracy, California, Sam Matthews, a journalist with the *Tracy Press*, could still recall details of the visit.

"I could see a lot of people [had come to see the candidate]—close to 2,000. Many carried campaign signs and banners, mostly for Humphrey, and there were a whole bunch of red, white and blue balloons in the air."

Matthews wrote, “I can still remember seeing and hearing ‘the Happy Warrior,’ as Humphrey was sometimes called.”

He explained that “Humphrey, known as an impassioned public speaker, didn’t disappoint the crowd. He energetically called for the election of the Johnson-Humphrey ticket as a way to further the programs of Johnson and John F. Kennedy, whom Johnson had succeeded as president upon Kennedy’s assassination in November 1963. . . . After Humphrey ended his 20-minute talk, the train pulled out, heading to the next campaign stop.”[41]

For Matthews and countless other journalists, staffers, and candidates, whistle-stop campaigns created indelible memories that would stay with them for a lifetime.

ORIGINS

The first whistle-stopping politicians needed two obvious but essential things: locomotives to haul trains, and tracks to take them where they wanted to go. The first steam-driven locomotive was built in 1804 in England.[42] John Stevens designed and built America’s first steam-driven locomotive in 1825,[43] running it on a circular track on his estate in New Jersey.[44]

It took several years for a relatively small number of railroad tracks to be laid in the US. By the end of 1830, fourteen miles of track had been laid by the Baltimore & Ohio Railroad.[45]

It did not take long for someone to get the idea that they could adapt railroads to politics. Andrew Jackson became the first sitting president to travel by train in 1833, for a twelve-mile trip in Maryland between Ellicott’s Mills and Baltimore. He was met by a cheering crowd, a precursor of the thousands of railroad-station rallies to be held over the two centuries that followed.[46]

William Henry Harrison was the first presidential candidate to ride the rails, in 1836.[47] Although he lost the election, he went on to victory four years later and was the first president-elect to travel by train to his inauguration.[48]

The expansion of the railroad accelerated after the Civil War, as the country industrialized in the East and expanded toward the West. The nation's first transcontinental railroad system was inaugurated in 1869, linking railroad systems in the East to train tracks in the West.[49]

By the turn of the twentieth century, there were more than two hundred thousand miles of track.[50]

The term *whistle-stop* was coined by railroad officials to describe towns too small to merit regularly scheduled train service. If there were passengers to be discharged, the conductor would pull the signal cord, and the engineer would respond with two toots of the whistle.[51]

The unscheduled depot visits became known in railroad vernacular as "whistle-stop towns" and eventually simply as "whistle-stops." But that well-meaning shorthand description became synonymous with insulting ways to describe backward or undesirable communities, such as "hick town" and "jerkwater town."[52] Not wanting to insult small communities, railroad companies dropped the term altogether . . . at least for a while.

The term *whistle-stop* did not become associated with campaign trains until 1948, when President Harry S. Truman kicked off his now-famous national underdog train tour in Crestline, Ohio. Until then, the trains were referred to as *special trains, campaign trains, specials,* or variations of those words.

Cartoon by Gibson Crockett, *The Campaign of '48 in Star Cartoons, Washington Evening Star-News*, 1948.

In 1948, Senator Robert Taft (R-Ohio), referring to Truman's campaign train tour across the country, said during a speech in Philadelphia that Truman should not go around the country "blackguarding [attacking] Congress at every whistle-stop."[53]

Taft, in turn, was criticized by the Democrats for denigrating the cities and towns Truman visited by train as "whistle-stops."[54]

Sensing a PR opportunity, the Democratic Party jumped into action. The Democratic National Committee surveyed officials in thirty-five cities where Truman had campaigned by train, asking, "Was it nice of the Senator to call you a whistle-stop?" Of those who replied, 73 percent did not approve of Taft's comments; more than 25 percent wanted more information.

Los Angeles mayor Fletcher Bowron countered Taft's perceived slur, saying, "The term hardly applies. Anyone who could have been in Los Angeles last Monday [when Truman's campaign train paid a visit]—a perfect day in June, with Southern California sunshine and blue skies—and witnessed nearly 1,000,000 good American citizens lining the streets to welcome their President would have both whistled and stopped."[55]

Truman first used the term *whistle-stop* in a speech at the Greater Los Angeles Press Club on June 14, 1948. He described the City of Angels as "the biggest whistle-stop I ever saw."[56]

But it did not take too long for the term *whistle-stop* to come back into vogue and lose its pejorative meaning. In little more than two election cycles (four years), no one seemed to mind when the Associated Press began its story about Truman campaigning in New York City for Democratic presidential candidate Adlai Stevenson this way: "Whistle stopper Harry S. Truman lends a hand to Adlai Stevenson here today in the biggest 'whistle-stop' of them all."[57]

The meaning and use of *whistle-stop* continued to evolve. In addition to referring to campaign trains, it is often used to describe a series of quick and brief visits to various locations or destinations.

BREAKING DOWN BARRIERS

For decades after the introduction and growth of railroads in the early 1800s, it was not considered appropriate for those

A Herblock Cartoon, © The Herb Block Foundation, used under license.

running for the White House to use trains to get there. Indeed, it was frowned upon to seek the office in any public way, shape, or form. The presidency was supposed to seek the man, not the other way around.[58]

Stephen A. Douglas, who ran in Illinois for the US Senate against Abraham Lincoln in 1858, ignored that tradition when he conducted a whistle-stop campaign train tour.[59] To let townspeople know he was on the way to speak to them, Douglas mounted a brass cannon on a flatcar at the back of the train. The weapon was fired by a two-man crew in semimilitary dress as the train approached communities.[60]

Lincoln, by contrast, could not afford his own private railroad car and had to ride from town to town on a public day coach.[61] Sometimes he had no choice but to ride freight trains in order to get to his destination. On one occasion, while Lincoln was riding with others in the caboose, the freight train was sidetracked so the Douglas campaign special could speed by.

"The passing train was decorated with banners and flags, and carried a band of music which was playing 'Hail to the Chief,'" according to Lincoln biographer John W. Starr Jr.[62]

On other trips, Lincoln rode on the same train as Douglas but as a regular fare-paying passenger.[63]

"The Douglas campaign was the forerunner of just about every presidential campaign that followed," observed Bruce Chadwick, author of *Lincoln for President.* "The work was so prodigious that no candidate tried it again until 1896, when William Jennings Bryan campaigned throughout the nation."[64]

Andrew Johnson was the first incumbent president to campaign by train when he made what would later become the traditional "swing around the circle" by rail to speak to voters in New York City, Chicago, St. Louis, and Washington, DC.[65]

But according to Ejler Jakobsson in a 1956 article for *Railroad Magazine*, Congress criticized Johnson for lowering the dignity of the office, and he did not win his party's nomination. "Still, he is credited today for having carried on the campaign tradition," Jakobsson noted.[66]

President Ulysses S. Grant rode the rails so often that he was criticized and questioned by Congress. "The question even came up as to whether executive acts performed outside the White House were legal," according to Bob Withers.[67]

Grant was ordered by a House resolution to account for actions taken away from the capital, Withers wrote.

"The angered president cited chapter and verse to prove that he was not constitutionally bound to exercise his duties of office at the seat of government. He supplied statistics to show how much time his predecessors spent out of town and listed the acts they performed while they were away.

"The Democratic Congress' curiosity seemed satisfied when Grant pointed out that the president who spent the most time away from Washington was [Thomas] Jefferson, the party father."[68]

In 1896, Democratic presidential candidate William Jennings Bryan became the first national office seeker to conduct an early version of what became the modern whistle-stop campaign train tour. The "Silver-Tongued Orator" traveled by rail an estimated eighteen thousand miles in one hundred days. He delivered six hundred speeches at hundreds of train depots in twenty-seven states and was seen by about five million people.

According to Keith Melder, associate curator in the division of political history in the Smithsonian Institution's Museum of History and Technology (now known as the National Museum of American History), "Other candidates had spoken briefly and shaken hands from the rear platforms of their trains, but

Some politicians set records for how many speeches they gave from the back of trains. In this 1896 illustration from *Puck* magazine, presidential candidate William Jennings Bryan is standing at the rear of a caboose, holding a bellows labeled "16 to 1," blowing paraphrased fragments from speeches at rural citizens as the train passes. Accompanying him are several newspaper reporters. Bryan traveled more than eighteen thousand miles, through twenty-seven states, and spoke to millions of people. (1896 illustration by John S. Pughe for *Puck*. Courtesy of the Library of Congress, Prints & Photographs Division, LC-DIG-ppmsca-28841.)

never before had a presidential aspirant made the 'whistle-stop' technique into a formal feature of the contest. For more than fifty years after the campaign of 1896, 'whistle-stop' oratory and campaign trains were nearly synonymous with presidential struggles. . . .

"Bryan, in 1896, was seemingly indefatigable: he rode dreary trains for hundreds and thousands of miles, and for days on end. Often, he was awakened in the small hours of the morning to wave from his observation platform to enthusiastic crowds gathered at tiny country depots along his route. For much of the trip, he had no special accommodations—just ordinary sleepers and day coaches—but toward the end of the campaign the

Democratic National Committee provided, out of its meager funds, a private car for the candidate. He had the good fortune of being able to sleep anywhere and, apparently, at any time," Melder noted.[69]

Some communities came to expect that politicians would make at least a token appearance at their train station when they were traveling in the region.

In 1905, the small town of Temple, Texas, was unhappy to learn that President Theodore Roosevelt would not stop in their community even for a minute as his train took him to a reunion of the Rough Riders in San Antonio.

In response, the city council passed an emergency ordinance that required all presidential trains that traveled through the town to stop for ten minutes. In the spirit of compromise, however, the council agreed that Roosevelt's train only had to make a five-minute visit.

When it did stop, more than two thousand people, including schoolchildren, listened to his speech.[70]

CHASING TRUMAN

President Truman's whistle-stop campaign train did stop in Temple in 1948. "I was going to stop, anyway, so you didn't need any ordinance to get me to stop," he told the crowd. "Your congressman says I promised him to come here just before I took office way back in January 1945."[71]

Truman faced criticism for traveling around the country on his campaign train, condemning the "do-nothing Congress" because it failed to act on key measures and issues.[72]

"At first, the critics referred to my tour as a 'one man circus' and called it less efficient and less dignified than the campaign

Harry Truman was giving 'em hell—Thomas Dewey was not.

Cartoon by James T. Berryman, *The Campaign of '48 in Star Cartoons, Washington Evening Star-News*, 1948.

being put on by the Republicans," Truman wrote in his memoirs. "But as the crowds grew larger and larger and more people flocked to my train than showed up around the [Thomas] Dewey train, our opponents began to get worried."[73]

When Truman conducted another whistle-stop train tour in 1950, Republicans charged that it was a "quarter-million-dollar junket" for political purposes that would be paid for by taxpayers.

Democrats defended the trip, saying that Truman had a

A Herblock Cartoon, © The Herb Block Foundation, used under license.

responsibility to "discuss current problems and issues face to face with the voters as the opportunity permits during the trip."[74]

A lawsuit filed in 1952 to prevent Truman from going on a national campaign train tour was dismissed by a district court judge in Washington, DC.

Andrew J. Easter, a draftsman, charged that Truman was not devoting himself fully to his presidential duties and "spends a great amount of his time in speech making and traveling to different parts of the United States," according to the *Evening Star*,[75] and was "depriving the citizens of the United States of America of his abilities, time and undivided attention."[76]

Easter's request for a restraining order claimed that Truman could use the twelve days the tour would take to "sieve out undisclosed corruption, incompetence, mismanagement, and wastefulness from government."[77]

Republicans were not happy about Truman's whistle-stop campaign train tour in 1952 in support of Democratic presidential nominee Adlai Stevenson.

GOP chairman Arthur E. Summerfield described the tour as "a degrading and disgraceful spectacle that will make votes for Ike Eisenhower.

"The American people will not be fooled by the big lie technique of the 1948 campaign. It worked once, but it will not work again," he predicted in a speech at the National Press Club.[78]

In 1984, Democratic presidential nominee Walter F. Mondale criticized President Ronald Reagan's plans for a two-hundred-mile whistle-stop train tour in Ohio. "Let's get it straight," Mondale stated. "Ronald Reagan is no Harry Truman. He should spend less time impersonating Truman and more time listening to what Harry Truman said."[79]

When President George H. W. Bush made a similar train tour

in northwestern Ohio eight years later, Democrats labeled it as the "On the Wrong Track Tour '92" because he would be going "into [a] safe haven where he doesn't have to face the issues."[80]

In 1996, Republican Party chair Haley Barbour alleged that taxpayers funded 90 percent of the costs of President Clinton's whistle-stop campaign trip to the Democratic National Convention, and said that Republicans would file a complaint with the Federal Election Commission over the matter.

Barbour thought that the train tour was really "a continuous campaign trip with many stops," and the Republicans wanted the government to be reimbursed for the costs associated with the trip.[81]

The *Washington Post* reported that Kansas Republican senator Robert Dole mocked the Clinton campaign train trip to the convention, labeling it the "Status Quo Express." Dole noted that his staff had calculated that the trip would cost taxpayers $12 million per mile in campaign promises.

"I believe they're on the wrong track. We are going to give them another track: a track back to Little Rock," Dole said.[82]

RECORD HOLDERS

In 1903, Theodore Roosevelt planned a tour of the midwestern and western states, which was dubbed the "Great Loop Tour" because of its route.

But it was not a typical whistle-stop train tour. That's because its goal was advocacy rather than campaigning, according to Michael F. Blake, author of *Go West Mr. President: Theodore Roosevelt's Great Loop Tour of 1903.*

Roosevelt "was adamant that his speeches be devoid of any partisan rhetoric, nor would he meet solely with Republican

This campaign-train-related illustration from a *Puck* magazine cover refers to news accounts that President Theodore Roosevelt refused to shoot a bear while on a hunting trip in Mississippi. The drawing shows a family of bears dressed as humans near railroad tracks. The youngest cub is crying; a train labeled "Presidential Special" has just passed, with Roosevelt standing on the back of the last car holding papers labeled "Speeches." The mother bear indicates that Roosevelt is on a campaign tour rather than a hunting expedition. (Illustration by John S. Pughe for *Puck* magazine, April 15, 1903. Image courtesy of the Library of Congress, Prints & Photographs Division, LC-DIG-ppmsca-25732.)

officeholders in the various cities and towns," Blake wrote. "He happily shook hands with Democratic mayors or senators, just as he would Republicans."

The president took a hands-on approach to the journey, writing his own speeches about good citizenship, the importance of a strong navy, and his recently signed immigrant legislation.[83]

The tour "would be the longest, most elaborate cross-country journey ever taken by a president of the United States," presidential historian Douglas Brinkley explained in his book *The Wilderness Warrior: Theodore Roosevelt and the Crusade for America.* "The trek served as an appealing way to present Roosevelt's conservation policies to all regions before the 1904 presidential election. Emphasizing America's natural wonders, the adventure crystallized Roosevelt's already potent belief that the Far West, in all its wildness and rawness, was the least exhausted part of the country."[84]

Roosevelt "traveled light when it came to his train," Blake noted. "Whereas most presidential trains pulled at least eight cars, Theodore's had only six: two for baggage and four sleeper cars." (The baggage cars carried both winter and spring clothing for the party.)

"All the cars were electrically lit and equipped with all the conveniences a traveler would need. The president's car, called Elysian (traditionally the last car of the train), was 'the handsomest ever placed on the tracks by the Pullman Company.'" His car was fitted with an observation parlor, three staterooms, a dining room, kitchen, and servants' quarters. The kitchen was supervised by "the best chef in the employ of the [Pullman] company."[85]

President Franklin Roosevelt holds the record for whistle-stop tours. He made 399 train trips, traveled 350,000 miles, and delivered hundreds of speeches along the way.[86]

Lady Bird Johnson campaigned 1,680 miles through the South in 1964 to help reassure Dixie that her husband, Lyndon Johnson, had not forgotten his southern roots. It was the first time that a First Lady had gone on a whistle-stop tour by herself.[87]

"For her, the train was a sentimental necessity because she did not want any region of this country to feel that it was the forgotten region, and she went there to say so," recalled Liz Carpenter, staff director and press secretary for Lady Bird Johnson.[88]

Not everyone thought she should go, however.

"Kenny O'Donnell, who had been Jack Kennedy's principal political advisor and had stayed on to help in the 1964 campaign, turned up his nose at the whole thing," Carpenter said. "He sat sphinxlike in meetings with me—half laughing at the whole idea and obviously feeling that neither the South nor women were important in the campaign.

"'But we must go,' Mrs. Johnson insisted. 'We must let them know that we love the South. We respect them. We have not turned our backs on them. I don't think there's much chance of carrying it for Lyndon, judging by the letters I get from my Alabama cousins. But at least we won't lose by default.'"[89]

Mrs. Johnson did go, of course. She made forty-seven speeches along the way, and welcomed on board about sixteen hundred local politicians, dignitaries, and other VIPs.[90]

The shortest known whistle-stop tour was conducted by Dick Tuck, a well-known political prankster who ran for the California State Senate to represent Los Angeles County in 1966. Riding on the historic Angels Flight Railway,[91] his campaign tour traveled about six hundred feet[92] in about four minutes—round trip—up and down a hillside in downtown Los Angeles.

Some cities were more likely to be visited by whistle-stopping politicians than others.

Dick Tuck, a Democrat and political jester, strikes the pose of a typical candidate as he rides the Angels Flight Railway on April 13, 1966. The cable-car line runs slightly more than three hundred feet up and down a hillside in downtown Los Angeles. Tuck, then forty-two, wanted to be a California state senator from LA. His whistle-stop trip set a record for being the shortest in history. (Photo by Ed Widdis for the Associated Press, used under license.)

Take Willard, Ohio, for example.

Located in the southwest corner of Huron County, Willard was an important terminal on the old Baltimore & Ohio Railroad line, where trains carrying politicians would stop for engine changes.

Among those who delivered a short talk from the back of their train when they stopped briefly in the city were Herbert Hoover, FDR, Dwight D. Eisenhower, and Harry Truman.[93]

NAMING THE TRAIN

Starting in the early twentieth century, whistle-stop trains were often named for the candidate they carried or reflected a theme of their campaign.

The train of socialist presidential candidate Eugene Debs, for example, was called "The Red Special,"[94] and Gerald Ford's was "Honest Abe,"[95] while Bill Clinton's 1996 train was labeled "The 21st Century Express,"[96] and his presidential rival, Bob Dole, called his train the "Balanced Budget Express."[97]

Trains named for the person they carried included the "Lady Bird Special" in 1964,[98] the "Dewey Victory Special" in 1948,[99] and the "Dick Nixon Special" in 1952.[100]

Sometimes reporters would come up with their own name for or description of the trains they covered, such as Democratic vice-presidential candidate Lyndon Johnson's "Cornpone Special"[101] in 1960 (a reference to his southern roots) and Adlai Stevenson's "Ghost Train"[102] in 1952 (a reflection of the fact that the candidate was not on the train trip).

In a nod to his wife, who accompanied him on the campaign trail during his first presidential run, Nixon called his train the "Pat and Dick Nixon Special 1960."[103]

Sometimes the trains carried inspiration or aspirational

messages, such as the "Believe in America Tour" of the John Kerry–John Edwards ticket in 2004,[104] George W. Bush's 2000 "Change the Tone Tour,"[105] and Biden's "Build Back Better Express" in 2020.[106]

And then there was the "Joe Smith Special" in 1956.[107] The train on which Democratic presidential nominee Adlai Stevenson rode for a time was not named for a real candidate, but rather for the average people that the name "Smith" symbolized.

It was also a dig at Republicans.

As told by the Associated Press, at the 1956 Republican National Convention, a delegate from Nebraska failed in his effort to have an open convention by nominating a mythical Joe Smith against Vice President Richard Nixon.

The chair of the convention told the delegate to "take your Joe Smith and get out of here."

Democrats seized on the slight to Joe Smiths as a way to raise funds. A Democratic Party official said that the mythical Joe Smith "typifies the essential difference in the political philosophies of the two parties. The Democrats are interested in the average American citizen—in his human rights. The Republicans are interested in his property rights."[108]

Republican senator Barry Goldwater of Arizona was his party's nominee for president in 1964. The name of his campaign train—"Baa Hozhnilne"—certainly stood out from all the others. Goldwater's staff explained that the name was Navajo for "win over" or "be victorious."[109]

THE FERDINAND MAGELLAN

One of the most famous railroad cars ever to be part of a national whistle-stop campaign tour was the "Ferdinand Magellan." It was a standard-issue Pullman car that was converted through a collaboration between the Pullman Company and the Association of American Railroads, and the only one earmarked for use by the president.[110]

The car was rebuilt to White House specifications in 1942, when President Franklin Roosevelt's press secretary and the chief of the White House Secret Service detail recommended that additional security precautions be taken when he traveled around the country by rail.[111]

The car was the idea of Michael Reilly, who headed Roosevelt's Secret Service detail but pointed out that he "had a hard time convincing the Boss that the railroad car was not being built for him but was being built for his office and for the railroad companies' own protection and peace of mind.

"He capitulated eventually, saying, 'Well, if they are going to build it, let's make it a little more comfortable.'

"With that," Reilly said, FDR "took the diagram I handed him and wrote out: 'Take out 3 feet of kitchen-pantry; add 3 feet to observation room.'"[112]

The "Ferdinand Magellan" measured eighty-four feet long, fifteen feet high, and ten feet wide[113] and cost the government a whopping ten dollars. That was quite a deal, considering the Pullman car cost about $250,000 to fix up.[114]

It was "a model of comfort and safety," Robert J. Donovan, author of *Conflict and Crisis: The Presidency of Harry S. Truman*, observed. "There were five staterooms, among them the president's private quarters, the amenities of which included a shower. Toward the rear of the car was a living area, walls paneled with limed oak. A green carpet bore a sofa and several overstuffed chairs.

"Viewed from the outside the most striking feature of the

car was a canopied rear platform adorned with the presidential seal. Attached to the back railing was a lectern from which stemmed a microphone connected with loudspeakers overhead," Donovan noted.[115]

The car, called POTUS (president of the United States)[116] whenever it was part of a train, was entitled to the right-of-way over all other railroad traffic.[117]

"Extra heavy doors with complicated double locks are at each end of the car," United Press reporter Merriman Smith observed. "Included in the equipment of 'the private,' as the car is called, are double galleys for the preparation of food, a dining room large enough for twelve, five staterooms, and a comfortable living room. The President's stateroom comes complete with a shower, lavatory, and toilet.

"Next to the President's car is a compartment car for ranking staff members, and then next in line is the diner. The President has all his meals in 'the private.' His galleys are used only to fix coffee and late-night snacks, most of his food coming from the dinner kitchen."

Smith described how the private railcar had been specially fortified.

"The under part of the car is heavily shielded with steel to make it bottom-heavy in the event an assassin tried to bomb the train. The heavy weight would make the car sit down rather than turn over.

"The windows are three inches thick and can stop a .50 caliber machine-gun slug at point-blank range. The windows, because of their thickness, are tinted a slight green which has the same effect as a color filter on a camera. The countryside can be seen through the windows in true color value regardless of glare or reflection."[118]

Taxpayers have certainly gotten their money's worth from Magellan over the years. Not only did President Roosevelt put the car to good use, traveling fifty thousand miles in it,[119] but so did his successors, including Presidents Harry Truman (twenty-one thousand miles); Dwight Eisenhower (about a thousand miles); and Ronald Reagan (two hundred miles).[120]

KEEPING UP

Presidential campaigns usually incorporated new technologies and methods of communicating and connecting with the public as they became available, practical, and affordable.

The train on which Abraham Lincoln rode to his inauguration in 1861 carried a portable telegraph.[121]

President Woodrow Wilson had a new typewriter on his 1919 cross-country train tour to promote America's participation in the League of Nations.[122] The train also carried several motion-picture photographers who documented the trip.[123]

In 1923, President Warren Harding installed loudspeakers on the rear of his train and placed speakers inside the press car so reporters could listen to his remarks without going outside.[124] Crowds along the way often came out to see the "newfangled" loudspeakers, and the telephone that could be plugged into the overhead lines, as much as they did to see and hear the president.

"This gadget fascinated Harding, who often adjusted it personally," Ejler Jakobsson wrote in an article for *Railroad Magazine*. "Harding called this feature his 'Lifesaver'—ironically enough, on a strenuous trip which led to his death."[125]

In 1928, Democratic presidential hopeful Al Smith was the first whistle-stopping candidate to introduce a modern motif.

His eleven-car private train featured showers, a barbershop, and duplicating equipment to print advance copies of his speeches for journalists.[126]

Truman's train carried a teletype machine, which enabled typed messages to be sent over an electronic channel. In 1948, he ordered one of the machines to be installed on the train of his opponent, Thomas Dewey. The Democratic incumbent wanted to ensure that his Republican rival had access to the latest news about important developments overseas.[127]

There was at least one time when a candidate's campaign staff regretted a convenience it had provided for reporters on the train.

Jody Powell, press secretary to Democratic presidential nominee Jimmy Carter, recalled how a photocopier on Carter's 1976 whistle-stop tour of New Jersey and Pennsylvania overshadowed press coverage of the colorful campaign event.

By coincidence, news about an interview Carter had given to *Playboy* magazine became public the same day as the train trip. Powell admitted that he immediately regretted putting the copier on board. The machine, which was originally intended for duplicating news releases and speeches, was used instead by dozens of reporters to make copies of the controversial interview.

After all was said and done, it was the *Playboy* interview, not the whistle-stop train, that made the news that day.[128]

PREMATURE OBITUARIES

In the mid-twentieth century, the lure of new and more cost-effective ways to connect with voters proved irresistible to many politicians, who began to favor airports, airplanes, and television studios over railroads, train stations, and rear-platform cars. But just when it was assumed that campaign trains were a thing of the past, they made a comeback.

There was an inherent disadvantage in "discussing the big questions of this campaign from the rear end of a train," Woodrow Wilson told a crowd in Michigan from the back of his train in 1912.

"It can't be done," he observed. "They are too big, that is the long and short of the matter. . . . By the time you get started and begin to explain yourself, the train moves off. I would . . . rather make your acquaintance than leave a compound fracture of an idea behind me."[129]

Truman's opponent, Thomas Dewey, had his doubts about the value of campaign trains. As he put it, "The strain on the candidate's health outweighs any possible profit," and he wondered whether voters "really want that type of heroic efforts from their candidates," Sidney Shalett wrote in a 1952 article for the *Saturday Evening Post.*

The campaign trains that year "may be the last of their type," he speculated. "For some years, political pundits have entertained major doubts as to whether votes are won or lost through this type of cross-country stumping," Shalett noted. "Others doubt whether this gypsy like process of rolling across the country, greeting people at every stop, and being nice to the coattail riders who want to be seen on the platform with Mr. Big permits a candidate to display a high degree of brain work in his speeches.

"Indeed, if Truman hadn't been so successful in 1948, it is likely that serious consideration would have been given this year to curtailing the whistle-stop 'Victory Special.'

"The main drawbacks are that you can't whistle-stop in a four-engine transport, and the logistical problems of hauling by

"Those Darn Train Whistles Again!"
H.S.T.
HERBLOCK
©1952 THE WASHINGTON POST CO.

air 100-odd correspondents who trail a major candidate are appalling," Shalett concluded.[130]

"Campaigning by air has serious deficiencies," Robert Bendiner, author of *White House Fever*, pointed out. "To haul the candidate and his staff, plus a hundred correspondents and the usual boarding parties, calls for a small fleet of planes and a continuing exercise in logistics.

"Airports offer a poor counterpart to the whistle-stop, moreover, since only the most faithful will travel fifteen miles from town to hear the candidate, and they can't hear much for the noise when they get there," he explained.[131]

"Despite all the obituaries written by the new generation of television and airplane political strategists, there is something about [a] railroad political caravan that no flying machine or magic lantern (television) can replace," James Reston, a nationally syndicated columnist, observed in 1956.

"It is substantial, as a Presidential nominee should be. It doesn't disappear in a cloud at the end of the city. It comes downtown with a roar and flourish, political style, and it's all wrapped up in the history and symbolism of the Republic," he said.[132]

When Republican president Dwight Eisenhower announced in February 1956 that he would run for reelection, he made a point of saying that he would not campaign by train due, in part, to his ongoing recovery from a heart attack the year before. Although he would continue to travel and be in touch with people, he would not do it, he stated, "on such an intensive basis that I must violate the restrictions within which I must [now] work.

"All of this means also that neither for renomination nor reelection would I engage in extensive traveling and in whistle-stop speaking, normally referred to as barnstorming. I had long ago made up my mind, before I ever dreamed of a personal heart attack, that I could never as President of all the people conduct the kind of political campaign where I was personally a candidate. The first duty of a President is to discharge, to the limit of his ability, the responsibilities of his office," he said.[133]

Four months later, the Republicans announced that rather than spending money on train trips, they would use it to buy more television and radio advertising. But Democrats saw value in continuing to use whistle-stop campaign trains to get to 1600 Pennsylvania Avenue. "I lean to whistle-stop campaigns because they give the candidate an opportunity to be very close to a greater number of his fellow citizens," said Paul M. Butler, chair of the Democratic National Committee. "That should be the objective of government: Staying close to the people."[134]

There was obviously a difference of opinion between the nation's two political parties on whether to whistle-stop or not to whistle-stop. This led the *New York Times* to publish an article about which campaign strategies and techniques each party preferred to use in order to win the White House.

Campaign train advocates thought voters preferred to see a candidate in the flesh, not on the tube; that candidates were better able to address local political issues and problems and accumulate political IOUs if they were traveling through a region; and that campaign trains helped "keep the faithful converted (and) keep the party workers fired up." They felt that "nothing does this like having the nominee come to town and greet local leaders on the train platform."

In the same article, Republican leaders countered that campaigning on TV was more effective, efficient, and cost-effective than campaigning by train. But that view was not held by all GOP political operatives. Vic Johnston headed the staff of the Senate Republican Campaign Committee and was a campaign aide to Ohio Republican senator Robert Taft Sr. in his 1952 White House bid. As Johnston observed, "We just can't conceive here in Washington what an effect a campaign train has, with its carnival atmosphere, the reporters hopping off the train and running back along the tracks to the rear car, the flashbulbs popping. This is big stuff in a small town."[135]

Like a well-intentioned New Year's resolution, the Republicans' decision not to campaign by train did not last long. Other Republicans, including Richard Nixon, Henry Cabot Lodge Jr., and Barry Goldwater, followed suit in their races for the White House.

Whistle-stopping worked so well in Harry Truman's uphill battle for the White House in 1948 that he recommended the tactic to another candidate seeking higher office: Lyndon Baines Johnson.

"You may not believe this, Lyndon," Truman said, "but there are still a hell of a lot of people in this country who don't know where the airport is. But they damn sure know where the depot is. And if you let 'em know you're coming, they'll be down and listen to you."[136]

In 1988, as whistle-stops continued to take a back seat to air travel and the airwaves, the *Washington Post* published what turned out to be another premature obituary for campaign trains.[137] The newspaper declared that the term *whistle-stop* was obsolete and had been replaced with "tarmac takeoffs," a reference to candidates who maximize "their television time by touching down at as many airports as possible each day, speaking before the cameras at each of them, and then moving on without ever having gotten farther into the host city than the airport."

The *Post*'s editorial claimed that the term *whistle-stop* had "recently retired to a condo in Florida after a long and active career in political journalism."

But several political campaign events that year showed that an important political term and the American tradition it represents were both a long way from retirement.

As I observed in a follow-up article published by the paper, "There is no denying that television, jet planes and computers dramatically changed the way in which politicians seek votes. But those who think that these 'newfangled' campaign tools forced the retirement of whistle-stop trains are asleep at the switch.

"Tarmac campaigns notwithstanding, it is not unusual for a jet-age politician to go on a whistle-stop campaign tour to reach voters and attract press coverage. . . .

"Are whistle-stop trains a thing of the past? Can the very word be classified as a retired political term? Hardly! The whistle stop remains the healthy and active 'grand old man' of American political events."[138]

In 1988, Massachusetts governor Michael Dukakis conducted a campaign train tour in Illinois[139] and Pennsylvania[140] as part of his race for the White House.

Also that year, Jesse Jackson rode his "Rainbow Express" in his race to win the New Hampshire presidential primary.[141] The "Liberty Bell Express" train, which in 1987 traveled from Washington, DC, to Philadelphia, sought to generate publicity and drum up support for legislation that would grant statehood to the District of Columbia.[142]

One year earlier, Baltimore mayor William Donald Schaefer conducted a whistle-stop train tour in his successful campaign to become the governor of Maryland. His tour was briefly interrupted when a man who claimed to be a presidential candidate yelled obscenities and dumped papers on the podium on the back of Schaefer's train.[143]

And in 1984, President Ronald Reagan campaigned from the back of his "Heartland Special," which retraced Truman's 1948 whistle-stop tour in western Ohio.[144] Reagan traveled on the "Ferdinand Magellan" for the two-hundred-mile journey, the same railcar used by Truman and Franklin Roosevelt.[145]

CHAPTER 2

The Traveling Circus

> The logistics of organizing a "Victory Special" . . . is only slightly less complicated than planning the spring tour of Ringling Brothers' circus.[146]
>
> —Sidney Shalett, *Saturday Evening Post*

Sometimes a politician had direct input about where his train went and where it would stop, and decisions could be subject to the advice and preferences of political leaders, organizations, and operatives. But often, just keeping the whole campaign from going off the rails was a journey of its own.

When Vice President Theodore Roosevelt "negotiated the details of his campaign tour in South Dakota in 1900 with party leaders, he consistently stated a preference to make one or two major stops in each state where he would address large crowds," John M. Hilpert, author of *American Cyclone: Theodore Roosevelt and His 1900 Whistle-Stop Campaign*, noted. "In this model, he would rely on newspapers to carry his message to the remainder of each state's population. However, state committees preferred multiple stops to heighten the excitement by showing off the Republican celebrity in as many places as possible.

"Eventually, party leadership selected a strategy that combined the two approaches, thus significantly elevating the level of effort expected of Roosevelt," Hilpert said.[147]

The planning of President Woodrow Wilson's 1919 national whistle-stop campaign train trip to promote America's participation in the League of Nations was the responsibility of Joseph Tumulty, Wilson's secretary.

Tumulty charted "the course of the train in long diagonal swoops through the Midwest and far West, where opposition to the president was strongest, avoiding the East and West, where the League was popular," according to Alden Hatch, the biographer of Wilson's wife, Edith.

"Tumulty also had the task of coordinating arrangements for the speeches, parades, banquets, receptions, and hotel space with advance agents and pro-League citizens in each locality with whom he prepared detailed schedules called 'maneuver sheets,'" Hatch wrote.

"It was a complex business. Everyone wanted as much of the president's time as possible, and he had so little time. To keep him on a schedule and still avoid slighting any important local politicians or organizations was an extremely delicate feat of political social tightrope-walking. Tumulty managed it with great dexterity.

"Routing the train was an equally complicated operation which White House aide Edward Smithers worked out with the executives of the railroads involved," Hatch observed.[148]

Grace Tully, President Franklin Roosevelt's personal secretary, recalled that in planning his rail trip, the president "would first call in [a member of his staff] and the head of the White House Secret Service. . . . He would then inform them where he wanted to go and discuss with them the best route and facilities to use.

"The crews of Presidential trains were carefully chosen by the railroad companies providing the service," she explained.[149]

Because Roosevelt was paralyzed from the waist down as a result of polio, special arrangements had to be made for him to board and leave the train.

"Through most of his White House term he used a special ramp, about twenty feet in length and hooked at a stop to the rear platform, for boarding and leaving.

"By the combined ingenuity of [staff and Secret Service] and some Navy engineers, an elevator was designed during the war years to facilitate this loading problem under certain circumstances," Tully observed.[150]

But despite the most careful planning by staff, mistakes happened when politicians campaigned by train.

When Dwight Eisenhower stopped in Carmi, Illinois, in 1952, his campaign train overshot the station by several hundred yards, and people had to run to catch up with it. And then, the train stopped short of the depots at the next two stations.[151]

Lady Bird Johnson detailed in her memoir the planning and attention to detail that went into her 1964 campaign tour of the South on behalf of her husband, President Lyndon Johnson.

"The original schedule lasted ten days and covered fourteen states," she said. "We met for three hours. First, by my insistence and after much discussion, we whittled the trip down to four days. Next, we discussed whether the tour should end in Tallahassee, Florida, or go through Mississippi, Louisiana, and into New Orleans.

"I am anxious to concentrate heavily on North Carolina and give Virginia more stops than we had planned. We all agreed that we should bear down on Georgia. It was a profitable, long session, and I only found when it was over how dead tired I was."[152]

After the plans were finalized, and two days before the trip was formally announced, Mrs. Johnson called Liz Carpenter and told her, "Before we put this out in the newspapers, let's make the courtesy calls," Jan Jarboe Russell wrote in her book, *Lady Bird: A Biography of Mrs. Johnson.*

> By then, Lady Bird was a pro, having learned at the hands of her husband, the master politician. She understood that politics is a parlor game and that she needed to show all the players the cards in her hand—before they read about her trip in the newspapers—and do it in a personal enough way to persuade them to join her game.
>
> On September 9, she worked the telephone for eleven straight hours, calling every governor, senator, and congressman in eight southern states. Hour after hour, her message to each person that she reached was similar. "I'm thinking of coming down and campaigning in your state, and I'd love your advice," she told them disarmingly.
>
> Of course, the trip was already planned down to the last detail. Yes, she pretended to solicit their opinions. This was Lady Bird's own version of the Johnson treatment, a variation of the one that Southern women had used for generations to manipulate supposedly stouthearted men.[153]

In her memoir, *Ruffles and Flourishes*, Liz Carpenter, Lady Bird Johnson's press secretary, provided a behind-the-scenes look at the work that went into organizing the "Lady Bird Special."

Weeks before the event, accompanied by Secret Service agents and members of the Johnson campaign staff, Carpenter would make an inspection tour of the proposed route.

> Small Southern towns are made to order for Whistlestops. The depot is still downtown, right in the middle of the Main Street. J. C. Penney is on one side and International Harvester, with its shiny red tractors, on the other. A cotton gin is down the street. . . .
>
> These were sleepy little towns when our advance group went through, but it didn't take long for word to spread that strangers were in town from Washington. The routine was the same. Joe Moran would get the depot master and figure out the exact spot for the train to stop. Bill Brawley would call the local politicians. Jack Hight would touch base with the civic leaders. The Secret Service would scout the KKK situation. I would go into the depot and telephone the newspaper editor to get his advice. . . .
>
> Their advice was invaluable. They had their fingers on the pulse of their town. They could measure how much goodwill the Democrats had in the town.[154]

Weeks or months of careful planning were required to help ensure effective and successful campaign train tours.

In 1968, US senator Gaylord Nelson, a Democrat from Wisconsin, and Bronson La Follette, the Democratic nominee for governor of Wisconsin, spent three days seeking votes from the back of a campaign special. The route covered about half the state in a circle roughly between Milwaukee, Marshfield, Eau Claire, and Madison.

The trip, originally suggested by Nelson, took more than a year to plan and required a half dozen campaign aides to coordinate. The journey cost the campaign $18,000, which was eventually paid for by the Democratic Party of Wisconsin because other candidates were included on stops along the way.

To entertain the passengers on board and the crowds at each stop, the train carried a Dixieland band. Every time the campaign special pulled into a depot, the band rushed from the train to join the crowd on the platform near the observation car.

Warren J. Sawall, a member of Nelson's staff, recalled that three weeks before the train trip, he and other campaign aides drove the entire circuit from beginning to end with the trainmen who would be assigned particular segments of the tour.

"At each spot, we met the local coordinator, persons I had recruited during the previous several months. We marked out the exact spot where the train could stop on the platform, went over the program, and worked on procedures for building the local crowd.

"After a few days of rest and consideration of the problems that were still unresolved, I drove the entire route again the week before the event and followed up on what we had done on the first trip," according to Sawall.[155]

Bill Richardson, who was a Democratic member of Congress from New Mexico in the 1980s and '90s, traditionally staged an airplane blitz of his district with other candidates before

Election Day. In 1990, however, he told his staff that he wanted to do something different to generate more press coverage and remind voters of the old traditions of the Democratic Party.

A member of Richardson's staff suggested a Truman-style whistle-stop tour of the district, which Truman had visited in 1948.

Richardson took a hands-on role in helping to raise money for the train, offering advice on the route and seating arrangements, and serving as the master of ceremonies at each stop.

He encouraged other congressional candidates not to rely entirely on television spots. "Get back to the old days and old ways [of campaigning]," he pointed out. "The train gives you media, it gives you organization, and the public loves it."[156]

Bill Clinton's 1996 campaign train tour through five midwestern states, on his way to the Democratic National Convention in Chicago, dwarfed the tours of his recent predecessors, including Ford, Reagan, and George H. W. Bush, Amtrak noted.

"We're viewing this as the granddaddy of all of them. The penultimate, the most ambitious," said Mark Wasserman, an assistant vice president of Amtrak. The logistics were "incredibly complicated," he observed.

That's because four different railroad companies were involved, and because of the security-related precautions that had to be taken.

Clinton's thirteen-car train included "locomotives and two passenger cars," Gene Gibbons of Reuters reported. "A fourth train composed of two locomotives and two cars carrying more security people [brought] up the rear, and helicopters [scouted] the perimeter. Freight trains that normally travel the same right-of-way [were] being re-routed or delayed, rail officials said."[157]

In an effort to take full advantage of the photogenic nature of the campaign train, Democratic officials noted that "Harry Thomason, the Hollywood producer and close friend of the Clintons, [had] a central role in planning the trip, images of which [would] be beamed" to the Democratic National Convention.[158]

Indeed, Clinton's campaign train tour was the idea of Thomason and fellow Hollywood producer Mort Engelberg, according to the *Washington Post.*

Convention delegates received updates of the train ride from aerial shots, video-tracking maps, and live footage of Clinton's speeches along the way.[159]

A lot was riding on the success of the trip.

"The Clinton-Gore campaign is counting on the train ride to raise the pitch of enthusiasm by the time Clinton arrives at a convention that offers little other suspenseful drama," the *Washington Post* observed.

"This will give the delegates an update on the ride and a feeling of excitement and anticipation," said Gary Smith, another Hollywood producer who was working on the convention.[160]

In the rest of this chapter, we'll take a look behind the curtain at the blood, sweat, and tears involved in creating the traveling show of a whistle-stop campaign.

RAIDING THE WAR CHEST

The cost to rent a train car or conduct a full-scale campaign train tour steadily rose over time.

In the early 1900s, "the custom was that the president would purchase a drawing room at the regular fare and the railroads would provide a private car attached to a special train," pointed out Alden Hatch, the biographer of Edith Wilson, President Woodrow Wilson's wife.

On Wilson's 1919 campaign tour to build support for the US's participation in the League of Nations, the railroads "lost no money because over a hundred reporters accompanied the President, and their fares brought in a substantial sum," according to Hatch, author of *Edith Bolling Wilson: First Lady Extraordinary.*"[161]

Eugene Debs's "Red Special" campaign train cost $20,000, which he raised from contributions.[162]

In the 1930s and '40s, a campaign train could cost national political parties between $1,500 and $3,000 a day.[163]

It could be a challenge to collect what was owed by some of the passengers.

As Gordon Gordon noted in *Railroad Magazine*, "The conductors aboard these specials report no trouble with the correspondents, but the politicians often try to duck them, especially if they are riding the train only for a day or so.

"After one 10,000-mile campaign journey, a conductor reported he has worked harder at being a detective than at his job. The railroads themselves may often be stalled on their pay for as long as four years."[164]

In 1952, the estimated tab for each of Truman's train tours was $25,000.[165]

Republican presidential nominee Richard Nixon's 1968 train trip, which covered only 247 miles,[166] cost $100,000, about the same amount that the Democratic National Committee paid for Jimmy Carter's train in 1976.[167]

President Bill Clinton's 1996 train tour probably exceeded $750,000, according to White House spokesman Mike McCurry.[168]

Of that total, the Clinton campaign was reported to have paid $113,000. "News organizations are paying tens of thousands more to ride along and report the trip," Reuters wrote. "But these figures are dwarfed by the always-staggering cost of presidential security and communications arrangements."

McCurry stated that he didn't know the overall cost of the trip but acknowledged that the $113,000 price tag was low. "Obviously it costs considerably more than that to support the president when he travels."[169]

CONTROLLED CHAOS

Like snowflakes and fingerprints, no two political whistle-stop trains were alike. Each reflected the personalities of the candidates and the staff that it carried. Each had its own traits and peculiarities. And each made its own unique contribution to American political lore. Associated Press reporter Jack Bell describes several of the campaigns he covered:

> With Willkie in 1940, the whole operation could be described with one word—"chaos." Yet there was a spirit about it that was lacking on the more sedate and orderly special train that carried Eisenhower to his appointments with the people.
>
> The Dewey travels, and later those of Eisenhower, were model operations, so far as the press was concerned, because of the presence of [knowledgeable staff]. Riding about the country with Truman, however, always involved sheer exasperation, mixed with exuberance and a touch of exhaustion thrown in. Despite the efforts of patient [staff members], the advance texts of Truman's speeches seldom came out on time.

> There would often be a last-minute scramble, with [staff members] arriving at the press work car to provide some partial notes on the forthcoming talk only minutes before the train was to arrive at the city where the major address was scheduled. And then Truman sometimes disregarded his advance text and talked about something else.[170]

Richard H. Rovere, who traveled for a time on two whistle-stop campaign trains in 1948, wrote that "everything I've seen on the Dewey campaign train is slick and snappy. This is in strong contrast to the genteel rowdiness and good-natured slovenliness of the Truman campaign, at least when and where I observed it.

"Campaign trains become, in their few weeks of existence, compact social organizations; they develop their own mores and their own institutions. One of the most remarkable—indeed, almost weird—features of life on them is the way the spirit of the leading passenger, riding in the last car, seems to dominate and mold the spirit of the entourage.

"It's understandable that this should happen to the staff of the candidate, but it actually affects the newspapermen," Rovere observed.[171]

STEADY AS SHE GOES

The speed at which campaign trains traveled to their next destination could depend on the preferences of the politicians they carried.

"The candidates' taste as to speed have often been paradoxical," journalist Robert J. Donovan observed. "Thus, Herbert Hoover liked the train to go fast. Franklin Roosevelt insisted that his go slow. Harry S. Truman did not care how his train went just so it kept going."[172]

Truman biographer David McCullough said that "Truman liked to go about eighty" miles per hour.[173]

"Travel with FDR was, even in the context of the 1940s, amazingly leisurely," United Press reporter Merriman Smith reflected later. "Mr. Roosevelt delighted in a slow-speed train. He knew the various roadbeds of the country better than some railroad men. And he knew that reducing the rate of speed meant an easier ride. He also wanted the opportunity to sit by the window of his private car and study the passing countryside.

"He loved to astound his guests with amazingly detailed knowledge of the geography through which he was passing. He kept before him a small, neatly folded road map on which he followed the progress of the train," Smith recounted.[174]

But there was another reason why the wheelchair-bound FDR preferred slow train speeds.

"Train speed above thirty miles an hour forced the President to brace himself with extra care—a tiring requirement. As a consequence, daytime trips for the Boss were always set up within this thirty-mile-an-hour limit. At night, extra speed up to seventy miles was sometimes ordered," Tully noted in her memoir.[175]

But the train's speed could create some challenges.

President Franklin Roosevelt's 1944 train trip from Washington to San Diego "was so slow that the batteries on the sleeping cars would not recharge themselves sufficiently, and the train had to stop every two nights to pump power into the batteries from the Diesels in the radio car," according to UP reporter Merriman Smith.

"In fact, the trip . . . was so slow and boring," Smith remembered, that "I rode through most of Oklahoma atop the engine cab waving to astonished track walkers who never before saw a man riding on top of an engine."[176]

The slow pace of Roosevelt's train could cause a ripple effect and impact the schedules of other trains that ran on the same track.[177]

Not every aspiring candidate could use campaign trains, even if they wanted to.

First there had to be a railroad that went where they wanted to go. Then they had to be able to pay for, plan, and promote the trip.

But the lack of a train or tracks did not always prevent some candidates from staging campaign-train-style events.

In 1978, Wisconsin gubernatorial candidate Lee Dreyfus went on a seven-week, twenty-six-hundred-mile tour of the state in a sixteen-year-old school bus that was made to look like a campaign train.

The Republican candidate spoke to people from a rear platform, which was equipped with a public-address system, railing, and bunting.

The front of the "train" featured a cowcatcher, smokestack, and train whistle. The inside of the vehicle had a "dining car," sleeping accommodations, and a press room for journalists who were invited to accompany Dreyfus.[178]

Dean Gallo's 1984 campaign for Congress in New Jersey included a trolley-style engine and car decorated as a whistle-stop train.[179]

In 1992, Vermont Republican Timothy Philbin "set off from a Statehouse parking lot in a small bus painted with a red, white and blue eagle and fitted with a speaking platform and loudspeakers" that played a recording of a locomotive whistle, the Associated Press reported.[180]

THE

DREYFUS FOR GOVERNOR

... CAMPAIGN WHISTLE STOP SPECIAL

IS COMING TO TOWN

MEET LEE DREYFUS

A lack of railroad tracks in some states led some politicians to improvise when conducting campaign-train-style tours. Republican gubernatorial candidate Lee Dreyfus campaigned across Wisconsin from the back of a converted bus in his "Red Vest Whistle-Stop Special." As shown in this poster promoting the tour, the bus had a rear platform, speakers, and signs about his candidacy. The name referred to Dreyfus's trademark piece of clothing—a red vest. (Image courtesy of the Library of Congress, Prints & Photographs Division, Yanker Poster Collection.)

LOGGING MILES

Whistle-stopping candidates often kept grueling and strenuous schedules in order to meet and speak to as many people as possible.

In 1896, Democratic presidential candidate William Jennings Bryan made 570 speeches, spoke about 80,000 words a day, and covered 18,000 miles in twenty-nine states.[181]

President Theodore Roosevelt traveled 21,209 miles in 1904 and made 673 speeches.[182]

In 1908, President William Howard Taft racked up 114,500 miles and made 418 whistle-stop speeches.[183]

Politicians did not always speak to friendly audiences at train stations. This illustration from *Puck* magazine shows President William H. Taft speaking in 1909 from the back of a railroad caboose to a large crowd of skeptical Midwesterners. One man is holding a sign that says "We're from Missouri, also Wisconsin, Minnesota, Nebraska, Dakota & Iowa. Show us!" Taft is holding papers behind his back titled "Notes for speech how new tariff will benefit the West." (1909 illustration by L. M. Glackens for *Puck*. Courtesy of the Library of Congress, Prints & Photographs Division, LC-DIG-ppmsca-26410.)

Franklin D. Roosevelt set the record for train travel by presidents—more than 240,000 miles on almost 400 trips[184]—which included 50,000 miles on the "Ferdinand Magellan," the specially built Pullman car.[185]

LONG HOURS AND HARD WORK

"It was quite a campaign. I worked my staff almost to death," Truman wrote about his September 1948 train tour. "I believe that at one time or another I put them all to bed, and despite its long hours and hard work I gained weight during the campaign. I worked the reporters very hard too."[186]

The pace got more hectic as the tour continued. "As the campaign gathered speed," Truman remembered, "I stepped up my schedule of the whistle stops. In all, I traveled about 31,700 miles and delivered more than three hundred speeches—356 to be exact.

"I was used to hard work, and my job was cut out for me. I campaigned for thirty-five days and averaged about ten speeches every day. On one single day I delivered sixteen speeches," he noted.[187]

"The work went on from seven in the morning until past midnight day after day until they lost all sense of time, until every day became merged with every other day, and everything became a blur," historian David McCullough wrote in his book *Truman.*

Margaret Truman "would remember the world beginning to seem like an endless railroad track. She would sit by the window and take idle snapshots of the passing countryside—telephone poles whizzing past empty plains, country roads that seemed to lead nowhere," according to McCullough.[188]

He observed that "for everyone riding the Truman train, the

A Herblock Cartoon, © The Herb Block Foundation, used under license.

campaign had become an unimaginable ordeal—interminable, exhausting in a way comparable to nothing in their experience."[189]

One staff member "suffered from arthritis and heart trouble, yet worked twelve, fourteen hours a day, knowing how much Truman counted on him. 'For years afterward,' Clark Clifford said, 'I'd sometimes wake up at night in a cold perspiration thinking I was back on that terrible train.'"[190]

Truman recalled that a typical day on his campaign train tour would start at 5:00 a.m. Then, "the first time where there was a stop, I'd get off and take a walk. And, of course, they had to hold the train as long as I wanted it held. I was President."[191]

McCullough wrote that "the candidate, who bore the main brunt, seemed indefatigable, his outlook entirely positive. Between speeches, he could lie down and go immediately to sleep, however pressed others were, however rough the roadbed. 'Give me twenty minutes,' he would say.

"'Strain seemed to make him calmer and more firm,'" Truman staff member Jonathan Daniels said. "'At no point in the entire campaign did any of the staff, or the press, or his family ever see Truman show a sign of failing stamina or failing confidence.'"[192]

Different candidates handled the pressure of whistle-stopping differently.

"Ike has had a hell of a time," Eisenhower aide Homer Gruenther observed. "He is pressed too much, but these whistle-stop campaigns demand stops in almost every city. We stop about every thirty-five minutes, and he talked from five to fifteen minutes. It is generally five. But he no more gets off the platform and seated, than it is time to get up and give another talk. . . . Almost every day, he throws off more steam than the train. But he does a pretty good job laughing outside while he is steaming inside. I know very well when he is saying, 'Senator, it is great to have you with us,' he is saying inside, 'You son-of-a-bitch, what in the hell are you doing on this train?' Sometimes, though, he almost reverses these thoughts."[193]

PERSONAL PRIORITIES

"One of the first things I discovered on the campaign train was that I was cut off from my customary sources of information and intelligence," Truman aide Ken Hechler said in his book, *Working with Truman: A Personal Memoir of the White House Years.* "I couldn't switch on radio or television to find out what was happening in the world. There is scarcely time during a ten-minute stop to jump off and get a newspaper. If the President wanted a fact or figure checked before using it, I couldn't pick up a telephone and go right to an accurate source—I had to take enough material along to supply the answer immediately. At some stops, I jumped off the train, made a beeline for a shop that might have a pay telephone, and made a quick long-distance call to double-check some obscure fact we had to verify.

"Being out of touch with the outside world produced embarrassing situations also, despite the up-to-date communication system managed by the United States Army Signal Corps in a railroad car filled with elaborate equipment and coding devices for classified messages," Hechler admitted.[194]

Whenever President Franklin Roosevelt traveled by trains on weekends, the Catholic passengers on board would rise early on Sundays to attend church. One morning when they returned from services, Roosevelt was sitting up in bed in silk pajamas, enjoying a second cup of coffee and some cigarettes. He told the passengers as they reboarded the train, "Well, one of us is wrong!"[195]

BETWEEN STOPS

The time it took for a train to travel from one station to another provided candidates and their staff with an opportunity to rest, catch up on their work, or prepare for the next scheduled depot rally.

"Between stops, Truman read intensively an evolving work called 'The Book,' a compendium prepared by one of his aides in which local personages, projects, and local lore were briefly sketched," *White House Fever* author Robert Bendiner said.[196]

Eisenhower aide Robert Cutler remembered that campaign songs about the candidate and his wife, Mamie, would play on the train's loudspeakers between stops. At one point, Eisenhower could not concentrate on his work because of the music. Cutler said that "word would come from the Candidate, seated in the rear parlor and hard at work with (another colleague) and me on the night speech: 'Turn that darn thing off! It's driving us crazy!'"[197]

On one occasion, a politician had to deal with an unfolding crisis during his campaign trip.

Richard Nixon had no sooner started his tour of California in 1952 than he learned from Republican Party headquarters in Los Angeles that an article would be published the next day about allegations that he had improperly used what became known as the "Nixon Fund," a hidden political stash of about $18,000 that he'd collected from supporters in California.[198]

"It still did not seem serious to me, but I decided to talk the matter over with four of my advisors in the lounge of my private car," Nixon recalled.

"The consensus that night among our little strategy group was to ignore the attacks, on the theory that answering them would simply give them more publicity and would play into the hands of those making the attacks. This, I knew, was generally sound political strategy.

"'Let's wait and see what they do,' I said.

"We did not have to wait long. The next morning the attack began."

Reflecting on the event in his memoir *Six Crises*, Nixon wrote, "I was worried not about the campaign fund story but rather about the split-second timing we needed in order to make ten whistle-stops a day on our tour of the Central Valley of California and into Oregon and the state of Washington."[199]

The Democratic-leaning *New York Post* carried the first reports of the fund—somewhat sensationalized accounts that, in Nixon's words, "let me have it with both barrels," the *Washington Post* reported. "An avalanche of coverage followed, and soon the 'secret fund' was the central issue of the presidential campaign.

"Though legal, the previously undisclosed nest egg caused such a stir that Nixon was nearly forced from GOP presidential nominee Dwight D. Eisenhower's ticket. Some of Eisenhower's staff and key party elders wanted Nixon to step down; former GOP presidential nominee and New York Gov. Thomas E. Dewey personally urged Nixon to resign.

"Nixon saved himself with a dramatic if maudlin television appeal that became known as the 'Checkers speech,' so named because of a cocker spaniel dog given by a supporter to his young daughters which Nixon swore never to give up, come what may in the political wars," the *Washington Post* reported.[200]

During Bill Clinton's 1996 campaign train tour, the Democratic presidential candidate "stood glued to the observation car platform for miles, shouting 'hello's' and 'thank you's' into a microphone for pockets of Ohioans who gathered trackside for a glimpse of their president," the Associated Press reported.

"Whenever the whim struck him, Clinton reached for the lever above his head that blew the booming train whistle. 'I love this,' he enthused."[201]

ALL IN THE FAMILY

Whistle-stopping politicians sometimes brought their wives and children on their campaign train tours and introduced them at trackside rallies.

Antoinette Hughes, the wife of 1916 presidential candidate Charles Evans Hughes, was the first spouse of a candidate to go on an extended train tour.

Hughes's biographer Merlo J. Pusey observed that "she tried to shield him from visitors when he was worn out, curtailed his talking when his voice was overstrained, and pulled his coat-tail when she thought he had spoken long enough. She won the heart of everybody. Tall, slight, and dressed in good taste . . . she impressed thousands as the ideal companion for a presidential candidate.

"As she sat at a tiny table in the 'Constitution,' pouring grape juice for the men of the press, Hughes tenderly waved his hand toward her and exclaimed, 'Gentlemen—the greatest asset of the Republican Party.'"[202]

"Lou Henry Hoover dutifully accompanied her husband [Herbert] on his campaign tours, although she limited her role to waving at the crowd [from the back of the train] and chatting with dignitaries who joined them on the platform," according to historian Donald A. Ritchie. "Always a crowd pleaser, she elicited warm applause but made no speeches and followed the unwritten rule that First Ladies granted no interviews," he noted.[203]

James Roosevelt often accompanied his father on campaign train tours, including FDR's 1932 cross-country trip. As he recalled in his memoir,

> One of my campaign chores was to appear on the rear platform at the midnight to 6 A.M. stops and try to explain to the faithful few who gathered even at those hours that Father had to sleep some time.
>
> One morning in Seattle, after coming out at 2 A.M., I decided to stretch my legs on the platform. I was accosted by a tall, thin, determined female, who said:
>
> "You're that Roosevelt boy, ain't you?"
>
> "Yes, ma'am!" I admitted, flashing her my best eager-beaver campaign smile and extending my hand.
>
> "Young man," she said, ignoring my hand, "I came here to see your Pa. Now you just go right in that train and fetch him out!"
>
> I tried to explain how weary Father was and how cruel it would be to awaken him. The more I talked, the madder she got, and finally she began hitting me on my naked head with her umbrella. I turned tail and ran.
>
> She was in hot pursuit, still whamming me with the umbrella, when [Secret Service agent] Gus Gennerich came down the platform and rescued me. Pa had the story from Gus before I even awoke that morning and thought it was the funniest incident of the campaign.[204]

Republican presidential nominee Wendell Willkie's "family included his wife, Edith, his son Philip, and two brothers, Edward and Fred. Fred was on the Special only for a few days," Mary Earhart Dillon wrote in her book *Wendell Willkie: 1892–1944*. "Mrs. Willkie became a favorite with the crowds that met the train for platform speeches. Frequently she was called for by the crowd before it was quite time to present her. Although she never spoke a word, her gracious smile and friendly manner were highly satisfying. Edward was the official greeter of visitors aboard the Willkie Special when the candidate was otherwise occupied."[205]

"As a regular finale to his whistle-stop act, Harry Truman would ask the crowd: 'How ja like to meet ma family?' First, Mrs. Truman would be presented as 'the boss.' And then Margaret, often as 'the boss's boss,'" wrote Robert Bendiner, author of *White House Fever.*

And "in his 1952 whistle-stopping, Eisenhower would often beckon his wife to the platform and say something like 'And folks, here's my Mamie.' Mrs. Willkie was often greeted by a band rendition of 'Let Me Call You Sweetheart.'"[206]

Eleanor Roosevelt did not enjoy campaigning as much as her husband Franklin did, and thought it was in poor taste to go out and electioneer for him, journalist Bess Furman, reported.

Furman, who traveled with Eleanor Roosevelt for two weeks in 1936, asked what her rules were for campaign trains. Mrs. Roosevelt listed six:[207]

1. Always be on time.
2. Never try to make any personal engagements.
3. Do as little talking as humanly possible.
4. Remember to lean back in the parade car so that everybody can see the president.

5. Be sure and not get fat, because you will have to sit three people in the back seat (of the car).
6. Get out of the way as quickly as you can when you are not needed.

"Eleanor thus boarded Franklin's train anticipating a full ration of anonymity," according to presidential historian David Pietrusza, author of *Roosevelt Sweeps Nation: FDR's 1936 Landslide and the Triumph of the Liberal Ideal*. "This was, after all, Franklin's show. And alongside Franklin on his rear platform, there was only so much room—and never any shortage of local politicians lusting to fill it (a detail to which Franklin paid immense attention)."

But, as Scripps-Howard columnist Ruth Finney documented, the "crowds wanted Mrs. Roosevelt. If she failed to appear on the platform, they shouted for her until she did appear, and they cheered her just as heartily as her husband, sometimes more heartily. She smiled and waved but made no speeches. She never does when her husband is about."[208]

Pat Nixon accompanied her husband, Richard, on his 1952 campaign train trip.[209] She handed out autographed menus to the children who had crowded around her coach at one depot.

"She was still smiling and waving to the hundreds of children and adults standing in the [railroad] yards as the train gathered speed," a reporter wrote.[210]

LBJ's wife and daughters accompanied him on all or portions of his train trips when he ran for vice president in 1960.[211]

Chelsea Clinton, Bill and Hillary Clinton's daughter, who "until (then had been) carefully shielded from the exposure of public life, made her political debut . . . on her father's whistle-stop train trip" in 1996, Reuters reported.

"Chelsea, 16, was at President Bill Clinton's side as he rode the rails through parts of West Virginia, Kentucky and Ohio, and was introduced at every stop. She even worked rope lines, shaking hands with excited fans," the wire service said.[212]

IS THERE A DOCTOR ABOARD?

The stress, strain, and hectic pace on the whistle-stop campaign trail could take a toll on candidates and staff and, on occasion, resulted in health issues while they were on the train.

As First Lady Edith Wilson wrote in *My Memoir,* toward the end of August 1919, "when there was apparently no more [President Woodrow Wilson] could do to get the [Treaty of Versailles] ratified by the Senate, he said that as a last resort he must go to the country to explain to the people what failure to ratify would mean. His hope was that an aroused public opinion would force the Senate to yield.

"The proposed trip was opposed by Dr. [Cary] Grayson [President Wilson's personal physician], who did not think the president could draw further on his strength without risking disaster. They had several talks, very serious talks, the Doctor pointing out the effect of the heat and discomfort of a month on the train, the perpetual strain of speaking and handshaking, the endless luncheons, dinners, parades and receptions—in short, all the noise and excitement and absolute denial of rest or privacy that attend a president wherever he goes.

"'Yes,' my husband said, 'all that is true; but I feel it is my duty, and my own health is not to be considered when the future peace and security of the world are at stake.' . . . To this neither Dr. Grayson nor I could find an answer."[213]

Woodrow Wilson went on the national campaign train trip the

next month, in September 1919. But the tour's intense schedule—eight thousand miles in twenty-two days—cost Wilson his health. He suffered constant headaches during the tour, finally collapsing from exhaustion in Pueblo, Colorado, in late September.[214]

In her memoir, Mrs. Wilson pointed out that there was "never a moment to relax and rest. And so on across the continent. From one city to the next a small local committee would accompany us, which meant constant entertaining even on the train. . . . I could not remain blind to the physical sacrifice he was making and must wonder if it were not too great. . . . Doctor Grayson's disregarded warnings against attempting the tour haunted my sleep."[215]

Dr. Howard Markel wrote in an article for *PBS NewsHour* that "on September 26, the president's private secretary, Joseph Tumulty, announced that the rest of the speaking tour had been canceled because the president was suffering from 'a nervous reaction in his digestive organs.'"[216]

Wilson's train, the "Mayflower," "sped directly back to Washington's Union Station. Upon arrival, on September 28, the president appeared ill but was able to walk on his own accord through the station. He tipped his hat to [the] awaiting crowd, shook the hands of a few of the people along the track's platform, and was whisked away to the White House for an enforced period of rest and examination by a battery of doctors," Markel said.

As with Woodrow Wilson, some of Franklin Roosevelt's associates advised him not to go on his 1932 campaign train tour. "They knew Republicans were casting doubts on his health and stamina and were afraid that nervous exhaustion or even a slight accident en route might play into their hands," according to Paul F. Boller Jr., author of *Presidential Campaigns* and an emeritus professor of history at Texas Christian University.

"Well, I'm going anyhow," FDR told advisor James Farley and publicity director Charley Michelson. "I'm not going to take a doctor along either," he stated firmly.[217]

Franklin Roosevelt loved a crowd and relished public speaking, but even he found the pace could be grueling, historian Richard Ellis observed. "Barely an hour would go by before the train would pull into another station where another enthusiastic crowd awaited, expecting their president to appear, wave, smile, and speak," Ellis noted.

Toward the end of one campaign train tour, Roosevelt told Henry Cabot Lodge Sr. that the trip had been "very severe" and had him "feeling jaded and tired. . . . Now, thank heavens, I have little more than a week left."[218]

Months after completing one tour, Roosevelt admitted to a friend that as much as he "liked and respected . . . [the] many thousands of mostly friendly and often enthusiastic citizens . . . I could not [to] save my neck, differentiate one town from another or one crowd from another."

He said that the grueling schedules of appearances and speeches "were very hard and rather monotonous. . . . Much though I liked them and glad though that I was there to see them, it was inevitable that I should begin repeating myself unless I wished to become merely famous."[219]

Mary Earhart Dillon, author of *Wendell Willkie: 1892–1944*, told the story of when the Republican presidential candidate's voice was husky as his train left Chicago. "The first day of the campaign tour had been a long, fatiguing strain. He had refused to use a microphone as he was unused to the instrument and considered it an obstruction to his methods of speaking.

"The next principal objective was Coffeyville in Kansas, with train speeches along the way. . . . With each back-platform speech, Willkie's voice became more strained until by the time he reached Rock Island, he could only whisper to the crowd: 'The spirit is willing, but the voice is weak.'" Dillon continued:

> As his throat condition became worse, so did the anxiety among his associates on the Willkie Special. They pleaded with him not to speak to the crowds that gathered at the railway stations but merely to wave them a greeting.
>
> Willkie protested that the people had come to hear him talk, and he did not want to disappoint them. Meanwhile, a telegram had been sent to Dr. Harold D. Barnard, a Hollywood throat specialist, who was flown from California by Robert Montgomery, the movie star and a warm friend of the candidate, and who met the train on Sunday in Kansas City. When the eminent physician confronted the patient, he was greeted by a cold glare.
>
> "Lean back and open your mouth," said Dr. Barnard.
>
> "Go to hell and take your tools with you," growled Willkie in a raspy whisper.
>
> Dr. Barnard looked at him a moment and said calmly, "Personally, I don't give a damn. But that throat of yours right now is the only way some twenty million Americans can express themselves. Lean back!"
>
> Willkie looked at the doctor, suddenly grinned, and opened his mouth. Dr. Barnard relieved anxiety on the Willkie Special by his announcement that there was no throat infection but only some

Concerned aides watch as a doctor examines a politician aboard his campaign train. (Cover illustration by Peter Arno for the *New Yorker*, September 20, 1952.)

> badly strained vocal cords. He ordered the patient not to speak again until he reached Coffeyville.[220]

Candidates often maintained a frenetic pace and would use every opportunity to connect with their audiences.

About Dwight Eisenhower speaking from the rear platform, one of his aides observed, "This guy never misses anyone. He waves to the right, then to the left, then he turns around and waves to the rear, and finally looks up and waves to people in windows or perched on roofs. If he sees a nose sticking out beyond a post, he waves."[221]

Eisenhower's pace on his October 1952 campaign train tour could have been a contributing factor to a health scare he had while the train was traveling through central Pennsylvania.

His aide, Robert Cutler, recalled the time when Eisenhower—"after five prior informal talks on that day—suddenly experienced a sense of exhaustion.

"His high color faded; his strong voice slackened. [Major General Howard McCrum Snyder, Eisenhower's personal physician] immediately put him to bed, not to be disturbed until arrival at Pittsburgh. Everything was canceled—work, visitors, another appearance on the rear platform. . . . The indisposition was very slight, suddenly appearing and disappearing."

Cutler noted that "the incident raised a red flag. The Candidate's short informal talks were somewhat reduced in number."[222]

DANGEROUS SITUATIONS

Sometimes the train itself posed dangers to politicians and the people who came to see them at depots.

After President Theodore Roosevelt's train arrived at the railroad station in Lake Mills, Wisconsin, in April 1903, the train unexpectedly moved backward into the crowd that had gathered to hear Roosevelt speak from the rear platform. People immediately scattered to safety.

"While some were slightly bruised in the scramble, no one was seriously hurt," according to one news account.[223]

On October 4, 1912, when he was governor of New Jersey, Woodrow Wilson "had a narrow escape from what could have proved a serious accident. A freight locomotive 'sideswiped' the rear cars of the train which was bearing the Presidential candidate," the *Brooklyn Daily Eagle* reported.

"The engine ripped through the rear cars of the Wilson train and damaged the car in which the Governor was sleeping. Curiously enough, Governor Wilson did not know of the accident until this morning. He did not even wake, in spite of the fact that the crash aroused nearly everyone else on the train. The observation car was badly splintered. So were several other cars, including the sleeper, which accommodated the Wilson party."[224]

One presidential candidate was almost killed by his own campaign train.

In 1916, Charles Evans Hughes narrowly escaped being run down at the railroad station in Oswego, New York, when a limousine carrying him and his wife stalled on the railroad tracks. "Suddenly, the locomotive pushed its way around the curve [and headed toward the Hugheses' car].

"There were frightened cries, and men, tearing off their coats, waved them as a warning to the engineer. The chauffeur of the Hughes car worked frantically to back out of danger," the *Harrisburg Telegraph* reported.

"Fifty men in the crowd, regardless of personal danger, bent their shoulders to the task of pushing the automobile from the tracks and the engineer of the train jammed on the brakes. He got the train under control with twelve feet to spare.

"During the excitement, Mr. and Mrs. Hughes sat quietly in the closed car, making no effort to get out. When the excitement was over, Mr. Hughes shook hands with the chauffeur and told him not to worry about the incident. The crowd cheered."[225]

Some trains could be dangerous for the crews that operated them. That was certainly the case in Woonsocket, Rhode Island, when "the engineer of Governor James M. Cox's special train was compelled to jump from the moving locomotive today when the flue burst, flooding the cab with scalding steam," the *Evening News* in Harrisburg, Pennsylvania, recounted in 1920.

"With great presence of mind, the engineer threw on the emergency brakes before taking the plunge, the train coming to a stop within a hundred yards of a regular passenger train close behind flagged by a trainman."[226]

The month before, in September 1920, Governor James M. Cox's train derailed near Maricopa, Arizona. Cox escaped uninjured, and members of the governor's party crawled through the windows of the coaches to safety, according to one newspaper.[227]

More than thirty years later, a different kind of accident disrupted a candidate's rally at the train station in New London, Connecticut.

"A platform collapsed a moment after Gov. Adlai E. Stevenson stepped onto it today, throwing three movie stars to their knees and jolting some of Stevenson's staff," the United Press wrote on October 27, 1952.

"The shaky wooden platform split in the middle and dropped a foot. The Democratic Presidential nominee fell just before it gave way. . . . Humphrey Bogart, his wife, Lauren Bacall, and Robert Evans didn't move fast enough and were thrown to their knees but were not hurt.

"The microphones were moved to a new spot and Stevenson began his speech with a reference to the crowded conditions that caused the platform's collapse.

"'It looks,' he said, 'like everybody is trying to get on the Democratic platform.'"[228]

A few days later, his campaign train backed up suddenly into a crowd of Stevenson supporters at a train station in Silver Spring, Maryland. Reporters dubbed it a "ghost train" because the candidate—Illinois governor Adlai Stevenson—was not on it. He had been forced to return to Illinois to deal with a prison riot.[229]

The United Press said that the train "overshot its scheduled stopping place by about 100 feet. When the crowd . . . rushed toward the back platform, the train suddenly backed up, causing dozens of persons to scramble for safety. No one was hurt."[230]

In 1968, the campaign train of Illinois Democratic US Senate candidate William G. Clark came to an abrupt halt when it struck and killed a dump truck driver at a railroad crossing outside Normal, Illinois. Tire marks indicated that the driver "veered at the last moment in a vain attempt to avoid being struck," according to one news report.[231]

Fast-forward to 1996, when "a 20-foot-tall speaker stand toppled into the crowd of 40,000 waiting to see President Clinton in Michigan City, Indiana, injuring at least a dozen people.

"The victims, at least two of whom were bleeding profusely, wore neck braces as they were carried out of the crowd on stretchers," according to the *Tampa Bay Times*. "The spectators were hurt when the portable stand, made of gray metal and holding two [public address] speakers . . . fell as the crowds waited for Clinton's train to arrive for its last campaign stop before the Democratic convention in Chicago."[232]

DECEPTIONS

On some occasions, stand-ins deceived people into thinking they had seen or heard the president or a presidential candidate.

On President Benjamin Harrison's cross-country train trip in 1891, a Pullman conductor made an apparently impromptu decision to present himself as the president of the United States when he thought Harrison had retired for the evening.

"The train halted for a few moments in a section of Arkansas woods and a crowd of hillbillies [as reported by the *Pullman News*] demanded a speech."

The conductor "thanked his fellow citizens of the great state of Arkansas" in a few words, and they, nothing wiser, applauded lustily. As the train moved ahead, a slight noise behind him caused the conductor to turn. To his embarrassment, he discovered Harrison in short sleeves convulsed with laughter.

The conductor's apologies were cut short by Harrison's assurance that "no president could have done better."[233]

Socialist presidential candidate Eugene Debs would often speak to any crowd who wanted to hear him. The grueling pace eventually took its toll while he was on the campaign trail in 1908.

Debs's biographer, Ray Ginger, wrote, "He was now so weary that he could hardly crawl out of his berth, and the sound of his voice had scarcely died out before he was back in bed. His throat felt raw and tired; a metal band seemed to be tightening across his forehead. Day after endless day, Debs drove himself out on the rear platform to smile and wave at the adoring hundreds. . . .

"But the time finally arrived when he just could not stand the pace. It became obvious that Debs would never finish the trip unless he conserved his energy."

Debs's brother Theodore and campaign aide Stephen Reynolds devised a scheme to help provide the candidate with some needed rest. Ginger recounted:

> Theodore was almost a dead ringer for his brother, except that he was nine years younger. When a crowd in a station yard at night began to shout for Debs, Theodore turned up his coat collar, pulled down his hat brim and stepped onto the back platform. Reynolds hastily announced that "Comrade Debs is quite tired; we are now behind schedule; we have a very important meeting in the next town; Comrade Debs will not speak." Then Theodore quickly stepped back into the coach. A few days of this favored treatment gave Debs a chance to partially regain his strength. The accustomed fire came back into Debs' voice.[234]

Early one evening in 1908, William Jennings Bryan's train approached Newport, Kentucky, just across the river from Cincinnati. Among those on board was Congressman Albert Berry, who represented the region and was anxious for constituents to see him campaigning alongside Bryan.

But as the train approached the depot, Berry was told that Bryan had just taken off his shirt and was busy working on a speech. The alarmed congressman claimed he would be ruined

This 1908 cartoon from *Puck* magazine shows 1908 presidential candidates William Jennings Bryan and William H. Taft debating from the rear of a railroad car while whistle-stop campaigning. The surrounding vignettes show the politicians shaking hands, kissing babies, awarding prizes at county fairs, tossing a medicine ball, and so forth. (Illustration by John S. Pughe for *Puck* magazine, August 12, 1908. Image courtesy of the Library of Congress, Prints & Photographs Division, LC-DIG-ppmsca-26297.)

politically if Bryan failed to speak on his behalf, especially after he had appeared at other stops earlier that day.

A reporter on board the train heard Berry's laments and decided to go to his rescue. The correspondent, whose build and facial features resembled the candidate's, borrowed Bryan's hat and placed it on his own head.

As the train pulled slowly into the station, Congressman Berry escorted the reporter out to the back platform, where they were greeted by the crowd with a roar of applause. It's doubtful that any of the townspeople had ever seen Bryan in person or knew what he sounded like, but all were familiar with the newspaper pictures that showed him wearing a broad-rimmed hat.

The reporter went on to deliver a brief speech similar to the one he had heard the candidate deliver before. Bryan, who had approved the charade, kept out of sight in his private railroad car.[235]

Journalist Bernard Asbell recalled that "on FDR's 1936 campaign train tour, the Democratic presidential candidate admitted he was tired of sitting by the window of his railcar and waving to the crowds at every town the train passed through. That's when he asked White House usher William D. Simmons, 'How would you like to be President for a while? Only for a little while. Maybe an hour or two.'

"With a flourish, [Roosevelt] turned over his cigarette holder to Simmons and showed him how to wave a big, open-fingered hand in the Rooseveltian manner and how to smile a big, open-jawed smile," according to Asbell.

"'Fine! Fine!' the President said again. 'Now, every time we pass a town, just sit there and wave. I'm tired. I'm going to take a nap.' And he wheeled out of the lounge."

All across Arkansas, "Simmons sat by the President's window. At each town, the train slowed, not too little, nor too much, just enough so the local townsfolk could experience the incomparable thrill of seeing" someone who appeared to be Franklin Roosevelt waving to them, Asbell said.[236]

Tom Evans, an aide to then-Senator Harry Truman, remembered that on Truman's 1944 whistle-stop tour of the country, "we couldn't stop in the smaller towns, of course, and Senator Truman gave me the job of standing outside on the back of the platform and waving at the people as we went through.

"Of course, I'm much taller than Truman, but I do have gray hair, and I wear glasses, and I can wave. And we went through so fast that people never knew the difference. But that was the big job I had in the campaign of 1944," Evans recalled.[237]

Similarly, people who thought they saw Dwight Eisenhower wave to them from his 1952 campaign train as it sped by could have been fooled into believing it. That's because Eisenhower aide Gruenther claimed that he was "a stand-in for Ike when [they went] fast. . . . I wave with Mamie [from the rear platform] to the crowds and they're thrilled to have 'seen Ike,'" he recalled.[238]

MISSED CONNECTIONS

Sometimes, despite the best-laid plans, a campaign train sped right by a town or train depot where people had gathered expecting to hear from the candidate.

That was the case in October 1952, when vice-presidential candidate Richard Nixon's eighteen-car train did not stop as expected in Merrillan, Wisconsin. "A crowd of 600 persons converged on Merrillan Friday afternoon hoping to hear a whistle-stop talk by Sen. Richard Nixon, but had to be content with the whistle," the *Marshfield News-Herald* reported. "The train did not stop."[239]

Something similar happened on the Kerry-Edwards campaign in 2004. "I was sitting up in the small lounge at the back of our car when I heard it, the growing sound of cheers and screams," Elizabeth Edwards (wife of vice-presidential candidate John Edwards) wrote in the campaign's blog diary. "We raised our hands to wave, but the engineer hadn't slowed down, and by the time we had waved even a little to the signs and cheers and camera flashes, it was dark again. We sat frustrated—but we know we were not as frustrated as the people of Lawrence, Kansas, who stood until 1:00 a.m. for the train to pass through."[240]

To help make up for the snafu, the Kerry-Edwards campaign

arranged for John Kerry's running mate to return for a campaign rally in a local park, with the train as a backdrop. A heavy rain forced the campaign to hold an indoor event instead, at a former factory.[241]

Sometimes planned campaign train trips were canceled or postponed.

In 1972, a whistle-stop train tour in Rhode Island to promote the reelection campaign of Senator Claiborne Pell was canceled because his marquee guest—Mrs. Jacqueline Onassis—announced she could not attend because of a court case.

"Mrs. Onassis said she deeply regrets the decision but feels the appearance in this campaign activity could be detrimental to her lawsuit in the [Ron] Galella case," according to a Pell spokesperson. Galella was a photographer involved in a New York court battle with Onassis over his right to photograph her.[242]

John Anderson had to scrap a planned five-day whistle-stop tour in several states during his 1980 run for the White House. An Anderson spokesperson announced the tour was canceled because of "a large number of complicated problems" involving the logistics of the trip.

The Associated Press said, "The whistlestop tour was intended to emphasize Anderson's repeated campaign theme that the big cities of the Upper Midwest and Northwest need help to avoid bankruptcy. It was also intended to give Anderson some much-needed television coverage at a time when his standing in the polls [had] fallen."[243]

"The Anderson campaign [had] been pinched for money lately, but it was not clear if canceling the trip was related to a general drop off in contributions," the news outlet observed.[244]

Anderson eventually overcame the challenges of doing a train tour, which he conducted just days before the election.[245]

Sometimes candidates' family members had a direct hand in helping make a campaign train tour possible.

Jay Tunney, the son of boxing champion Gene Tunney, the younger brother of former US senator John Tunney, and a Democrat from California, recalled, "I personally spent the last nine months of my brother John's 1970 senatorial campaign in New York City raising badly needed money."

Nonetheless, Tunney said, "I was involved from a distance in helping with the decision to put in place a campaign train in the Central Valley of California so we could show the candidate 'real time' to the voters in what had become an increasingly TV dominant political campaign culture."

He noted that "the train tactic was of course borrowed from Truman, the Kennedys, Pierre Salinger and Gov. Pat Brown. [It] was successful mainly because John exuded a sincerity and warm friendliness with people that everyone appreciated. He never cut people off or made them feel as though they weren't worthy of their own opinions. He was a very kind guy."[246]

In 1982, Iowa State Representative Jean Lloyd-Jones, a Democrat, had to cancel a planned campaign train tour because the trip would be too costly. The railroad company was going to charge $9,750 to operate the train.[247]

Wisconsin governor Tommy G. Thompson suggested that President George H. W. Bush do a cross-country whistle-stop campaign train tour leading up to the start of the Republican National Convention in Houston, Texas.

"Go on a train from Washington, DC, to Houston . . . go to listen to America," Thompson advised.

But the trip never happened. "It got vetoed by Secret Service," Thompson lamented. "The campaign said it would be too costly, too hard."[248]

Former senator Adlai E. Stevenson III, the Illinois Democrat whose father campaigned for president by train in 1952 and 1956, recalled he'd "considered whistle-stops once or twice in my own career, but we always found the logistical difficulties overwhelming."[249]

President Truman's 1948 national train tour almost had to be canceled in the midst of the tour in Oklahoma City.

"We ran out of money," Truman recalled, "and some of them got in a panic again and said we'd have to call off the campaign and go back to Washington, but we raised it. We never had much, but we raised enough to finish the trip. And then we got enough money for a second trip."[250]

VIPS

To help attract crowds, movie stars, other celebrities, and politicians were often invited to ride along on whistle-stop trains and appear at depot rallies. Some VIPs would board the campaign special when the train entered their state or congressional district. They would depart after conferring with the candidate in private or appearing with them on the back platform.

A guest on one of Franklin Roosevelt's campaign trains in 1936 was Lyndon Baines Johnson, who later became president himself. "'I've just met the most remarkable young man' Roosevelt later told White House aide Tommy Corcoran. 'Now I like this boy, and you're going to help him with anything you can.'"[251]

In 1948, Johnson, who by then was a member of Congress, also appeared on Harry Truman's rear platform.[252] Truman endorsed Johnson in his Senate race, urging Texans to vote for all Democrats in the November election, "and a Democratic senator in the form of Lyndon B. Johnson."[253]

Johnson "boarded the train at San Antonio and stayed all day," Truman aide Clark Clifford remembered. "Truman would call him out every time we stopped at the end of his speech and say, 'Now here I want you to meet your next senator' and hold [Johnson's] hand up. I'm satisfied that that was one of the great contributing factors to Johnson's election."[254]

Jane Dick, vice chairman of the Volunteers for Adlai Stevenson organization, told of the time when Hollywood stars Lauren Bacall and Humphrey Bogart "had offered to do anything they could for Stevenson—not just as entertainers, but as workers. It was decided that one of their most useful contributions would be to ride on the campaign train. The advance publicity that they were aboard was practically guaranteed to attract large crowds to our whistle stops. They willingly agreed, and their regular appearances on the observation platform functioned just as they were supposed to."

Unfortunately, the two movie stars were so successful that crowds wanted to see them instead of the candidate and made it difficult for the train to stay on schedule.

Citing these issues and concerns, Stevenson's staff asked Bacall and Bogart to leave the train tour.

"The Bogarts, of course, understood at once, and quietly disappeared," Dick recalled. "They remained loyal and valuable campaigners to the end."[255]

But other celebrities did not appear to overshadow the politicians they were riding with, including comedian Bob Newhart and movie stars Gregory Peck, Peter Falk, and Dorothy Provine, who were on Governor Edmund G. Brown's campaign train in 1966 when he ran for reelection. The stars would take turns introducing local and statewide politicians, and Peck would introduce the governor.[256]

Actress Shirley MacLaine accompanied Senator George McGovern on his 1972 campaign train tour of central California.[257]

One of the VIPs on the 1978 campaign train tour of US senator Howard Baker, Republican of Tennessee, was "Rosebud," an antique steam engine that pulled the train. The engine was used in the evacuation of victims of the 1889 flood in Johnstown, Pennsylvania.[258]

"Rosebud's" starring role in Baker's whistle-stop tour was featured in news coverage, ads, and posters.

But Baker's train was stranded when a train ahead of it derailed. Baker had to travel the final hundred miles of his trip by automobile. "I bet I'm the only man who ever misplaced an entire train," he joked later.[259]

Racing legend Richard Petty and entertainer Jimmy Dean campaigned with North Carolina governor Jim Martin in 1998.[260]

Civil rights icon Rosa Parks was President Bill Clinton's guest on his 1992 campaign tour and appeared with him on the train's rear platform.[261]

On his 1996 whistle-stop tour, Reuters reported that Clinton was "introduced at every stop by a different 'local hero.' These have included a female Gulf War veteran, a paralyzed former policeman who was shot in the line of duty, and in Arlington, Ohio, a local preacher and anti-smoking activist."[262]

THE WELCOMING COMMITTEE

"In 1904, Teddy Roosevelt made a whistle-stop political trip through the Southwest including the Indian Territory (now Oklahoma)," according to former ambassador William T. Pheiffer.

Everyone's Meeting the

BAKER SPECIAL

Featuring Senator Howard Baker
and ROSEBUD the Steam Engine

Clinchfield Railroad's famous antique steam engine, Rosebud, will pull the 1978 Baker Special campaign train statewide Oct. 30-Nov. 2.

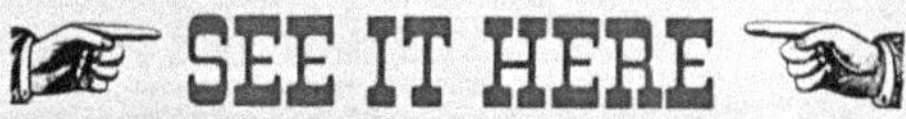

4:00 p.m. Monday, Oct. 30th

Old Southern Railway Station
Depot Avenue
(Across from Regas Parking Lot)

FREE REFRESHMENTS!!

20 Paid for by Re-elect Senator Baker Committee/David McClung, Treasurer

Publicity and marketing were used to encourage people to see politicians when their campaign trains stopped at local railroad depots. This poster promoted one of the trackside rallies of US senator Howard Baker (R-Tennessee) during his whistle-stop tour of the Volunteer State in 1972. Baker visited twenty-eight cities over four days as part of his reelection campaign. (Re-Elect Senator Baker Committee.)

> My Dad was then the U.S. District Judge for the territory and, as the highest-ranking federal official therein, he headed the delegation which welcomed President Roosevelt on the arrival of his presidential train at our hometown of Purcell.
>
> After the usual amenities, the President invited the delegation to be seated for some chit-chat. My Dad seated himself on a bench on which, alas, the train attendant had carelessly left a sheet of flypaper coated with adhesive on both sides.
>
> When the delegation rose to leave at the conclusion of the talkfest, the bench rose with my Dad, to his great discomfiture and to the unrestrained mirth of the President. It required about half an hour for Teddy Roosevelt and his aides to extricate him from the fly trap, which necessitated the removal of his pants and his prized frock coat, which was surely the only one in the Territory.
>
> For the remainder of his days, my Dad was known locally by the unflattering sobriquet of "Flypaper Bill."[263]

William McKinley apparently did not hold visiting delegations in very high esteem, calling them "about the most annoying incidents of such trips. . . .

"These committees, always larger than they should be, and rarely of any use whatever, meet the train [far away from the train station]. They swarm into it and into the seats of those already entitled to travel by that train; they tumble over each other; they blunder into the car of the principal man on the train, and then do a great deal of gawking and obstructing. . . .

"When the town is reached from which this sort of reception committee was dispatched, it will have a new committee ready from the next town beyond, with more men whose curiosity and appetite must be satisfied before they alight and join in turn the shelters on foot and in the carriages. . . . [In short], it does not give any convincing impression of welcome; it creates a very unpleasant and uncomfortable notion of a beastly and unnecessary crush," McKinley observed.

"The idea of traveling 12,000 miles with a reception committee is enough in itself to make the most suave and patient of men pause," he concluded.[264]

Politicians might be welcomed by people on horses or donkeys[265]—or even by a woman riding an elephant and draped in an American flag.[266]

Democratic presidential candidate Edmund Muskie was greeted by a supporter who asked him to sign a stuffed parrot.[267]

It was not unusual for people to bring their babies and lift them up so the candidate or officeholder could hold or kiss them.[268]

In 1952, a man lifted his two-year-old son up to Republican vice-presidential nominee Richard Nixon through the candidate's open railcar window while it was stopped at a train station in Elroy, Wisconsin.

"Nixon took the child in his arms but just then the train started to pull away," according to the Associated Press. "The boy's father yelled excitedly, 'Hey, that's my kid you've got.'

"Nixon spotted a policeman running alongside the slowly moving train and handed him the child for a safe return to the anxious parent."[269]

Some individuals made it a habit to greet visiting politicians.

Each of the three times that Alfred Landon's campaign train

People were not the only ones who would come to meet whistle-stopping politicians. In this 1908 photo, a woman draped in the US flag and riding an elephant greets President William Howard Taft when his train stops in Northfield, Minnesota, on September 26, 1908. (George Grantham Bain Collection. Courtesy of the Library of Congress, Prints & Photographs Division, LC-USZ62-101136.)

stopped in Corydon, Iowa, he was met by W. P. Allred, a ninety-year-old veteran of the Civil War.[270]

Ninety-five-year-old Henry Griffel shook President Truman's hand when his train stopped in Burlington, Iowa, in 1950. Griffel had shaken the hand of every president for the previous sixty-four years, starting with Grover Cleveland, who was president in 1884.[271]

Some people who came out to see and hear whistle-stopping politicians would arrive wearing clothing that made them stand out from the crowd. They included a woman in a dress adorned with "I Like Ike" lettering[272] and cowboys in chaps and waving ten-gallon hats.[273]

Whistle-stopping politicians would often receive gifts from the welcoming committee or appreciative citizens when they arrived at railroad stations.

In 1896, William Jennings Bryan received home-baked apple pies.[274]

Four years later, Teddy Roosevelt was given a pair of golden spurs in Nebraska from the National Convention of Republicans clubs and the Republicans of Nebraska.[275]

In 1940, Wendell Willkie was presented with fruit, candies, livestock, and even a live forty-two-pound turkey.[276]

In 1948, Truman was given an Angora goat that wore a sign saying "Dewey's Goat," a reference to Truman's opponent. Although Truman wanted to use the goat to help trim the White House lawn, the president had to leave the animal at the station because there was no room for it on his campaign train.[277]

Democratic presidential candidate Adlai Stevenson received a bolt of cloth from a woman admirer as he was standing on the rear platform of his campaign train in Reading, Pennsylvania. A United Press photographer captured the moment, just as Stevenson lifted the material and his face was momentarily hidden behind the gift. The photo was captioned "Peek-A-Boo Candidate."[278]

As Stevenson's train traveled throughout California, "at most stops he was presented with gifts of local products, such as in Madera, where he received salted almonds and fruit."[279]

That same year, 1952, Stevenson made a campaign stop at a railroad station in Crestline, Ohio—the same station where, in 1948, Truman delivered what was the first to be labeled a "whistle-stop speech."

A local Democratic official there gave Stevenson a trophy: a

A local farmer proudly presents a watermelon as a welcome gift to a whistle-stopping candidate. (Cover illustration by Perry Barlow for the *New Yorker*, August 14, 1948.)

replica of the railroad station adorned with a big brass whistle on top. A card noted that it was from Crestline, "birthplace of the whistle-stop."[280]

On a campaign train tour four years later, reporter Mary McGrory wrote that Stevenson "in the course of one morning, received a box of jellies, celery, a basket of apples, [sheets] of paper, peanut brittle, cereal, and a football."[281]

On campaign stops in Minnesota in 1952, Richard Nixon received butter and other products from local farms, onions and potatoes, and even a bagged pheasant. "We're really getting the loot today," he told residents.[282]

In Wisconsin, Nixon was presented with a 150-pound wheel of Swiss cheese. "This is the largest piece of cheese I have ever seen," Nixon said.

"In the dining car, [the cheese] was the subject of considerable thinking by the Nixon aides," according to one newspaper account. "Apparently, it was a campaign problem which had not been encountered before by the assistants to the senator.

"What in hell do we do with all that cheese? was the campaign question of the moment.

"'We might slice enough out of it to feed all the people on the train and send the rest of it to the White House,' was the none-too-hopeful response of an obviously junior assistant."[283]

Lady Bird Johnson received so many gifts of flowers, peanuts, and homemade cookies, pies, and jellies during her campaign train tour in 1964 that her staff made special arrangements to leave them at towns along the route.

"Because the train couldn't carry all the gifts heaped upon Mrs. Johnson at each stop, we set up a little-known operation," her press secretary, Liz Carpenter, wrote in her memoir, *Ruffles and Flourishes*.

> When Mrs. Johnson received flowers, her secretary, Mary Rather, would then take them and walk nineteen cars through the train to a window by the engine. By previous arrangement, a police car would be waiting. She would toss the bouquets to the police car, including nicely written notes from the First Lady.
>
> The policeman would dispatch the flowers to hospitals in the town. This obviously accomplished two things: (1) It furnished an opportunity for Mrs. Johnson to share the flowers with many people, and (2) It disposed of the mounting mound of flowers which gave the train's hospitality car a distinctly funereal appearance.
>
> All over the South, Mary would gather up the roses, attach the notes, wait a decent number of towns, and then go running back through the train and pass the bouquets to the waiting policeman.[284]

Democratic presidential candidate Jimmy Carter received a large horseshoe-shaped loaf of Italian bread from a politician in Trenton, New Jersey. The bread was so heavy that it collapsed under its own weight and hit Carter. The candidate was not injured, and photos of the mishap were published by several newspapers.[285]

CHAPTER 3

Trackside Speeches

The exuberant [Franklin] Roosevelt loved a crowd and excelled as a rear-platform speaker, whereas Hoover usually looked like he would rather have been somewhere else.[286]

—Donald A. Ritchie, *Electing FDR: The New Deal Campaign of 1932*

Before the advent of planes, social media, websites, and traditional mass media outlets, many presidential candidates relied on campaign trains to reach voters. The politicians rode the rails to connect with people at train depots across the country. There, speaking from the back of a train, they'd talk to crowds numbering in the hundreds or thousands of people who had traveled from around the region to hear what they had to say.

A campaign train "is a sensible vehicle that is in touch with life," observed James Reston of the *Cincinnati Enquirer*. "It gives a candidate time to put a few thoughts down on a piece of paper before the next stop and, equally important, it gives him something to think about."[287]

The trains had certain advantages over other forms of political campaigning.

"One big advantage of the campaign train, of course, is that the railroad usually runs into a part of a city or town, so voters who bother to take a trip downtown can see the candidate in person without too much trouble," a newspaper noted. "Airports, on the other hand, require long-distance driving, either on the part of the candidate or the spectators, if a nominee is to be fittingly displayed to the public."[288]

As one newspaper editorial observed, "When a presidential candidate gets out of the TV studio and into the small towns [on a campaign train], he is moving a lot closer to the American people. He talks directly to them, and they to him in a way no amount of air touring and television exposure could duplicate.

"This is how it should be in a system of government which depends, basically, on a free exchange of ideas between the President and the public. And that is the main reason we commend the whistle-stop."[289]

MAKING AN ENTRANCE

When Stephen A. Douglas campaigned by train when he ran for US Senate against Abraham Lincoln in 1858, he had a brass cannon mounted on a flatcar at the back of the train to let townspeople know he was on the way to speak to them. A two-man crew in semi-military dress fired the weapon as the train approached communities. Ironically, Lincoln often traveled on the same train as a regular passenger.[290]

In 1891, President Harrison narrowly missed being hit by cannon fire intended to welcome him to a train station in Atlanta.[291] The explosion broke windows in the dining car of Harrison's train. Fortunately, the president was at the back of his train at the time and did not find out about the incident until later.[292]

Most of the speeches whistle-stopping politicians made from the back of trains were, by nature, only a few minutes long. Sometimes they took the form of a conversation between the politicians and the crowds that gathered to hear them.

A good example is one of the remarks that President Franklin Roosevelt made during his 1936 drought-inspection trip, as reported by Richard Strout of the *Christian Science Monitor*:

> To a shirt-sleeved and smiling group of 200 farmers and wives gathered at this little town, Mr. Roosevelt made his first rear platform appearances [on his 1936 drought-inspection] trip and bantered good-naturedly with the crowd. The scene was typical of such incidents.
>
> The crowd was waiting as the sleek, 8-car special pulled into the yards. It waited expectantly until the President, on the arm of Franklin Roosevelt Junior . . . came out. There was a flutter of applause; the President, in a brown seer-sucker suit, waved cheerily.
>
> "How are you all?" he asked. Everybody smiled.
>
> "Better since we've seen you," at last, one woman admirer got up the courage to say.
>
> Mr. Roosevelt tossed his head with a characteristic gesture and smiled.

Mysterious Figure Seen Near Presidential Train

A Herblock Cartoon, © The Herb Block Foundation, used under license.

> "Glad to see you have so many children," he observed to the crowd . . . with a gesture at several scores of barefooted urchins, some of them clad in a solitary garment. A minute later, he commented on the fact of recent rain. The rain motif is expected to be heard frequently from now on.
>
> "You're going to carry Ohio!" cried another voice.
>
> "Fine," said the president, "send me a telegram the night after the election."
>
> A bouquet of flowers is passed up.
>
> "I'll give them to my daughter-in-law, Betsy," Mr. Roosevelt remarked, with an introductory wave between the crowd and blond-haired Mrs. James Roosevelt.
>
> A minute later, the Roosevelts retired. The crowd gave a satisfied clap. "All aboard!" shouted the conductor.
>
> The long train pulled away, leaving a group to tell their descendants that they had once talked with the President.[293]

SPECIAL ARRANGEMENTS

Accommodation for Franklin Roosevelt's mobility-related needs is just one example of the care and attention to detail that campaign train planners paid to help ensure the success of depot- and trackside speeches.

As Walter Fitzmaurice noted in a 1947 article for *Trains* magazine, "The Special's engineer knows where he'll stand also. A Secret Service crew goes out over the route, stopping at each station and [marking] for the engineer the stopping point, which, when measured against the train's length, assures the widest space length around the Magellan at the rear. The [Secret Service] men also check bridge load capacities against the Magellan's weight and instruct local police in crowd control. All this is done weeks before departure day."[294]

A memorandum to the advance men—they were usually men in those days—who worked on Richard Nixon's 1960 whistle-stop train tour noted that the rear-platform speeches were "the most frequent train stops and require some special arrangements."[295]

The memorandum then laid out a step-by-step process for the events:

> The train should be stopped so that the rear platform is in the best position for the VP's speech. This is done, with the cooperation of local railroad people, by placing a stake at the point where the engineer is to stop the engine—calculating the length of the train from there back to the speaking point. Your job is to decide on [the] position of [the] rear platform. [The railroad staff] will do the rest.
>
> Location should be determined on the basis of the best place to assemble a crowd.
>
> The rear platform of the train will serve as the speaker's platform—and the local MC should be prepared to step right up onto this platform to introduce the top dignitaries. Then the top state or local candidate should introduce the VP—who will come out to the platform from the door to his car.
>
> The number of candidates and officials to be

> introduced should be held to an absolute minimum. . . . If there is a Republican mayor, he should be introduced, or perhaps serve as MC.
>
> The group to be introduced should wait at the foot of the steps to the rear platform and as each name is called, the individual goes up on the platform, waves, then down the other side. Only two or three people should remain on the platform when the VP comes out to speak. There isn't room for any more.
>
> Immediately at the conclusion of the speech, the train will pull out—so any presentations should be made before the speech, as soon as the VP comes out.
>
> There should, of course, be a band and decorating in the area.
>
> For the safety of the crowd, it is essential to provide rope barriers around the rear car of the train.[296]

The script for Harry Truman's 1948 whistle-stopping events followed a predictable format.

"The whistle-stop routine seldom varied," his daughter, Margaret Truman, pointed out in a biography of her father:

"As we pulled into the station, bands blare[d] out 'Hail to the Chief,' and the 'Missouri Waltz.' Dad, usually accompanied by three or four local politicians, would step out on the back platform of the train, and they would present him with a gift—a basket of corn, a bucket of apples, or some items of local manufacture.

"Then one of the local politicians would introduce the

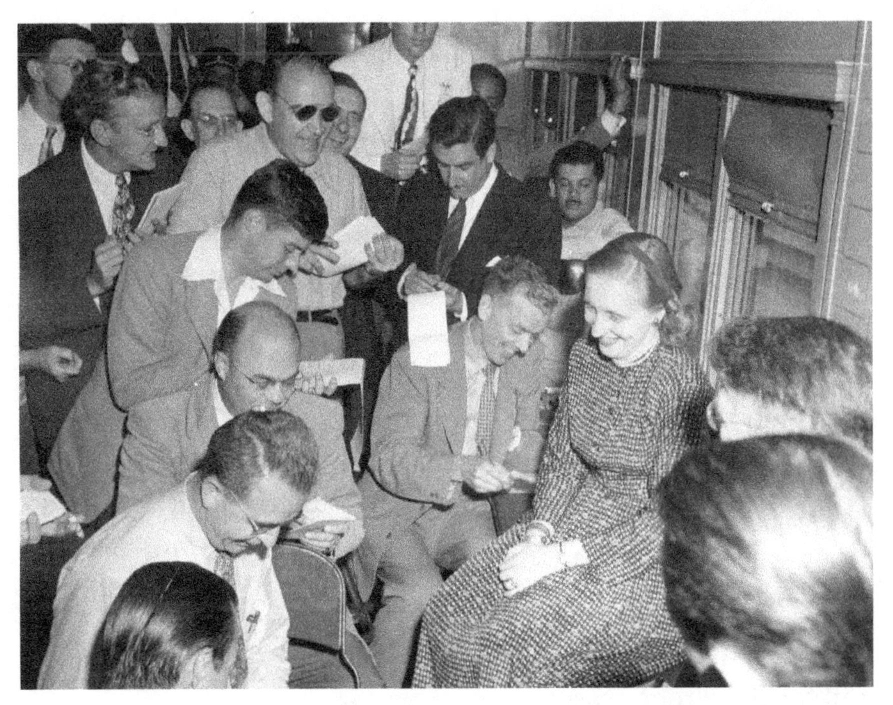

Margaret Truman (right) is surrounded by reporters on her father's campaign train. The train was headed west during Harry S. Truman's 1948 whistle-stop tour. (Photo by the US Department of the Navy. Courtesy of the Harry S. Truman Presidential Library & Museum, used by permission.)

President, and Dad would give a brief fighting speech, plugging the local candidate, and asking people for their support. But the heart of these little talks was a local reference, sometimes supplied by Dad spontaneously, more often by careful advance research on the part of the staff," she said.[297]

Historian Robert A. Caro noted in his book *The Passage of Power: The Years of Lyndon Johnson* that Lyndon Johnson designed the format of his 1960 campaign train tour himself:

> As the LBJ Special entered the outskirts of a town, its public address system would be switched on, and over it would come the stirring strains of "The

> Yellow Rose of Texas." At first the tune would be played at low volume, but as the train approached the town's center, where advance men would have gathered a small crowd, "the volume would be turned up to a point where the tune could be heard blocks away" [according to Johnson aide George Reedy].
>
> Record player and engine would stop simultaneously, a dark blue curtain that had been hung over the doorway onto the rear platform would be pulled aside, and the tall figure of Lyndon Johnson, waving a ten-gallon hat, would step through.[298]

One time a campaign train was stopped at the wrong place and for the wrong reason.

California governor Edmund G. Brown (father of future governor Jerry Brown) rode the "Progress Special" train during his losing battle for reelection in 1966 against his challenger, actor Ronald Reagan.

At a trackside gathering in downtown Inglewood, a Los Angeles suburb, the campaign special became the first whistle-stop train to receive a ticket when local police issued a citation to the engineer for blocking a traffic intersection.[299]

ADDING SOME COLOR

In informal talks from the rear end of his train in 1900, Theodore Roosevelt "got into the habit of repeating remarks that had gone over big the first time he made them,"[300] Paul F. Boller Jr., author of *Presidential Campaigns*, observed.

The Rough Rider had several ways of opening his campaign

Theodore Roosevelt campaigned by train several times throughout his political career, including in 1912 when he ran for president as the nominee of the Bull Moose Party, formally known as the Progressive Party. He's shown in this *Puck* illustration seeking votes from the rear of a caboose before a crowd of people who all have moose antlers sprouting from the sides of their heads—including, in the bottom right corner, a baby being held by its mother. (1912 illustration by Samuel D. Ehrhart for *Puck*. Courtesy of the Library of Congress, Prints & Photographs Division, LC-DIG-ppmsca-38463.)

speeches during his run for the White House on the Bull Moose, or Progressive Party, ticket in 1912. "In delivering a train-end talk he almost invariably addresses his audiences as 'Friends.' In his set speeches, the colonel greets his 'fellow citizens, men, and women of the State of--------,'" one newspaper reported.

Just like other candidates, Roosevelt would often say a few words about babies and children, a journalist reported. "Don't crowd the little bull mooses," he admonished supporters at one trackside rally.[301]

Richard Strout, a reporter with the *Christian Science Monitor,* observed that Herbert Hoover was much too shy for the part and often mumbled through his speeches. "It was embarrassing to watch him try to be carefree, jolly, and bouncy on the stump. He was not a good speaker at all.

"In fact," Strout recalled, "at one stop a small boy turned away in disgust after listening to Hoover speak and said to no one in particular, 'Speak up! Speak up!'"[302]

When Franklin Roosevelt campaigned by train in 1936, he sounded "to me like a bishop visiting the people of his diocese," according to Pulitzer Prize–winning reporter Marquis Childs and the author of *Witness to Power.* "He spoke of issues almost tangentially. How much better off we were than we had been four years before, he insisted. The pronouns were almost always we, us, you, and I. . . . This was part of his legerdemain—the smiling, kindly bishop sharing the blessings of his gentle rule.

"At each stop local references to recovery projects were carefully spliced into his text. Eleanor's appearance beside him on the back platform always drew cheers. Rarely did he speak of the opposition, but when he did, it was in condescending terms, as though it were a negligible matter that should be treated lightly."[303]

Journalist Bess Furman had two notebooks filled with notes, taken in October 1936, of the remarks FDR made to crowds who had gathered along the train tracks. "There was, of course, a certain sameness to them, but there was also spontaneity," she pointed out.

"Excerpts taken at random still hold their freshness. At Oelwein, Iowa:

> 'My friends, I am very glad to come here. I have never been in this part of the state before, so it was certainly time for me to come.

> 'I find it terribly hard after four years to try to make political speeches. I have been so tremendously engrossed in trying to bring things back—and that goes beyond party politics.
>
> 'Some of you here are railroad men. But after all, we're all tied in together. We won't have better railroads unless the farmers are prosperous and unless city dwellers have enough money to buy what the farmers produce. Merchants can't sell goods unless there is buying power.
>
> 'As I go through the country this year, I see, in comparison with 1932, great differences. In these four years, we have gained a view of the interdependence of farm people and industrial people. I've learned a lot that will stand me in good stead whether I go back to the White House or not, and incidentally, I get a tremendous kick out of it—Seems we are starting [to leave]—good-bye, good-bye!'"[304]

Biographer Mary Earhart Dillon observed that practically all of Republican presidential candidate Wendell Willkie's speeches were written on his train.

Dillon said that staff writer Elliott V. Bell "had explained when he first joined the Willkie Special that the proper way to write campaign speeches was for several writers to sit down with the candidate, discuss their ideas, and then separate to write drafts which the candidate must then go over to make appropriate changes.

"There must be continual discussion between writer and candidate [so] that each might understand the views and objectives

A politician waits nearby as campaign aides work on the remarks for his next trackside rally. (Cover illustration by Peter Arno for the *New Yorker*, September 21, 1940.)

of the other. [But] during the entire six weeks' tour, Bell talked with Willkie only five times, and then never under the condition that he had proposed.

"Accordingly, the staff wrote speeches based on the writer's own surmises of what the candidate wanted to say. Immediately after completion, all speeches were delivered to [aide Russell Davenport] who sought to 'improve' them. After [he] had partly ruined half a dozen good speeches by his fine writing, [another aide] upbraided [Davenport] and beseeched him to let the speeches alone. Davenport was highly offended."

Dillon noted that Willkie "continued to improvise, and thereby often ruined the sequence of ideas in an otherwise good speech. Rarely did Willkie read an address before giving it. This was partly due to the lack of time and the general confusion, and partly because he failed to understand the need for rehearsal.

"As a result, he frequently placed the emphasis in the wrong place, with the result that his audience would often cheer the wrong sentiments."[305]

To provide material for President Harry Truman's back-platform speeches, the Democratic National Committee established a research division to provide local color the candidate could use at each stop.

"The DNC had assembled a secret team of experts to supply Truman with such data," Truman historian David Pietrusza wrote in his book *1948*.

> Headquartered in stifling and noisy quarters on Dupont Circle in Washington, DC, its research division consisted of failed Philadelphia congressional candidate William L. Batt Jr.; Batt's friend and Americans for Democratic Action organizer,

> Johannes Hoeber, PhD; liberal veterans activist Kenneth M. Birkhead; Oregon-born natural resources expert Philip Dreyer; the ADA's Harvard-educated research director, David D. Lloyd; former *Kansas City Star* reporter and budding novelist Frank K. Kelly; and twenty-nine-year-old Senate Committee on Banking and Currency staffer John E. Barriere.
>
> "We won't be peddling any baloney," Truman had told them. "Facts—that's what people want, and that's what we'll give them."
>
> The original plan had been for various government agencies to compose Truman's whistle-stop addresses, but the results were dreadful, dry, lifeless statistical litanies. Soon enough, the research division became the speechwriting division.[306]

As the research division chief, Bill Batt, recalled, "We provided our [local data] through the [government's Works Progress Administration's] *WPA Guide*, which was our secret weapon, and we got a complete set out of the Library of Congress. . . . Between the *WPA Guide* and [Truman's own knowledge], there was an amazing collection of local background, so when he went into [poet] James Whitcomb Riley's hometown, he was quoting from Riley's poetry about the old swimming hole. I remember talking to newspapermen later who traveled on both the Republican and Democratic trains and were impressed by the fact that the President had something to say in each place and also had taken some trouble to brief himself on each area, while Dewey's speeches all came out alike."[307]

During Truman's campaign train tour across the country in

View of the press car on a campaign train. The reporters were traveling with President Harry S. Truman during the 1948 race for the White House. (Photo courtesy of the Harry S. Truman Presidential Library & Museum, used by permission.)

September 1948, Truman aide George McKee Elsey recounted in his memoir, *An Unplanned Life*, "I labored over the notes for the back-platform talks, which, while seemingly impromptu and off-the-cuff, were anything but. No matter how many 'whistle-stops' were scheduled for the day (and once we had fifteen), I varied the subjects so that Truman would be hitting on a different campaign issue at each stop. Knowing that Truman was highly quotable and that he would not be repeating himself, reporters would race from the press car to the rear of the train to hear his remarks."[308]

Truman would often ask the reporters on his train for advice and feedback about his speeches. "He literally took them into his confidence and noted afterward that many a suggestion made [when they played poker] cropped up later in his speeches with real returns to himself and the ticket," wrote Truman biographers Frank McNaughton and Walter Hehmeyer.[309]

"He asked the correspondents to criticize his speaking, and they did so without hesitation. They told him his delivery was halting and somewhat stodgy, that he did best when he was talking extemporaneously to crowds on the train steps. Thereafter, there was less of strained effort and more ease in Truman's speeches; less of the labored preparation and more of the impromptu delivery," the two authors recounted.[310]

One presidential candidate thwarted the best speech preparation efforts of his staff.

Wilson W. Wyatt Sr., the campaign manager for Adlai Stevenson's 1956 race for the White House, asked Phil Stern, one of the writers on the campaign, "to prepare a list of what I captioned 'whistle-stop vignettes.' They consisted of a dozen brief paragraphs on different subjects extracted from Adlai's speeches.

"I suggested that Adlai use one as the key point at each of his whistle-stops and pointed out that, after all, these were not scheduled to be major policy speeches. He completely agreed that that was a reasonable approach and would give him time to meet more of the political figures as he crossed the country."

But rather than use the carefully prepared vignettes, Stevenson would write his own speeches. "Adlai simply could not bring himself to be repetitious even though each audience was different," Wyatt said.[311]

INTRODUCTIONS

Alben W. Barkley reminisced about the time in 1932 when he campaigned with Franklin Roosevelt on board the "Roosevelt

Special." Barkley, who was running for reelection to the US Senate from Kentucky, introduced Roosevelt to the crowds who had gathered at railroad depots as they traveled across the Bluegrass State.

> One day, we pulled into Corbin, a sizable industrial town and railroad center . . . I pranced out on the rear platform, ready to make my little speech for Mr. Roosevelt. I saw, to my delight, that a huge crowd of many thousands was gathered. I felt that such an assemblage called for something special in the way of preliminary remarks.
>
> "My friends," I began, "It has been four years since I spoke in Corbin, so naturally, I cannot recall every individual in this great crowd by name.
>
> "But I can recognize that you are the same people I addressed here four years ago [because] after four years of Hoover, you are all wearing the same clothes that you had on four years ago!"
>
> The crowd roared, "Amen! That's the truth!" And FDR, who always loved a humorous dig . . . laughed with them. For years to come, I often heard him refer to the Corbin incident as a choice example of pertinent political satire.[312]

Introductions could sometimes go on too long, however. Journalist Arthur Edson remembered the time in 1960 when Senator Olin Johnston gave a long introduction to vice-presidential candidate Senator Lyndon Johnson. He "started out with a stemwinder and it went on and on about the Democrats and South Carolina, and the textile workers, and the price of cotton. [Johnston] finally sat down without having done what he got up to do—introduce Lyndon Johnson."[313]

BULLET POINTS

"For each whistle-stop talk, Ike liked to have a six-by-three-inch white card in his pocket, listing a half-dozen points in heavy black pencil," Robert Cutler, author of *No Time for Rest,* said. Dwight Eisenhower's campaign aide, Gabe Hauge, "would prepare these cards the night before, adding a few details about the particular town in order to give the Candidate an advanced 'feel' for his audience." Cutler continued:

> At 8 a.m., the Candidate would review these cards with Gabe and me, changing them to suit. Sometimes the Candidate used a prop to illustrate his text. A favorite prop was a piece of [lumber] about three feet long sawed almost through in two places, which dramatized the shrinking power of the dollar.
>
> The full [section of lumber] was the value of the dollar when F.D.R. became president; break off the first piece, you have the dollar's value at Roosevelt's death; break off the second piece, what remains of the [lumber] is the value of the dollar after the years of Truman's Presidency. The crowd got the point.[314]

The speeches that Lyndon Johnson made on his 1960 campaign train tour "were very southern in their delivery," biographer Robert A. Caro, author of *The Passage of Power: The Years of Lyndon Johnson*, observed:

> Old fashioned stump speeches, "real stemwinders": shouted out, and the points he wanted to make delivered in a bellow, so that his voice was continually hoarse, and as he shouted, his arms flailed, and he would raise an arm—or two—high above his head and jab a finger toward the sky. Among his gestures was one in which, a reporter wrote, "the Johnson hands went up beside his ears and wavered there like a television commercial on headache misery."
>
> And some of the points he made were unforgettable, for if Lyndon Johnson reading from a prepared speech was stilted and unconvincing, Lyndon Johnson without a speech . . . was still the Lyndon Johnson who had, in his early Texas campaigns, shown that in a state with a history of great stump speakers, he was one of the greatest of them all.[315]

UNSCRIPTED REMARKS

In 1932, Secretary of the Interior Hubert Work volunteered to speak on behalf of President Hoover when the campaign train stopped at a small town in California. A crowd gathered at the back of the train and called for Hoover to come out and speak to them.

In the midst of his remarks, Work stopped and turned to a colleague, asking, "Where the hell are we?" according to Secret Service agent Edmund Starling.

"Unfortunately, an employee of the local broadcasting company was holding a microphone against the rear of the platform, and the Secretary's question was perfectly reproduced. Everyone within an area of a quarter of a mile heard it, and with their typical western humor, the crowd roared with laughter."[316]

In spite of the advance work by staff, slipups by candidates did occur. "A dazed [Wendell] Willkie told one whistle-stop audience how glad he was to be 'near the town where Mark Twain was born' when he was already two states away from Missouri," according to Robert Bendiner, the author of *White House Fever*.[317]

When, in 1948, Republican presidential hopeful Thomas Dewey's train jerked away from the railroad station while Dewey was still speaking, he blurted out, "Well, that's the first lunatic I've ever had for an engineer. He probably should be shot at sunrise, but we will let him off this time since no one was hurt," recalled Lady Bird Johnson's press secretary, Liz Carpenter.[318]

Nationally syndicated columnist James Reston ended his account of the incident with this observation: "And the train took off with a jerk."[319] "Railroad workers and blue-collar laborers all over the country were properly aroused," former Truman aide Ken Hechler remembered. "Freight cars sprouted chalked slogans to drive the point home."[320]

Everywhere Dewey traveled after that night, he saw "Lunatics for Truman" written in the dust of hundreds of boxcars, United Press reporter Merriman Smith wrote.[321]

Truman quickly capitalized on Dewey's snafu, journalist Robert J. Donovan noted:

> The very next day, as it happened, President Truman's train rolled into a large railroad center in Indiana.
>
> Sensing his advantage before an audience

By the middle of the month, with everybody campaigning like mad, a collision seemed inevitable.

Cartoon by James T. Berryman, *The Campaign of '48 in Star Cartoons, Washington Evening Star-News*, 1948.

> composed largely of men wearing blue caps and overalls and carrying oil cans, he said, "Well, we have the finest crew on this train I've ever traveled with. I don't think there is any profession in the country that has fewer lunatics in it than the men and women who run the railroad."
>
> An appreciative audience yelled back, "Atta boy, Harry!"[322]

Dewey's running mate, Earl Warren, had a couple of slips of the tongue at whistle-stop depot rallies.

"At one stop, a member of his staff tossed some postcards with pictures of the Warren family on them into the crowds," Donovan reported. "The people broke through the police line to get them, upsetting the program. Warren bawled his assistant out in words that have no place even in the hottest political campaign. Unhappily for the candidate, the microphone was on, and every man, woman, and child in the place heard him."[323]

In at least one instance, the candidate did not know where he was or who he was talking to. A reporter who covered the 1956 Stevenson campaign train wrote that one early morning Stevenson "went on the rear platform and warmly greeted 'all of you fine people from Battle Creek.' Which was lovely, but we were not in Battle Creek!"[324]

Richard Nixon's 1952 vice-presidential campaign train tour got off to an inauspicious start in Pomona, California, when, as he recounted in a memoir, "Governor Earl Warren said, in introducing me, 'I now present to you the next President of the United States.' But the crowd loved it and he, in high spirits, laughed at his slip of the tongue."[325]

UNSCHEDULED STOPS

On President Truman's 1948 campaign train tour, he recounted that "we'd go on, and whenever the train got to a spot where there were enough people on the platform to be talked to, we'd stop, and I'd talk to them."

Truman considered "enough people" to be anywhere from ten to a thousand, and at times he would speak to audiences much closer to the small end of the scale. "They'd come out to hear me, and I talked to them," he said.[326]

Don Phillips, writing in *Trains* magazine, recalled that "one local official, irate that one of Nixon's trains in 1952 wasn't stopping in his town, pulled an emergency brake valve as the train sped through the outskirts of his town, bringing the train to a screeching halt at the station. Nixon had no choice but to give a hasty impromptu speech."[327]

EARLY DEPARTURES

At a train station near St. Louis, President Calvin Coolidge had just been introduced to fifteen hundred people who were waiting for him outside his railcar. Immediately after he was introduced, the train began to pull out of the station.

Coolidge, who had a reputation for being taciturn, only had time to say one word: "Goodbye."[328]

While Nixon was speaking from the back of his train in Tulare, California, in 1952, it started pulling out of the station before he was done.

"I cut short my remarks by calling out, come along and join our crusade," Nixon remembered, "and people ran down the tracks after the train. Like most candidates, I had an exaggerated idea about the importance of what I had planned to say if only a mistake hadn't been made in starting the train ahead of time."

He continued:

> I proceeded to chew out our staff and particularly Jack Drown, our train manager, for what I thought was a major error.
>
> Fortunately for everyone concerned, several members of our small staff combined had excellent intuition for politics with a sense of humor. As I was telling Jack "never let that happen again," [aide] Bill Rogers walked up and said, "I thought you planned it that way. Just as soon as the train started to move you finished your sentence and then spontaneously said to the crowd, 'Come along and join the crusade,' motioning for them to follow the train.
>
> "It gave a sense of participation and excitement which could never be conveyed by ending a speech on time and then waiting for the engineer to get up steam."
>
> I laughed and recognized that I had just experienced another example of the truth of one of Eisenhower's favorite admonitions: "Take your job, but never yourself, seriously."[329]

During Eisenhower's 1952 campaign, members of a crowd of twenty thousand people trampled and damaged public address wires as they waited for the candidate's train. By the time the damage had been repaired, it was time for the train to leave. Just as Eisenhower started speaking, it began pulling out of the station. "'Whoops!' he cried. 'They're taking me away!'"[330]

That year Eisenhower had two whistle-stop speeches end prematurely on the same day, in Saginaw and Lapeer, Michigan.

As reported by the Associated Press, in Saginaw, "The general still was talking as the train drew away from the disappointed crowd." Then later at Lapeer, "the train started before the general could get more than a few words out. He explained in exasperation, 'We're supposed to have three minutes, but this train has been acting up all day—I don't know what is going on here.'

"'I think it was just an honest mistake somewhere,' Eisenhower later recounted at another train-side rally."[331]

"Once, on a 1956 trip, the engineer mistook a 5-minute warning for a [signal to leave] and began pulling out as the mayor was giving a speech, flanked by Nixon and a local beauty queen," according to Don Phillips in an article for *Trains.*

"With the loudspeaker system on full blast, the mayor began shouting, 'Stop the train. My wife's on the platform, and she won't like me with this girl.' Nixon ordered the train to stop, but the mayor had a half-mile walk back to his wife."[332]

LEAVING ON CUE

President Franklin Roosevelt invariably insisted that the train should start to move as soon as he finished talking "so he could reach a dramatic climax and then have the train pull out of the station as he waved to the crowd," author Gordon Gordon recounted in *Railroad Magazine.*[333]

For railroad crews, this scripted ending was a challenge—at least at first.

"This posed a problem because maintenance crews often would be in the midst of icing or watering the train when he finished," Gordon wrote. "In later years, though, he became so expert at knowing exactly how long these operations would take that he could time his talks to the second. By the time the crew was ready, he would be winding up his address; they would know it and pull out, with his last few words dramatically coming from a platform that was slowly moving away from the crowd."[334]

CBS reporter George Herman recalled "one thing Lyndon Johnson used to do. Bobby Baker would stand next to Lyndon, and Lyndon would deliver a speech, a brief speech. At the end, he would kick Bobby Baker in the ankle, Baker would say into his walkie-talkie, 'Pull out,' and they would start the engine, and Lyndon would keep talking as the train rolled out of the depot, yelling, 'They're taking me away from ya! Bye, everybody! Vote Democratic! They're taking me away from ya!'"[335]

In 1960, California governor Edmund G. "Pat" Brown missed getting back on John F. Kennedy's campaign train that was touring California's Central Valley.

"Brown had introduced the candidate from the back platform in one of the Valley towns, then climbed down and began schmoozing with people in the crowd," *Washington Post* journalist David S. Broder remembered.

"Engrossed in conversation, Brown missed Kennedy's cue lines for departure . . . that staff members and reporters took as a signal to jump back aboard—and made an unsuccessful lunge for the back platform. As Kennedy joined the others laughing, the portly governor jogged down the track, puffing heavily until the train was halted so he could reboard."[336]

Sometimes a politician's parting words as the train pulled out of the station could be more memorable than his back-platform speeches.

"After speaking to about 500 people at the railroad depot

in Culpeper, Virginia,[337] Democratic vice-presidential nominee Lyndon Johnson bellowed as his train pulled out of the station, 'What has Dick Nixon ever done for Culpeper?'[338] Those final eight words were repeated in stories by news organizations around the country."[339]

While campaigning in Lansing, Michigan, Franklin Roosevelt apparently thought it was necessary to issue this request at the end of his speech and before the train pulled out of the station: "Ask the children who are under the train to please crawl out!"[340]

CHAPTER 4

Hecklers, Pranksters, and Protesters

> At almost all of the whistle-stops, [US senator Pierre Salinger, Democrat of California] was heckled by a few persons carrying Barry Goldwater banners or placards supporting Salinger's Republican opponent in the November election, former actor George Murphy.[341]
>
> —United Press International

Whistle-stopping politicians and their supporters discovered that campaigning via the railroad could be a double-edged sword. While trains enabled them to meet voters in otherwise hard-to-reach areas, the visiting trains also made it easier for people and organizations in those communities to express their displeasure with or opposition to the politicians.

SWING AROUND THE CIRCLE

In an effort to bolster public support for candidates in the 1866 midterm congressional election and promote policies to help transform and rebuild the South after the Civil War, President Andrew Johnson conducted an eighteen-day whistle-stop train tour. His trip was dubbed the "swing around the circle" because of the circular route it took from Washington, DC, through Maryland, Pennsylvania, New York, Ohio, Michigan, Illinois, Missouri, Indiana, and Kentucky, and back to the nation's capital.

Although Johnson was met by enthusiastic and appreciative crowds at the start of his journey, the reception he received worsened as the train made its way around the country. The heckling directed at him at several railroad stations was prompted by the unpopular policies he was advocating, his speaking style, and verified stories that he had been drunk when he was sworn in as Abraham Lincoln's vice president.[342]

If the goal of the demonstrations and heckling was meant to get under the president's skin, it worked. He often argued with hecklers at rallies, depots, or other venues, responding to their taunts and generally making matters worse for himself.[343]

As the trip progressed, Johnson made a series of PR stumbles, such as referring to himself as a martyr.[344]

A political cartoon captioned "Enthusiastic Reception of the President at Cleveland" depicts Johnson standing at one end of a train car and Ulysses S. Grant at the other. A crowd at the station rushes away from Johnson and mobs the military hero, chanting, "Grant. Grant. Grant. Hurray for Grant," while waving their hats in the air.[345]

Johnson's disastrous campaign train tour was mocked in a satirical song, whose lyrics included this chorus:

> You have swung around the circle,
> That you ought to swing, 'tis true;
> Oh, you tried to veto Congress,
> But I guess we'll veto you.[346]

ROUGH RIDING FOR A ROUGH RIDER

Republican vice-presidential candidate and New York governor Theodore Roosevelt attracted hecklers and protesters throughout a cross-country campaign trip in 1900.

In Waverly, New York, a large stone was thrown at his railcar and shattered the window where he was sitting. Although no one was hurt, Roosevelt mentioned the mishap in a speech and alleged that it was politically motivated.

He observed that "so long as the leaders of the Democrats were foolish enough and criminal enough to encourage that sort of political argument, so long was free speech in this country to be dangerously menaced."[347]

A few days earlier, dozens of boys gathered outside Roosevelt's dining car as it sat in a railroad siding in Norwich, New York. The boys shouted insults at the candidate and his guests as they ate dinner. According to the *Sun* in New York City, "beyond remarking that parental discipline seems to be below par in Norwich, the Governor paid no attention to them."[348]

On at least one occasion the former Rough Rider had to be restrained from jumping into the fray. Seeking refuge from a street brawl that had erupted after a nearby campaign appearance, Roosevelt's supporters escorted him back to the safety of his railroad car, even as projectiles continued to pelt the train. Instead of staying in the train, he was reported to have leaned over the railing of his car, gesticulated, and "laughed like a boy on a toboggan ride."

As his train left the station, the candidate's supporters cheered him on. Roosevelt later told a reporter, "This is bully, this is magnificent. Why, it's the best time I've had since I started. Wouldn't have missed it for anything."[349]

A BURNING ISSUE

Al Smith made history in 1928 when the Democratic Party unanimously chose him as its candidate in that year's presidential election. The four-term New York governor was the first Roman Catholic nominee, which also made him a controversial choice for his time. Among those who opposed his election was the Ku Klux Klan, a hate group known for burning crosses, lynchings, and the advocacy of anti-Catholic, antisemitic, white nationalist statements and policies.

To protest Smith's candidacy, the KKK burned a cross in the field next to the railroad tracks as his campaign train traveled from Kansas to Oklahoma City.[350]

HOOVER BALONEY

Seeking election to the White House in 1932, Democratic presidential candidate Franklin Delano Roosevelt blamed incumbent President Herbert Hoover for the Great Depression. At its peak, unemployment reached 25 percent, consumer prices fell 25 percent, and seven thousand banks—about a third of the banking system—failed.[351]

Hoover did not accept blame for the economic catastrophe enveloping the country. Indeed, as he campaigned from the back of his own train, the Republican standard-bearer claimed that "the forces of depression are in retreat" and that there was no need to defend the steps he had taken to help the country recover.[352]

Edmund W. Starling, who was the head of Hoover's Secret Service detail, later recalled that as the entourage left the train station in cars for a local appearance, "for the first time in my long experience on the Detail, I heard the president of the United States booed," and "we heard jeers and saw signs reading: Down With Hoover [and] Hoover: Baloney and Applesauce."

But the president was not being compared to food. He was being told that he was, in today's parlance, "full of crap," or worse.

Starling noted that "the President looked bewildered and stricken."[353]

Things did not get much better for Hoover when his train reached Elko, Nevada, and was pelted by rotten eggs and a man was arrested for pulling up spikes in an effort to derail the locomotive.[354]

Hoover eventually had had enough of being on the receiving end of the hecklers.

Before addressing a crowd of several hundred people in Elko, at the last rear-platform appearance before the 1932 election, someone yelled a taunt ("Raspberry!") at the first-term president.

Hoover shot back. "If that gentleman has an insult to deliver to the President of the United States, if he will come up here, I will take care of him," he said with a stern face.

Hoover's challenge was met with silence.

"It is a matter of respect for the office regardless of the man, and I am sure most of you agree with me," the president concluded.[355]

There was no response from the heckler, who "did not accept the challenge to present himself, and the crowd of 200 broke into a lusty cheer," the *Waterloo Daily Courier* in Waterloo, Iowa, reported.[356]

ROCKY ROADS

The safety of whistle-stopping politicians—and the trains they traveled on—has been an important consideration over the years.

And with good reason.

In 1932, an attempt to derail President Herbert Hoover's train in Nevada was thwarted by an alert watchman who "surprised and frightened away two men carrying sticks of dynamite near the railroad right-of-way," one newspaper reported. A railroad official claimed the men "undoubtedly had planned to wreck the Hoover train."[357]

That same day, a watchman who was guarding another railroad right-of-way for Hoover's train was attacked and injured, and twenty-two sticks of dynamite were found near the roadbed.[358]

"On another occasion a few weeks later, also at night, President Hoover's train sped along the Baltimore & Ohio near New Albany, Ind.," Herbert G. Monroe wrote in a 1945 article for *Railroad Magazine.* "Only two hours before, two motorists had purposely stalled their car across the rails with the idea of wrecking it and collecting insurance. They might have put across this shady deal, possibly wrecking the train also, had not the track been on the President's route.

"As it was, they had not figured on the extra-rigorous inspection that made an accident on the line at that time next to impossible."[359]

In 1940, a brick was thrown through a window of Wendell Willkie's campaign special as it was leaving a rail depot in Grand Rapids, Michigan.

Mary Earhart Dillon recounted in her biography of Willkie that the incident marked "the first time in more than a generation [that] an election campaign had become a matter of physical assault."

Congress passed a resolution condemning the incident. And President Franklin Roosevelt denounced as reprehensible the action of the person who threw missiles at the Republican candidate.[360]

"Hundreds of extra rail workers have been assigned to special details in connection with the campaign trains," wrote Bernard J. Losh of the *Dayton Daily News*. "Every foot of the track over which they roll is inspected periodically. Passenger trains are frequently put off schedule because of the rule that no other train may pass the president's (or candidate's) in either direction while it is moving. And when they are stopped, passenger trains may pass at no more than 30 miles an hour and freight trains are slowed down to 10 miles an hour or less."[361]

When President Franklin Roosevelt traveled by train across the country in 1942 and 1943 to tour factories and visit army camps, every inch of track was inspected, railroad switches were locked in place, and up to 150,000 soldiers stood guard on a single trip.[362]

"Even in peacetime, special security precautions were taken with regard to a Presidential train," observed FDR's personal secretary, Grace Tully. "The railroad company would check its track and roadbed in advance of a presidential schedule, overpasses and junctions would be guarded by railroad police, switches which might have broken a train in two would be locked, and a pilot locomotive was usually run about a mile ahead of the Presidential special. No following train was scheduled within a safe distance."

Tully noted that "each train was equipped with a telephone system which enabled the railroad company representative to communicate directly and immediately with the engine crew, and a special 'rear end safety' man was stationed to guard against the type of 'wrong-way' travel that cropped up in the Dewey campaign accident of 1948. A full detail of Secret Service men were always aboard, of course, and two of these were on twenty-four-hour duty in the President's car."[363]

In his story for *Railroad Magazine,* Monroe said that "standard Jersey Central instructions for guarding the President's safety cover more than four pages of single-spaced typing and call for such measures as specially selected coal; inspection of the entire right of way by supervisors, master carpenters, bridge inspectors, track foremen, and track walkers, to examine all bridges and all track conditions, and special protection at highway crossings where watchmen normally were not stationed at such hours."[364]

The Pullman car President Eisenhower campaigned from in 1952 outwardly resembled "any Pullman with an observation platform." But appearances can be deceiving, according to Ejler Jakobsson in an article for *Railroad Magazine.*

> But if you should try to blow it up and actually manage to raise its 285,000 pounds—twice the weight of the usual Pullman car—off the ground, it would land on its wheels.
>
> If you should fire at it with the most powerful rifle or machine gun available today, its 5/8-inch armor plate and three-inch bullet-proof windows would stop the bullets cold. If you should destroy

> a bridge under it and sink the car in a lake or deep river, it would remain upright and dry inside, while its passengers would probably get out with comparative ease and safety through submarine escape hatches built into its roof.
>
> You could not, through any means now known, gain entrance into the Presidential car through its battleship-bulkhead doors—unless permitted to do so by its occupant. Nor could you, according to the best current scientific and engineering opinion, employ a force that would overturn it.
>
> Furthermore, you would be surrounded instantly by an army of [S]ecret [S]ervice agents, bodyguards, and railroad police.[365]

Security inside the train—and out—has been a continuing concern for organizers of presidential campaign train tours.

When Massachusetts governor Michael Dukakis conducted a whistle-stop train tour in 1988, "squads of Secret Service agents patrolled the train and sat in a high observation car. A security helicopter paced the engines, and a truck capable of running on the rails sped along behind, carrying a squad of armed guards," the *New York Times* reported.[366]

CROWD CONTROL

Railroad crossings could be a safety hazard for crowds too.

"In big eastern cities, the boon of viaduct entry sometimes solved the problem; the President spoke from the vantage of an elevated right of way to his audience standing immobile in the street," Walter Fitzmaurice wrote in an article for *Trains*.

"But in small towns, two still pools of people, divided by the track before the oncoming train, became rivers on its arrival. They flowed along its moving sides, swirled at the rear, and still eddied around the Magellan's platform when it halted."[367]

"Our biggest concern—and my personal nightmare—in all of these whistle-stops was the possibility of someone getting hurt," Margaret Truman remembered. "A railroad train is a very odd, very dangerous contrivance. The average person has no idea that it operates under mysterious laws of physics which are uniquely its own. For instance, when a train brakes at a station, the cars bunch together, and then slowly roll back the length of their couplings.

"On a seventeen-car train, this means the last car may roll back as much as three or four feet. Invariably, as we stopped, [the crowd] would surge right up under the wheels. Once I tugged on an emergency brake that was on the rear platform to prevent a rollback. I was quietly reprimanded. Dad pointed out I was liable to start a panic in the crowd," she admitted.[368]

Then there was the time that Harry Truman took a hands-on approach to a potentially dangerous situation in a crowd.

At one stop in Oklahoma, "a young man on a very skittish horse was among the crowd," Margaret Truman recalled. But "the train terrified the animal, and he was obviously close to bolting. There was a real danger that he might have hurt or killed the rider, as well as many other people in the crowd."

Calmly, her father stepped down from the rear platform and approached the rider.

"That's a fine horse you've got there, son," he said. He opened the horse's mouth and studied its teeth. "Eight years old, I see." Then he handed the horse's bridle to the Secret Service, who escorted it away from the train.[369]

PROBLEMS WITH PICKPOCKETS

It was not unusual for rallies at train stations to attract the criminal element.

William Jennings Bryan discovered that for himself in 1896. At depot rallies, the Democratic presidential nominee would talk about his free silver platform, which advocated that the US should mint silver and gold coins at a ratio of 16:1. It was an inflationary measure that would have increased the amount of money in circulation and helped farmers who were in debt and needed more money.[370] To make his point that both types of money were acceptable, in a trackside speech in Lemont, Illinois, Bryan asked people to raise their hands if they had either silver or gold in their pockets. That's when pickpockets would move throughout the crowd to relieve people of their silver or gold.

Bryan eventually hired Pinkerton detectives to monitor the crowds at his rallies.[371]

Pickpockets were so prevalent that Bryan could sometimes spot them as he was making speeches from the rear platform of his train.

At one depot rally, "the next President was showing a knowledge that would do credit to an inspector of detectives," one newspaper noted, quoting Bryan's observation that "the way to catch them in a crowd like this is to spot them by watching the men who get way into the middle of the crowd at every station and have to break through to get aboard when the train starts."

Bryan spotted would-be pickpockets and pointed the men out to a colleague on the platform, the *Kansas City Times* reported in 1896. "They were just in the act of picking a man's pocket. The cry of pickpocket went up from the platform, and the two men ducked low and tried to crowd out of the mob. A dozen men grabbed them, however, and as the train pulled out, they were being marched off to the lockup."[372]

TURNABOUT IS FAIR PLAY

When he ran for the White House a second time, in 1900, William Jennings Bryan was apparently feeling confident about where he and his wife would be living after the election.

Speaking at a whistle-stop rally, Bryan told the crowd, "Friends, tonight my little wife will be going to sleep in a cramped hotel room on the other side of town. But next March, she'll be sleeping in the White House."

Not everyone agreed, however. After the cheering subsided, a man yelled out, "If she does, she'll be sleeping with McKinley," referring to Bryan's opponent.

There is no record of what Bryan may have told the man, but William McKinley did win the election that November.[373]

Margaret Truman, daughter of President Harry S. Truman, remembered that "he had his share of hecklers, but they never bothered him" in his 1948 underdog run for the White House.

"He would let them shout for a few minutes, and then he would say, 'Now give me a chance to be heard.' Fair play took over and in another sixty seconds he had the crowd with him." But "once some twelve and thirteen-year-olds got really raucous and ignored this approach. Dad waited another minute for them to shut up, and then he pointed to them and said, 'I think it's time you boys went home to your mothers.'

"The crowd roared, and they did a sheepish vanishing act," she concluded.[374]

In 1952, as Nixon's campaign train was pulling out of the

railroad station in Marysville, California, he was heckled about allegations that he had improperly used private funds to pay for political-related expenses such as travel and postage.[375] (See the story on page 53.) "Hold the train!" Nixon shouted angrily. When the train came to a halt, the vice-presidential candidate reminded the crowd about his work investigating communists and denied that he had done anything wrong by using the funds.[376]

The harassment persisted at almost every stop in Oregon the next day.

"Large crowds continued to turn out as hecklers transformed my speeches into sparring matches," Nixon recalled.[377]

But the emerging crisis had taken the edge off the campaign train tour for the Republican candidate. "The next morning, the 'Nixon Special' steamed through Oregon, but the original thrill and anticipation with which we had started was gone," Nixon wrote in *Six Crises*. "The train seemed like a prison with its inexorable schedule."[378]

At a campaign stop in Eugene, Oregon, Nixon "noted that the violence of the attacks was finally beginning to backfire. Those supporting me in the crowd were resentful of the hecklers. They were not only listening to what I had to say and believing it but also, they were willing to fight back, just as I was."[379]

SAFETY FIRST

Some pranks could have caused serious damage or worse.

That was certainly the case when Nixon ran for president in 1960 against Senator John F. Kennedy. Officials on Nixon's campaign train reported that a metal transformer box had been tied to a railroad trestle and found on the train's route to Illinois. The thirteen-by-three-inch fluorescent transformer weighed twenty-five pounds.[380]

The container apparently could have derailed the train, according to police and railroad officials. The FBI noted that the train was later rerouted.

"'We think it was just a Halloween prank,' reported Charles J. Flaherty, superintendent of transportation for the northern region of the Pennsylvania Railroad. Fortunately, as a precaution, patrol cars had been sent ahead of [the] vice president's train to check for such obstacles.

"More than 25 policemen were assigned to patrol the tracks until Nixon's train passed through Fort Wayne on its way to Illinois, where similar precautions were expected to be taken," the United Press International said.[381]

The incident capped a busy day of dodging objects on the campaign trail. Earlier in the day, eggs were hurled at Nixon twice, and a tomato was thrown once.[382]

That wasn't the first (or likely last) time eggs or vegetables were tossed at politicians by a dissenting citizen.

In 1948, someone threw and hit Republican presidential nominee Thomas Dewey with a tomato as he was speaking from the rear platform of his train in Mount Vernon, Illinois.[383]

In 1952, an egg hit the roof of the rear platform car on Democratic presidential candidate Adlai Stevenson's campaign train as it was leaving a railroad station in Indiana.[384]

United Press reported that Frances Baghat, mother of the twenty-two-year-old woman who threw the egg, observed, "It was a nice, fresh, brown egg. Not a rotten one," and missed Stevenson by a couple of feet.

Her daughter, Lola, explained that she objected to some of the Democratic Party nominee's comments.[385]

Democratic presidential nominee Adlai Stevenson speaks from his campaign train in Fresno, California, during his 1952 run for the White House. Politicians sometimes faced hostile or unruly crowds. In Indiana, someone threw an egg at Stevenson as his train was leaving a railroad depot. The egg missed him by a couple of feet, according to one news report. (Photo by Robert Lerner for *Look* magazine. Courtesy of the Library of Congress, Prints & Photographs Division, LC 52 1752 nn.)

SIGNS OF THE TIMES

Some signs that were displayed by people at trackside rallies made a bigger impression on whistle-stopping candidates than others. A case in point is the sign that 1968 Republican presidential nominee Richard Nixon said he saw as he campaigned by train in Ohio.

Nixon mentioned the sign in his victory speech on November 6. "I saw many signs in this campaign. The one that touched me the most was the one I saw in Deshler, Ohio, at the end of a long day of whistle-stopping . . . . It was almost impossible to see [at dusk], but a teenager held up a sign: 'Bring us Together.' And that will be the great objective of this Administration."[386]

Presidential candidate Barry Goldwater, the conservative

Republican whose economic proposals stirred controversy and debate, experienced his share of hecklers during his 1964 race for the White House. When his train pulled into the station at Athens, Ohio, protesters appeared to outnumber supporters. One person in the crowd carried a sign that read "Don't stop here, we're poor enough!"[387]

A few days later Goldwater was delivering a speech from the back of his train in a town outside Indianapolis. The campaign special had stopped next to a house with an apple tree growing in the backyard. While the candidate was making his remarks, a homeowner threw apples at the train, shouting, "That's what you'll be selling if he gets elected!"[388]

PRANKSTER-IN-CHIEF

If hecklers in the crowd could get under the skin of politicians, consider the mischief caused by the occasional prankster who managed to get on a candidate's campaign train.

Dick Tuck, regarded by many as one of the greatest pranksters in American politics, found a way to be a thorn in the side of a whistle-stopping politician.[389]

In 1964, Tuck was able to sneak Moira O'Connor, a young woman pretending to be a freelance magazine writer, onto Goldwater's presidential campaign train. Once on board, she slipped copies of the *Whistle Stop* under the doors of the passengers' compartments. The satirical newsletter, written by Tuck, ridiculed Goldwater and made fun of some of the controversial issues of the day. O'Connor was eventually unmasked, caught, and thrown off the train.[390] "If Tuck was still aboard, he was staying well out of sight as the train rolled through Ohio," David Wise of the Herald Tribune News Service reported.[391]

The supporters aboard the 1916 "Women's Campaign Train for Hughes" are cheered on at a railroad station. Their whistle-stop tour on behalf of Republican presidential candidate Charles Evans Hughes was not always welcomed when it stopped at cities across the country. (George Grantham Bain Collection. Courtesy of the Library of Congress, Prints & Photographs Division, LC-DIG-ggbain-22965.)

HECKLED BY PROXY

The whistle-stop trains of surrogates who campaigned on behalf of candidates and causes were not immune from hecklers and protesters.

The "Women's Campaign Special" was organized for and by women who supported Republican Charles Evans Hughes in his 1916 race for the White House against Democrat Woodrow Wilson. The train had a second and equally important but controversial mission: to advocate for women's right to vote.

Depending on the political climate in the region where the train stopped, Hughes's supporters, dubbed the "Hughesettes," would be greeted with jeers—or worse.

Frances A. Kellor organized the train and chaired the National Hughes Alliance Women's Committee, which sought to rally support for Hughes's candidacy. She recounted in a January 1917 article for the *Yale Review* that "paid hecklers were common" along the train's route. At one campaign stop, she reported, there was an attempt to drive automobiles through the crowd. In other cities, the train was met with derogatory banners or threats of splattered red paint and barbed wire.

Given the issues at stake in the election and the emotions they generated, Kellor acknowledged that "this opposition was to be expected."[392]

Lady Bird Johnson heard from Goldwater supporters when she campaigned for her husband, Lyndon, on the "Lady Bird Special" in 1964. As the first wife of a presidential candidate to conduct her own train tour, Lady Bird was the target of heckling because of her husband's support of civil rights legislation.[393]

Before she could speak to the crowd that had gathered at the train station in Columbia, South Carolina, a group of boys banged a drum and chanted, "We want Barry! We want Barry!" In response, she told the audience, "My friends, in this country we are entitled to many viewpoints. You are entitled to yours. But right now, I'm entitled to mine."

Her impromptu comments not only silenced the hecklers at the rally, but they also made national news and even prompted Goldwater's staff to denounce the boys' rudeness and to discourage future heckling of the First Lady.[394]

But the heckling continued by some of the same people from Columbia when the train arrived in Charleston. The taunts grew uglier, with hecklers using the N-word and calling LBJ a communist. The chants went on despite efforts by others in the crowd to silence them.[395]

"Me Too——If There's One Thing I Can't Stand It's The Whistle-Stop Call Of The Lady Bird"

A Herblock Cartoon, © The Herb Block Foundation, used under license.

Once, as Lady Bird Johnson's train pulled out of a station, a young Goldwater supporter carrying a placard chased the train down the tracks. One of Johnson's daughters, Lynda, who was standing on the rear platform, shouted to him, "You'll never catch us. We're in the 20th century and you're in the 18th!"[396]

Lady Bird's advisors on the train counseled her to take stronger action against hecklers. But she refused, telling them, "Look, I appreciate your kind words, but the effect is simply this. We are doing more talking about the hecklers than about the candidates. So, really, I can handle any ugly moment, and I do think it would be best if we each ignored the hecklers as much as possible in speeches."[397]

CONFRONTATIONS

Rather than ignoring hecklers, Hubert Humphrey, Johnson's running mate in 1964, confronted his.

While speaking at the train station in Tracy, California, Humphrey was met with sign-carrying supporters of the Barry Goldwater–William Miller Republican ticket.

According to one news account, as Humphrey spoke, one of the young people in the crowd carrying a Goldwater-Miller sign continued shouting comments at the speaker. Humphrey silenced the heckler by responding, "Listen, young man, you'd better get some manners."[398]

As he toured Nebraska on his campaign train in 1968, Robert F. Kennedy ran into his share of hecklers.

"Kennedy showed his tough side by never allowing a hostile sign or an insult to go unchallenged," biographer Thurston Clarke, author of *The Last Campaign: Robert F. Kennedy and 82 Days That Inspired America*, pointed out. "His rebukes were usually gentle but could be barbed. When a small-town mayor wearing a Nixon button introduced him, he said, 'I want you to know how pleased I am at the courtesy of the mayor wearing his Nixon button, to come up here and introduce me.'"[399]

As Democratic presidential candidate Edmund Muskie's train was making its way to Miami in 1972, "a genuinely savage person had boarded the train in West Palm Beach, using a fraudulent press pass, then ran amok in the lounge car," Hunter S. Thompson wrote in his book *Fear and Loathing on the Campaign Trail '72.*

Quoting news reports about the incident, Thompson noted that the intruder got "in 'several fistfights' and heckled the senator 'unmercifully' when the train pulled into Miami [and] Muskie went out on the caboose platform to deliver what was supposed to have been the climactic speech of his triumphant whistle-stop tour."

The heckler continued his tirade outside of the train, taunting Muskie as he was speaking from the rear platform. The presidential candidate cut his speech short because of the heckling, Thompson observed.[400]

Muskie tried his best to deal with the heckling by the intruder and others.

"Finally, Muskie's temper boiled," the *Tampa Tribune* reported. "When one youth called out, 'I've got a question,' he leaned over the railing, stabbed his finger at him, and said, 'No, you don't have a question. Your only intention is to disrupt this meeting and I'm not going to let you get away with it. I'm going to talk to these people, and I'm going to say it my way.'

"The crowd roared its approval and a Muskie press aide remarked, 'He's better when he gets mad.'"

Yippie leader Jerry Rubin told a reporter afterward that he was the person Muskie had chastised.[401]

Vice President Gerald Ford became president when Richard Nixon resigned in disgrace in 1974 because of the Watergate scandal. Running for election in 1976, the former Michigan congressman was campaigning by train in Flint, Michigan, where he bragged about the state's economy. A young man in the crowd disagreed and yelled at the president, "You blew it!"

Ford would have none of it, responding, "We blew it in the right direction, young man—and those of you who don't agree—and if you would go out and look for a job, you would get one."[402]

CHICKEN AND WAFFLES

When President George H. W. Bush sought reelection in 1992, his campaign train appearances in the Midwest were shadowed for more than a week by hecklers wearing chicken costumes and holding signs that read "Chicken George Won't Debate."

The "chicken offensive" was meant to call attention to and make fun of the Republican candidate's refusal to debate Bill Clinton, his Democratic opponent. Underneath the fifteen or twenty chicken costumes that followed Bush around the country were flesh-and-blood volunteers working under the direction of the Clinton campaign.

At one rear-platform campaign rally, Bush apparently could not take the ribbing any longer. "You talking about the draft record chicken or are you talking about the chicken in the Arkansas River?" he asked the bird in the audience, the *New York Times* reported. Getting no reply from the sign-holding feathered heckler, Bush pressed on. "Which one are you talking about? Which one? Get out of here. Maybe it's the draft? Is that what's bothering you?"

For whatever reason, the Republican president finally agreed to debate Clinton. Although the chicken did not claim credit for pushing Bush over the edge, fowl play was never ruled out by authorities.[403]

But Bill Clinton was not immune from protesters either.

"Some opposition popped up along the way" of his whistle-stop train tour in August 1996, according to Reuters, "but Clinton brushed it off like a bothersome fly. He thanked a group of people waving 'Dole-Kemp' signs for bothering to join Democrats at his rally.

"One sign offered a reminder of Clinton's most troublesome obstacle, the Whitewater financial scandal. It said: 'Two terms for Clinton—one in office, one in jail.'"[404]

Democratic running mates John Kerry and John Edwards faced a divided and raucous crowd when their campaign train pulled into Sedalia, Missouri, in 2004.

"Holding candles, flashlights and posters, the people of Sedalia engaged in a shouting contest: Some called out 'Four more years' and 'We want Bush,' while their neighbors chanted, 'Three more months' and 'Kerry! Kerry!' The candidates could barely get a word in," the *Chicago Tribune* reported.

"Posters held aloft competed for attention too. There were signs that read 'Give 'em hell, Kerry' and others that simply said 'W.'

"'Will you let us speak? Will you let us speak, please?' Edwards urged the jeering Republican section of the crowd."

The protesters continued, and Edwards then asked pointedly, "Are you guys really booing outsourcing of millions of America's jobs and doing something about it? My children are on this train. Show them some good Missouri manners, would you please?"[405]

CHAPTER 5

Meet the Press

Covering a Presidential election campaign trip . . . is about the hardest work there is in all [of] journalism. It means writing round the clock. It is not unusual for reporters writing for both day and night circulations [newspapers] to go two or three weeks with only two or three hours of sleep a night.[406]

—Merriman Smith, United Press

Abraham Lincoln taught reporters an early lesson about the importance of covering whistle-stopping politicians. The president-elect had indicated to journalists that he would not make any speeches before he left Springfield, Illinois, on the train trip to his inauguration in Washington, DC. Unfortunately for the reporters, Lincoln delivered impromptu remarks from the back of his train to a crowd of well-wishers who had come to the depot to see him off.[407]

After the train departed, the reporters on board surrounded Lincoln and asked for a copy of his speech. Because his comments had been impromptu, Lincoln promised he would do his best to write down whatever he could remember saying. The president-elect then dictated to an aide, after which copies were made and distributed to reporters.[408]

Campaign trains were a win-win for politicians and journalists alike. Candidates did not have to worry whether the press would come out to the depot to cover their speeches, while reporters knew that they would never be too far away from the politician, especially those who were crisscrossing the country.

For reporters, "The old campaign trains had many conveniences which the newest planes do not have," Carroll Kilpatrick, a reporter for the *Washington Post and Times-Herald* observed in 1956.

"Usually the train had that most welcome of luxuries: a shower. Correspondents had comfortable bedrooms or drawing rooms where they could put their typewriters on a table and where they could have some privacy.

"The diner usually operated almost 24 hours a day so that a correspondent could have a meal late at night after his work was done. Weekend breaks, so that the candidate could rest a bit in a hotel and get some laundry done, were welcome to the newsmen, too."[409]

Different journalists would cover whistle-stopping politicians in different ways.

Bruce Biossat, a reporter with the Newspaper Enterprise Association, traveled on Dwight Eisenhower's campaign train in 1952. He said that the journalists on a campaign train "usually fall into one of three categories, according to their work habits.

"The first stays in the press car, listens to the candidate spout over the public address system, pounds out his copy moments after the words are uttered, and thrusts his output at [a Western Union representative] a page at a time. The second leaps off the train at each stop, dashes back to the rear, and either stands close to the back platform or mingles with the crowd, observing and taking notes. This one writes his copy for the next stop—or maybe later.

"The third species waits for the official text of the speech," Biossat concluded.[410]

Associated Press reporter Jack Bell recalled that "since press association men worked in pairs, it was customary for one to remain at his typewriter and the other to get an estimate from local police of the size of the crowd, note any untoward incidents, and either dash to a phone to dictate his story or hurry back to the work car to bat out a few lines to be handed to Western Union before the train pulled out."[411]

Hobart Rowen, a reporter with *Newsweek* magazine, covered Harry Truman in 1952 as he campaigned by train for Democratic presidential nominee Adlai Stevenson. He remembered that "after a Truman-rear-platform speech, we would race to the press car and pound out our stories.

"Someone would yell, 'How big a crowd?' The *Washington Star*'s venerable Joseph A. Fox would stare out of a window for a moment, while we awaited his official call, and then sing out: 'Make it twenty-five hundred—no, three thousand.' And the rest of us would dutifully enter 3,000 in our stories."[412]

Traveling reporters were often issued press credentials, which some apparently balked at wearing.

"Correspondents aboard [the] Dewey train who have rebelled at wearing [the] huge buttons, which make them look like members of the Republican National Committee, now have a way of getting even," Drew Pearson noted in one of his nationally syndicated

Whistle-stopping candidates were often greeted by thousands of people at railroad depots and other trackside rallies. Democratic presidential nominee Adlai Stevenson speaks to a large gathering in Fresno, California, on September 17, 1952. (Photo by Robert Lerner for *Look* magazine. Courtesy of the Library of Congress, Prints & Photographs Division, LC-DIG-ppmsca-30526.)

columns. In small towns, "spectators seeing the buttons, rush up to newsmen, ask how the campaign is going, [and] are dismayed when reporters who look like GOP officials, say it looks 'very bad, very tough for our man up there,' pointing to Dewey."[413]

"The dry states posed a problem for those of the Fourth Estate who liked a drink or two after a hard day rewriting the same speech trying to make it look new," Jeremiah O'Leary, a reporter with the *Washington Times*, observed.

"One veteran, Jerry Green of the *New York Daily News*, used to tell of the special topcoat in which he had installed 10 little pockets, each capable of holding a half pint. You never knew when the train might venture into Iowa, Kansas, Virginia, North Carolina, Mississippi, or another state which enforced local dry laws, even on presidential trains," O'Leary said.[414]

Another challenge for reporters was that some politicians were more unpredictable than others about what they would say—or if, when, and where they would say it.

William Jennings Bryan "was a trial to newspapermen on his campaign journeys, for he frequently arose early in the morning to greet his admirers or make nearly impossible train connections. His long days of campaigning wore heavily on the reporters," according to Keith Melder, associate curator in the division of political history in what was then called the Smithsonian Institution's Museum of History and Technology.[415]

Reporters never knew when President Harry Truman was "going to make an impromptu speech from the rear platform of his car," Merriman Smith of United Press noted.

"The unscheduled platform appearances drive reporters daffy and make for many hours of nervous worry," Smith wrote. "A traveling White House correspondent never knows when the President is going to say something newsworthy. Thus, at each stop, the reporters boil out of their cars and race for the rear end of the train. The President comes out on the platform of his car, waves and acknowledges the cheers of the station crowd.

"And then he may speak. And the stop may last no more than three or four minutes. During that period, the newspapermen—the wire service reporters at least—must record the President's words, dash back to their rooms, bat out a few paragraphs, and hand them to a Western Union representative before the train pulls out."[416]

Halfway through Truman's 1948 national train tour, members of the traveling press were critical of the logistics for covering the candidate. Irwin Ross, the author of *The Loneliest Campaign: The Truman Victory of 1948*, noted that there were some unexpected challenges that made it more difficult for the fifty members of the press corps to cover the president—and for Truman to receive the most amount of coverage for his speeches.[417]

"Truman's prepared texts were often available only an hour or so before delivery; this meant that for the principal evening speech delivered on the West Coast, text would be available too late to be printed verbatim in the first editions of the morning papers in the East, where it was three hours later.

"Reporters were dismayed at the lack of a loudspeaker in the press car, which compelled them to dash back to the end of the train to catch the President's words at a brief whistle-stop. They were also not allowed in the last three cars of the train, where the Presidential staff worked and local politicians were received; a useful news source was thus cut off," he noted.

"The same lack of forethought also extended to such housekeeping details as laundry arrangements and baggage pickups; when the Truman train stopped overnight in a city, it was every man for himself," Ross observed.

There were no such problems on the train of Truman's Republican challenger, Thomas Dewey.

"Newspapermen were impressed by the smooth professionalism of the Dewey operation," according to Ross. "Prepared texts for speeches were usually available twenty-four hours before delivery, giving reporters plenty of time to mull over their stories.

"The press car and the two dining cars were equipped with loudspeakers, enabling newspapermen to hear Dewey's back-platform comments without stirring from their air-conditioned quarters. (Many reporters, of course, scrambled to the rear of the train to observe crowd reactions.)

"No housekeeping detail was overlooked, down to laundry, which was dispatched and retrieved within a few hours," Ross observed.[418]

"Next Stop, Wyoming—9 Votes"

ASLEEP AT THE SWITCH

On two occasions, a candidate's unexpected rear-platform speech literally caught the traveling press asleep at the switch.

Alice Dunnigan, a reporter for several Black newspapers, wrote in her autobiography, *Alone atop the Hill,* about the time she was on Truman's 1948 campaign train tour in Missoula, Montana. "The president and many of the reporters had retired since no other stops were planned for the night. But as the train reached this little college town, hundreds of students had gathered along the railroad track to see the president.

"The train came to a halt, and President Truman, dressed in pajamas and robe, briefly addressed the young people from the back of the coach. After his remarks, the students began asking questions. One yelled out loudly and clearly, 'Mr. President, what do you say about civil rights?' For much of this trip, President Truman had made no mention of the issue.

"The president quickly replied, 'I'll say that civil rights is as old as the Constitution of the United States and as new as the Democratic platform of 1944.' He then intimated that it would be renewed in the 1948 platform. That was one of the first of my big western stories, headlined 'Pajama Clad President Defends Civil Rights at Midnight,'" Dunnigan wrote.

She noted that two other reporters "missed the story because they were not out by the platform. They tried to prevail upon me not to file my story because it would make them 'look bad' to have missed it. I did not comply, and they probably filed stories anyway based on discussions with other members of the press."[419]

A similar incident happened four years later on Dwight Eisenhower's campaign train during his race for the White House. When the train made a scheduled early-morning maintenance stop in Salisbury, North Carolina, two hundred people had gathered there in the off chance that they would see the candidate. The crowd chanted, "We want Ike!"

Reporters, by now roused from their slumber, scrambled to record the surprise campaign appearance. Eisenhower, wearing pajamas and a robe, walked onto the rear platform of the train and leaned over the railing to shake hands with people. He was soon joined by his wife, Mamie. She was dressed in a negligee, and her hair was in curlers.

The Republican candidate told the appreciative crowd that he did not know that the train was scheduled to stop in their community. "My staff would give me the devil if they knew I was up. I'm supposed to be resting," he said.[420]

George Herman, a correspondent for CBS News, who covered Lyndon Johnson's 1960 campaign train, recalled:

> What would happen is, you would be sitting in the press car typing away, or listening to your tape recordings or making plans how you were going to deploy your troops at the next stop, and sort of subliminally in the back of your mind without your knowing it there would be music—and it would gradually increase, and you would hear "The Yellow Rose of Texas." And that was your warning that you were about to pull into another stop, and you'd better get your ass out of the press car and get out to watch the speech.
>
> Usually, if there was a text of the speech, you'd give the text to the cameraman with markings as to what you wanted and say, "If he departs from the text, film it all."

And then you would go out and work the crowd to see if you could find local political bosses, what they thought the odds were, and how they thought the vote in their town was going to go. [And then find] just plain people, to see if they had ever heard of Lyndon B. Johnson, and what they thought the Kennedy-Johnson ticket was going to do.

So, you tried to not stay and listen to the speech, because you had the text of it usually or had listened to that speech seventeen times already that day, and you knew what it was going to be, with a possible local variation.

Johnson, when he was campaigning, would speak in a soft, almost an undertaker's voice, and we were all so tired and [would] look down the line of the cameramen, and they would all be at their cameras, and the soundmen with their earphones on, dozing.

And then Johnson would say, "Folks, I'd like you all to meet my good wife. [Lady] Bird, come up here and say a word to these folks." . . . And Lady Bird would come up and say in a very high, screechy voice, "Friends . . ." and you'd look down the line and see all the soundmen wake up and snatch off their earphones![421]

REBUFFED

Herman said he'd heard a lot about covering whistle-stops before he was assigned to ride on Adlai Stevenson's presidential campaign train in 1956. He noted that the traveling reporters saw "crowds along the way waiting to wave at the candidate without ever knowing whether he would step out and wave back. And I must say that most of the press people waved back . . . you just did not want to disappoint them."[422]

Herman observed that Stevenson, an otherwise learned and erudite politician, was a babe in the woods when it came to understanding the impact of the mass media in an election year.

On one train trip, Herman promised Stevenson a five-minute story on the evening news if the candidate would only let a CBS cameraman take some pictures of him writing a speech, meeting with aides, talking with supporters, and so forth.

"Oh no," Stevenson replied, "that would be a gross invasion of privacy."

Herman remembered thinking, "If this man doesn't even understand television and politics, he doesn't understand America."[423]

ENDURANCE TEST

Liz Carpenter, press secretary to Lady Bird Johnson, recounted what it was like for the journalists who accompanied Johnson as she campaigned for her husband on the "Lady Bird Special" in 1964.

Carpenter thought that the most important decision she made when she organized the train trip was asking Dr. Janet Travell to minister to the 150 reporters who had signed up for the tour.

"For the press, the whole trip was a brutal physical endurance test," Carpenter wrote in her memoir, *Ruffles and Flourishes*. "I accused [Dr. Travell] of dispensing more drugs than I did press releases. There seemed to be an epidemic of laryngitis and sprained ankles."

And while the correspondents brought along their own occupational ailments—including stomach ulcers, hypochondria, and hypertension—they also acquired a series of minor injuries on board the swaying railroad cars and on the ground at depot stops.[424]

"But the reporters seemed to thrive on the pace," she remembered. "As the train would stop, they would jump off the cars, race down the side of the track to the back platform, record the happenings, the color, and the speech—and, if they were on a deadline, grab one of the phones we hooked up at each stop and dictate a story. Two toots of the [train] whistle, and they boarded again. We were off for the next stop."[425]

HAZARDOUS DUTY

There were other reasons campaign trains could be dangerous for reporters.

Associated Press reporters Jack Bell and Gardner Bridge were on board the Thomas Dewey campaign train in 1944 as it traveled one morning to Portland, Oregon, where the candidate was going to deliver a speech. The two journalists were seated in the press car and going over an advance copy of the candidate's remarks, when "suddenly, we weren't sitting at all," said Bell. "With a tremendous crash, the train stopped dead, and typewriters and chairs flew in every direction."[426]

"I should then like to say that when we picked ourselves up groggily from amid our first train wreck, we thought first of the presidential candidate and his lady and our duty to get off a story on this unprecedented happening to a campaign special. But we didn't," Bell admitted.

Instead, they made their way to a well-stocked bar in the

car, where miniature bottles of whiskey now covered the floor. "Automatically," he remembered, "Gardner and I reached out, picked up a miniature each, uncorked it, and swallowed the contents. Fortified with another of these windfalls, we made our way back through the train to find that Dewey and his wife had survived the wreck without major mishap."

Several reporters were hurt, including Bell and Bridge, who both suffered broken ribs. The journalists managed to escape from the railroad car, then interviewed the engineer about the accident. Their next challenge was to find a way to file a story about this late-breaking news. Bell managed to climb a steep embankment up to an adjacent highway and hitchhiked to a telephone, where he dictated the story. He beat the competition by more than fifteen minutes.[427]

"Dewey, sitting in the bedroom of his car, was shaken but not hurt by the collision; his wife struck her head against a wall," wrote David M. Jordan, author of *FDR, Dewey, and the Election of 1944*. "Luckily, the Deweys' engineer was able to slow his train down some before hitting the stopped train, and only the front car (the baggage and darkroom car used by the photographers) was severely damaged, although there was broken glass in cars further back."[428]

"Railroad men said they had no explanation for the wreck. They were in agreement it was the most 'stupid' wreck in railroad history," Charles M. Dean, a journalist with the *Cincinnati Enquirer*, reported.

"The crew knew the railroad had been blocked by a freight wreck at Castle Rock for 18 hours. Two giant freight engines were strewn across the right of way. The regular passenger train into which the special crashed was 'carrying signals' yet the special rushed around the curve a quarter of a mile north of Castle

Rock at 55 miles an hour. The engineer [thought that] if he had 'two more car lengths' he could have stopped in time. The only car damaged on the regular passenger train was the private car of a railroad official. Its occupants were uninjured because they 'knew how to take a wreck shock.'"[429]

The incident led someone on a train to write a theme song for the Dewey campaign train. According to nationally syndicated columnist Drew Pearson, "The Saga of E. A. Wells," sung to the tune of the immortal railroad song "Casey Jones," was about the engineer of Dewey's train that rammed another train.[430]

To commemorate the accident, the candidate, his staff, and the traveling reporters formed the "Castle Rock Survivors Association" and had their official group portrait taken at the rail depot in Tulsa, Oklahoma.[431]

Another reporter had a problem staying on the train. In 1948, the Truman campaign train was pulling into the depot at Berkeley, California. UP's Merriman Smith remembered that he "leaned far over the rail to get an early glimpse of the size of the crowd, reception arrangements, and so on. I already had a text of the President's remarks and wanted to file a story immediately."

But he said that he leaned too far, lost his balance, and "toppled off the train, landing on a steel guy wire."

Alarmed members of the welcoming committee thought he was dead. Smith wrote in his memoir that "to get me out of the way, they stuffed me into a telephone booth at the station. It turned out to be the only telephone within miles, and we got a ten-minute beat on the story."[432]

Reporters need not even be on the train to be imperiled. Frances Lewine of the Associated Press, who traveled on Lady Bird Johnson's campaign train in 1964, said that "as I was

Thomas Dewey, the 1944 Republican nominee for president (standing at the center of the train's rear platform), is joined in Tulsa, Oklahoma, by dozens of reporters and campaign staff for a group photo of the Castle Rock Survivors Association. The association was formed after an accident involving Dewey's campaign train in Castle Rock, Washington, in September 1944. (Photo courtesy of Gardner Bridge, an Associated Press reporter who was on the train and whose face is circled in the back right. The name of the photographer is not known.)

running up the tracks one day to get to the front of the car [to see] if there was anything going on there, I heard a large crash, practically within a half inch of me, and one of these 25, 50, or 100 pounds of cakes of ice [had] slammed off its little cart and missed me by inches."[433]

FILING STORIES

"For us broadcasters, there was a film to be handed to a courier who would be waiting for us, or a camera crew would be waiting there, and they would take the film back themselves. And for radio, there were telephones," recalled CBS's George Herman.

"There were many cases of missed connections and problems in getting copy or film back to headquarters. But it was not usually terribly important because if the candidate wanted to deliver a major policy address, it wasn't usually from the back of a train in those days."[434]

Writing copy aboard a campaign special was one thing. But trying to get it delivered to the home office could be quite another.

Merriman Smith of the United Press remembered that in 1946, Western Union's Carroll Linkins was "a traveling guardian angel" for reporters. Once journalists "hand their copy to him they know it is as good as in their offices," Smith wrote. "'Link' alerts Western Union representatives all down the line ahead of the Presidential train, and if there is no stop, he puts the copy in a weighted canvas bag and hurls it at the stationmaster as the train speeds through the town."[435]

Sometimes, however, it took more than Western Union to get a story filed. Smith described the time when "we were up in the boondocks of Northern California during the Truman campaign. The train was not due to stop for some time, and Mr. Truman had been saying some highly printable things about [Soviet leader Joseph Stalin]. . . . We had a big story and no way to file it."

He told a traveling United Press regional reporter that the only way to file the story was for him to jump off the train at the next station. As Smith described it later, the UP reporter "didn't much like the idea but finally agreed that if the train would slow down at the next town he would jump off. Then I got the White House transportation man to have the train slowed down, and the man jumped. He caught up with me about two days later. He said he didn't know how fast the train had been going when he jumped but that he had run for about a hundred yards before he could start rolling. United Press got about a 45-minute beat on that story.

"Press room folklore eventually had it that I wrapped the man in pillows and personally shoved him out the door," Smith wrote, "but this is [an] exaggeration. Actually, we were simply operating on an old principle—the theory of the expendable reporter."[436]

He was not alone in using creative ways to get his copy to his newspaper.

To file his story about Truman's comments on Stalin, journalist Robert Donovan remembered, "I wrote my story, then on top of it, I put a telephone number for the telegraph editor of the *Herald Tribune* in New York, and I attached a ten-dollar bill to it.

"When we stopped at the [next train] station, there were a lot of people milling around, and I had an idea. I was going to find a nice-looking middle-aged woman who looked responsible. I spotted this one lady. She was wearing a green plaid skirt, and I rushed right up to her—we did not have but a few minutes at that station—and I said, 'Ma'am, look, would you do something for me? Would you just take this and follow my instructions?'"

When the woman refused to take his money, Donovan told her, "Never mind, I don't have time to argue with you now. Would you just call this number [and] tell the editor who answers that I couldn't file. Then he will put you on a telephone recording device, and just read it to the device."

When he got back to San Francisco, he found a telegram informing him that the *Herald Tribune* was the only paper in New York that had made the big press run with the story!

"I never found out who that woman was," Donovan concluded. "I wish I had. I would have sent her a copy of the story."[437]

SWITCHING SIDES

Leo W. O'Brien, a reporter with the International News Service, "rode the campaign trains with Dewey so much that politics got in his blood," Sidney Shalett wrote in an article for the *Saturday Evening Post.*

"He would come back to the press car after the evening's work was done, mount a chair and make mock political speeches. Finally, unable to stand it any longer, he ran for Congress and was elected," Shalett noted.[438]

O'Brien, a Democrat, served in the House of Representatives for fourteen years.[439]

THE STORIES BEHIND TWO PHOTOS

The staff of whistle-stopping politicians usually took full advantage of the news-making nature of their trains and the backdrops they provided to generate favorable publicity about the politicians.

But that backdrop did not work out as intended for President Franklin Roosevelt in 1944.

After delivering his acceptance speech to the Democratic convention via radio from one of the cars on his train, FDR reread a few lines from his speech for the benefit of a newsreel cameraman and wire service photographer, according to Stanley Weintraub, professor emeritus of arts and humanities at Penn State University, in his book *Final Victory: FDR's Extraordinary World War II Presidential Campaign.*

But the photograph that was distributed by the wire service to newspapers across the country did not create the intended results. The photo showed "Roosevelt's mouth hung slack and

US President Franklin D. Roosevelt accepts the Democratic nomination for a fourth term in the White House via radio from a railroad car at a Pacific Coast naval base on July 20, 1944. The photo that was sent to newspapers did not show the president in a favorable light and raised concerns about his health. (Associated Press, used under license.)

gaping; flashbulbs had glazed his eyes and highlighted his haggard features," Weintraub wrote.

"Even worse, the brief newsreel shot at the same time revealed more of the hollow cheeks, gaping mouth, and loose shirt collar that evidenced serious weight loss," he noted.

"From the negatives, the local AP editor chose one with the President speaking, and another with his mouth closed. For transmission from Los Angeles, [AP photo editor] Dick Strobel chose 'the one with the open mouth, since it was more obvious that he was talking. I went into my office to write the caption while the darkroom technicians processed the print.'

"As soon as the cameraman, George Skaddings, saw the results, he rushed the picture back to Strobel. 'Hey, you better look at this,' he warned. . . .

"Yet there was no time to prepare a substitute image. The President was in San Diego, and in the East it was already two in the morning on the 21st. Final editions of the morning papers were being held for the wire photo. 'I made the judgment,' Strobel explained, 'to go with what we had.'

"For the anti-FDR press, the photo was a gift," Weintraub observed. "The image validated for the opposition that Roosevelt was feeble beyond his sixty-two years, demonstrably unfit to continue in office."[440]

The famous scene documented by photographers of Truman holding the *Chicago Daily Tribune* headline "Dewey Defeats Truman" was taken on the back of Truman's campaign train.

But the pictures were not taken on the night of Truman's come-from-behind victory.

Ben Cosgrove, in an article for *Life* magazine, said, "Of the countless politics-related photographs made over, say, the past century, one would be hard-pressed to point to a more famous image. . . .

"The reason for the picture's immortality? It's not the headline itself although that titanic error is, in its own way, rather marvelous—the screw-up was the result of an early press time and a poor prediction. Instead, the picture endures because of the look of unabashed, in-your-face delight in Truman's eyes. . . .

"A full two days after the election, the president was on his way back to Washington from his home in Independence, Mo., when his train stopped in St. Louis. There, someone handed Truman a two-day-old copy of the *Tribune*. (One version has a staffer serendipitously finding the paper under a seat in the station.)

"Maybe Truman had already heard about the Republican-leaning *Trib*'s embarrassing snafu, but he had not yet held a copy in his hands. Perhaps this was the first time he had any

At the train station in St. Louis, President Harry S. Truman holds up a copy of the *Chicago Daily Tribune* that erroneously reported Thomas Dewey's victory in the 1948 presidential election. (Photo by Pierce Hangge for the *St. Louis Globe Democrat*. Courtesy of the Harry S. Truman Presidential Library & Museum, used by permission.)

inkling of how huge and how hugely mistaken the headline actually was. However it shook out, in [photographer W. Eugene] Smith's photograph of that priceless moment [that appeared in *Life* magazine], Truman's elation upon coming face to face with the dead-wrong assertion of his defeat is positively palpable."

Similar images of Truman were taken by other photographers and published in newspapers and other publications.

"Seeing the image today, in the world of the 24/7 news cycle, it's hard to believe that the photograph was *not* made on election night," Cosgrove noted. "After all, in an age of 24/7 news, when more and more media consumers get their breaking news via tweets and friends' Facebook posts, two days can seem like a lifetime."[441]

AN INFORMED PRESS

The staff of whistle-stopping politicians often prepared and distributed information to reporters about the upcoming train trips.

For example, journalists on George McGovern's 1972 tour of central California received a press-briefing kit that included when and where the train would stop, a recap of the history of whistle-stop trains, a biography of the candidate, and profiles of the areas where the train would stop or travel through.[442]

Reporters and other passengers on Earl Warren's 1948 campaign train tour received *Daily Travel Notes*, a mimeographed newsletter with information about the day's scheduled stops and updates about the VIPs on board and transportation arrangements when the candidate left the train for a campaign event.[443]

HELPING HANDS

AP reporter Jack Bell wrote, "There was an uncertain element of timing and chance [to covering campaign train speeches] as I found out one hot day in San Bernardino, California, when Dewey, then the GOP nominee, made some unexpected remarks. In a telephone booth, dictating the story to Los Angeles, I looked out and saw the train beginning to move while the candidate still was speaking.

"No reporter who is traveling with a presidential candidate can afford to be left behind, watching his assignment and his home on wheels moving out of his reach. Cutting off in the middle of a sentence, I shouted, 'Train's going,' and hung up.

"Racing out to the tracks, I sprinted to catch up with the cars that were gathering speed.

The *McGovern Victory Special*, a thirty-four-page press information kit, was distributed to the reporters who accompanied Senator George McGovern (D-South Dakota) on his June 1972 campaign train trip in California. (McGovern Northern California Headquarters.)

Daily Travel Notes

DEWEY - WARREN
1948 CAMPAIGN

Published En Route on Governor Warren's Special Train

September 16, 1948 — Number III

SCHEDULE FOR TOMORROW

Ar.	Helper, Utah	MST	2:00 AM
Lv.	" "	"	2:10 AM
Ar.	Grand Junction, Colo.	"	6:10 AM
Lv.	" " "	"	6:20 AM
Ar.	Glenwood Springs, Colo.	"	8:20 AM
Lv.	" " "	"	8:40 AM
Ar.	Minturn, Colo.	"	10:20 AM
Lv.	" "	"	10:25 AM
Ar.	Malta, Colo.	"	11:40 AM
Lv.	" "	"	11:50 AM
Ar.	Salida, Colo.	"	1:00 PM
Lv.	" "	"	1:20 PM
Ar.	Royal Gorge, Colo.	"	3:00 PM
Lv.	" " "	"	3:05 PM
Ar.	Canyon City, Colo.	"	3:20 PM
Lv.	" " "	"	3:30 PM
Ar.	Pueblo, Colo.	"	4:30 PM

(Lv. Pueblo 4:00 AM Saturday)

PLATFORM TALKS

Platform talks are scheduled at Malta, Salida and Canyon City. The Governor may make an appearance on the rear platform at other operation stops if local conditions warrant it.

UTAH VIP'S

The list of prominent Utah Republicans to board at Ogden as listed in the Sept. 15 Daily Travel Notes should be corrected as follows:

Additions: S.C. Stewart, committee member.
Deletions: E.K. Moffatt, Fred L. Finlanson, J.A. Ottenheimer.

PROMINENT REPUBLICANS BOARDING IN COLORADO

Grand Junction

Congressman Robert Rockwell
Ralph Carr, former governor
Leon H. Snyder, National Committeeman

Glenwood Springs

Judge Charrwin, county chairman
U. S. Senator Eugene Milliken
David Hamil, candidate for governor
Will F. Nicholson, candidate for U. S. senator
Congressman J. Edgar Chenoweth
Chris Cusak, candidate for congress
William L. Lloyd, state chairman
Alma K. Schneider, national committeewoman
Lt. Gov. Homer Pearson
Mary Retter, county vice chairman

Royal Gorge

Lee Blackwell, county chairman
Grace Ireland, county chairwoman

The first page of the *Daily Travel Notes*, a mimeographed newsletter published from the campaign train of California Governor Earl Warren during his 1948 whistle-stop train tour as the Republican vice-presidential nominee. (Dewey-Warren 1948 Campaign.)

"On the back platform, Paul Lockwood, Dewey's assistant, saw my plight, hurriedly opened the gate to the steps, and cheered me on. I managed to grab the railing and swing aboard with Lockwood's help just as the engineer put on a burst of speed."[444]

One day in 1904, when President Theodore Roosevelt's campaign train made a brief scheduled stop in Bloomington, Illinois, a journalist "got off to buy some stationery, but the special pulled out before he could get back on," Ejler Jakobsson wrote in *Railroad Magazine.*

The reporter "ran at top speed, puffing and straining, but the gap between him and the last car kept widening. He was about to give up when Roosevelt, standing on the rear platform, leaned over, reached out, and helped the galloping reporter onto the speeding train.

"'I just had to make it because Teddy expected me to,' the reporter recalled afterward. 'With a final spurt, I grasped his outstretched hand and was dragged up the steps. There I lay for a few minutes, utterly spent. But for Teddy's help, I would never have caught the train.'"[445]

The staff on Republican presidential nominee Wendell Willkie's train "had a habit of pulling the cord as soon as the candidate was aboard and, as far as the correspondents were concerned, it was every man for himself," journalist Sidney Shalett recalled in a story that was published in the *Saturday Evening Post.*

"One day Willkie was amiably riding through southern Ohio enjoying the scenery, when he saw two carloads of people speeding along and frantically waving. Willkie, surmising that they were supporters come to get a glimpse of him, enthusiastically waved back.

"At the next stop he found out that the two cars contained correspondents [who had been] left behind after the last speech.

'We had to get state troopers to help us catch that train,' Jim Wright, Washington correspondent for the *Buffalo Evening News*, said. 'I'll never forget that ride in an open car at 83 miles per hour!'"[446]

In 1923, reporter Stephen T. Early (who later became a press secretary for President Franklin Roosevelt) was arrested as a communist agitator for trying to reboard President Warren G. Harding's campaign train in St. Louis. But "it was a short-lived arrest, for it was not long before the Secret Service explained the error and the St. Louis police released the wire service reporter to continue the trip," Linda Lotridge Levin wrote in her book, *The Making of FDR: The Story of Stephen T. Early, America's First Modern Press Secretary.*[447]

Bonnie Angelo, a reporter with Newhouse News Service, noted that "so far as the press was concerned, one of the greatest hazards [in riding campaign trains] is missing the train. It is very easy to happen because we are not allowed to jump out of the back platform. You have to run about five cars forward as the train pulls into town and the music starts playing. You leap off, and it is quite a leap down, I may say.

"You are not necessarily in a [train] station. You are maybe out where there is a [two- to three-foot] drop down. In any case, you get down and go leaping like rather ungraceful gazelles across railroad ties.

"You finally get up to the end of the train, and then the time comes, and a little whistle—the two-minute [warning] whistle—is blown.

"Then you have two minutes to get back. And you have two fears. Fear one is that you may miss the train. But if you decided to go ahead and make it, you may miss a sort of wonderful last line [by the politician]."[448]

BLOWING THE WHISTLE

It took a future chief justice of the United States to come up with a solution to the problem of frequently stranded reporters.

Earl Warren, whose father worked on the railroads, was Thomas Dewey's running mate in 1948. Warren instructed his staff to blow a police whistle two minutes before the train was scheduled to leave so that reporters and staff members could have enough time to board. The practice was later adopted by other candidates, who had the engineer blow the train whistle as the official warning of pending departure.[449]

But this solution did not work all the time.

Loye Miller, a correspondent for *Time* magazine, recalled that in 1964, Senator Barry Goldwater's whistle-stop train left unexpectedly, immediately after he delivered a speech in Athens, Ohio. About a dozen reporters were stranded at the station. A horrified look crossed Goldwater's face as he recognized several familiar faces among the people who were frantically waving their arms.

A reporter, parodying one of the candidate's own campaign slogans, yelled out, "In our hearts, we know we've been left!"[450]

When Robert F. Kennedy campaigned by train for president in the Midwest in 1968, he would often paraphrase at the end of his speech a quotation from George Bernard Shaw. Whenever newsmen heard Kennedy tell his audience "'As George Bernard Shaw once said . . . ,' they knew he was winding up and it was time for them to get back aboard," Jules Witcover, author of *85 Days: The Last Campaign of Robert Kennedy*, remembered.

"But at one of the train stops, he omitted the cue ending, and several members of the press corps were stranded. En route to the next stop, Warren Rogers of *Look* magazine was dispatched as an emissary to make sure the omission didn't happen again.

"The candidate laughed and agreed: from then on, there were few campaign speeches anywhere that didn't close with 'As George Bernard Shaw once said'—and with a mad scurrying for the train, or the press bus, or the airplane."[451]

For those reporters who could not make it back to the train on time, the Western Union representative, who charted the train's course on a big US wall map, would affix "a gold star at the point where a comrade vanished," Bruce Biossat, a reporter with the Newspaper Enterprise Association, wrote.[452]

Despite the best efforts of campaign staff, reporters were often left stranded at the train depot when a candidate's train pulled out earlier than anticipated.

Liz Carpenter, Lady Bird Johnson's press secretary, would hand out information sheets to reporters in case they were left behind when Mrs. Johnson's train left the station. They were told that "a whistle will blow two minutes before the train starts moving. We hope we won't be scattering you over the countryside but the train does not wait. In case you get left, look for the advance man. He can easily be identified as the happiest man at the depot because all of his problems have just left. See if he can work out your transportation to a nearby town. If he can't, just take out residence, register and VOTE!"[453]

Los Angeles Times reporter Don Irwin remembered that Nixon's 1968 whistle-stop campaign train tour in Ohio "produced an item for the annals of campaign coverage.

"Two correspondents for the same New York newspaper left opposite sides of the train as it stood on a track that ran along Main Street in London, Ohio. Both reporters bolted for telephone booths. The train pulled out ahead of schedule and they were left looking at one another across the empty tracks.

"Like other newsmen before them, the stranded journalists hired a cab to race the train to the next stop. In the Jet Age, catching up with the campaign can be a much costlier exercise," Irwin concluded.[454]

NOT WELCOME HERE

Some of the difficulties faced by reporters on and off campaign trains reflected social problems encountered by major segments of the population, including segregation and discrimination.

Traveling on President Truman's 1948 whistle-stop train tour, journalist Alice Dunnigan,[455] the first Black woman to travel on a campaign train, experienced what she called "a racial incident" in Cheyenne, Wyoming. As she and a group of other reporters were walking behind Truman's motorcade on the way to a hotel, she was grabbed by one of the military officers guarding the procession and ordered to "get back there behind those ropes."

A fellow reporter came to her aid and explained that she was a credentialed member of the presidential party. "After this civilian reprimand, the military officer stepped back in rank, without a word, and the party moved on without further interference," Dunnigan recounted in her autobiography, *Alone atop the Hill*. "As far as I was concerned, the incident was closed as the president and his group moved on according to schedule."

A few days later, Truman, who had been told about the incident, made a surprise visit to Dunnigan's train compartment and asked if she was being treated all right on the trip.

"When I assured him I was, he said, 'That's good. But if you have any further trouble, let me know,'" Dunnigan wrote.

"Needless to say, it boosted my ego to know that the president of the United States would show personal interest in an insignificant newspaperwoman and would take time out to express his concern."[456]

James L. Hicks, a Black reporter on Adlai Stevenson's 1952 campaign special, was denied a hotel room at a campaign stop in New Orleans. "Hicks and the other white reporters, too, were vocally indignant. A lot of bad feeling and bad publicity resulted," UP reporter Merriman Smith recalled.

Black reporters on Dwight Eisenhower's train that year didn't have this problem, however. The staff scheduled the stops so that Eisenhower and his staff never had to spend a night in a segregated southern city.[457]

HIGH-PRESSURE LOAFING

Traveling reporters usually spent much of their time in a press car located in the middle of the train. The press car was often a run-of-the-mill and sometimes rundown Pullman passenger car.

AP reporter Jack Bell explained that "a Pullman car—usually the vintage of 1890—was converted into a press work car by the simple expedient of ripping out the interior installations, building wooden tables along each side, and plunking some folding chairs down in the resulting aisle.

"From these quarters reporters turned out millions of typewritten and dictated words that kept a candidate and his ideas before the country."[458]

A darkroom for photographers was at one end of the car, with offices for Western Union's traveling staff at the other.[459]

AP reporter Gardner Bridge, who traveled on Thomas Dewey's campaign train in 1944, observed that "riding a presidential campaign train across the country and back as a news reporter was a constant shift between high-pressure loafing and high-pressure working.

"High-pressure loafing is the kind that is never free from worry. You thought you had an hour or two to sit around and relax, but you immediately started thinking of things to do—boning up on the country ahead, checking statistics on the country behind, rinsing out your socks, sorting your laundry, writing a letter home."[460]

UP correspondent Merriman Smith observed that "the challenge for reporters [during World War II] was to survive the crushing boredom of custodial coverage. Newsmen took up poker, stamp collecting, and practically anything to help make the long hours of train travel pass more quickly.

"All sorts of minor feuds and contests developed between the correspondents during the lengthy trips with President [Franklin] Roosevelt, who was rarely aware of what was going on in the cars ahead of his private quarters."[461]

Journalist Richard L. Strout recalled that campaign specials were "little worlds on rails, equipped with the latest refinement of press and electrical broadcasting machines, in which journalism is carried on at high speed between station stops."[462] He noted that "the trains generally carried 20 reporters, perhaps an equivalent number of cameramen and motion-picture operators, a crew of stenographers, mimeographers [operators of machines that made copies of documents written on stencils], electricians, and a retinue of political leaders besides the candidate's own family."[463]

In a 1944 story, Bridge described the interior of the press car he traveled in on Thomas Dewey's whistle-stop campaign that year.

"On one wall is a large map of the United States, with the train's course traced in red crayon. Other walls are plastered with bulletins on arrival and departure times, copy 'drop off' points, etc. One sign that puzzles members of the visiting press reads simply 'do not hate each other' in large type. It is a relic of a photographers' feud that sprang up early in the trip but soon died down. The sign was kept there just as a reminder."[464]

Traveling with politicians and their staff could have its drawbacks, *Washington Star* columnist Mary McGrory, who rode on one of Richard Nixon's whistle-stop campaign trains, remembered. According to McGrory, Nixon's secretary Rose Mary Woods once poured a drink on her. The reporter noted that Woods "took an exception to me, and as I remember, tried to pour a glass of scotch down my back. Very bad vibes."

What prompted the incident? McGrory said, "[Nixon] came into the club car and [Woods] said that I did not rise up to greet him or something like that. My memory is that I did, but anyway, it was not sufficient."[465]

LIVING CONDITIONS

On some campaign trains, especially presidential specials, journalists traveled in relative luxury. Richard L. Strout, a reporter for the *Christian Science Monitor*, covered President Franklin D. Roosevelt on his cross-country rail journey in 1936. The nation's chief executive wanted to see for himself how a historic drought was impacting the country.

In a memorandum to himself, Strout described what it was like to live on the train.

"This is unlike the normal train journey in that there is no expectation of arrival; the voyage will continue for almost two weeks so that it is more like a running hotel on wheels. There is no packing and unpacking of bags, no ticket collection, nothing resembling a public train. The Presidential Special is its own moving world, like a circus."

Strout noted that living conditions on board could be relatively luxurious. "The compartment is like a ship's stateroom; wash basin, toilet bowl under a seat, a ventilating fan which is not required with the air conditioning; green plush covers, a green metal door, carpet on the floor. The berth is wider than normal and moderately comfortable."

But because of security precautions that were taken on presidential trains, Strout observed that this form of travel could be disorienting. "There is no way of telling, as I ride in the dark, where I am, what time it is, whether it is day or night; whether it is raining, snowing or sunlight outside; nor even what direction I am going. I am in a metal cubicle. Later I find out that the train is running in an opposite direction from what I had supposed."[466]

"Sharing a compartment or drawing room for two or three weeks with a man one detested would be a ghastly experience," Merriman Smith recounted. "It happened to one reporter I know. He hated his roommate who was extremely fastidious about his personal hygiene. So, the first reporter got even with him by not bathing or changing his clothes. The drawing room began to smell like a poorly ventilated gymnasium and finally the object of the campaign pleaded to be transferred to another room. He was."[467]

DIRTY LAUNDRY

One of the largest problems on any campaign trip was limited access to laundry and shower facilities. Depending on the train, reporters often had to go for several days between showers and clean clothes. As a result, atmospheric conditions on board some campaign specials were so unbearable that Pullman porters burned incense inside the cars.[468]

It often paid to plan ahead.

Journalist Robert Donovan remembered that reporters aboard the Truman campaign special would send their dirty laundry ahead by plane to the hotel in the next city where they were scheduled to stay. "If you were going to be in Minneapolis two nights from now, and you were in Florida today, well, you would fly the laundry ahead to Minneapolis and pick it up there."[469]

It could be challenging to bathe or shower on a regular basis—and that's why it helped to be creative.

Truman aide Dewey Long recalled that when the candidate's train stopped one night in western Kansas to take on water for the locomotive, the president's staff, Secret Service detail, and other members of the traveling party took an impromptu shower under the water tank by pulling its release chain.[470]

Bess Furman, who traveled aboard one of Franklin Roosevelt's campaign trains, shared an anecdote about a fellow AP reporter who lived in Wyoming and became an instant hero to the traveling press corps. When the train stopped in Cheyenne, Furman's colleague invited the twenty whistle-stopping journalists and nine photographers to his house so they could take turns using his bathtub.[471]

CBS reporter George Herman said that reporters had to "rent some rooms with showers because you couldn't take a shower or bath on the train, and after three days on a train with no bath or shower, you get a little ripe. The usual practice was to rent a block of rooms at a hotel for two or three hours, run in and shower, and then leave."[472]

Providing bathing facilities "was an extremely well-planned aspect of the Goldwater train," Loye Miller of *Time* magazine said. "Every other night, we stayed in a hotel, which did a great deal for the atmosphere aboard our train."[473]

"[This was] essential . . ." Liz Carpenter, Lady Bird Johnson's press secretary, wrote about her time on the Lady Bird Special. "[After] three nights, well, we were pulling into Tallahassee for the night, so it became very apparent that if we wanted an unsmelly press, the thing to do was to rent six rooms and 150 towels! Which we did."[474]

PLAY IT AGAIN, SAM

Because train travel could be challenging and grueling, reporters and candidates alike were often happy to know that they were on their way back home. When Theodore Roosevelt announced to the press corps that after thirty days of whistle-stopping, he would not be giving any more speeches on that trip, the journalists broke out in song, chanting, "We are going home! We are going home!" and imitating Roosevelt's speeches, voice, mannerisms, and gestures.

Hearing the ruckus, Roosevelt emerged from his private compartment and joined in the fun, even mocking himself in a high falsetto voice.[475]

If this was the first time that the reporters traveling with a whistle-stopping politician broke out in song, it was not the last.

Richard Strout, a reporter for the *Christian Science Monitor*, told of the time he and colleague Tom Stokes traveled with Truman's 1948 presidential campaign: "We were sitting in one of the press drawing rooms of the Campaign Special one day between whistle stops, laughing at Truman's folksy phrases. He kept repeating that he was going to California 'fur to get me a degree.' Simultaneously the doughty little warrior was disclaiming charges of corruption and was telling audiences that the Republicans had nothing on him—'they couldn't prove a thing.'

"Suddenly Tom, if I remember aright, began drumming with his hand. 'Why, it's poetry!' he exclaimed. And then he uttered in kind of a sing-song voice what I shall always consider to be a positive example of simple inspiration: the actual Truman phrases put together—

"'They can't prove anything. They isn't got a thing on it.'

"'I'm going down to Berkeley fur to get me a degree!'

"Of course, Tom put it to the tune 'Oh Susanna' and it quickly blossomed into the song of the trip."[476]

In 1968, while Robert Kennedy and his wife, Ethel, were traveling on his campaign train in Indiana, several of the reporters who regularly covered Kennedy were busy in the club car composing their own version of "The Wabash Cannonball," recalled Jules Witcover in his book *85 Days: The Last Campaign of Robert Kennedy.*

"Among the lyricists were [Warren] Rogers, Dave Broder, Dave Halberstam of *Harper's* magazine, Jack Germond of the Gannett Newspapers, and Dave Breasted of the *New York Daily News,* who just happened to have his guitar along.

"Before the train had reached Fort Wayne, this singularly motley crew had seven verses whipped up, all dedicated to the candidate. He and Ethel came into the press car, a pack of aides behind them, and were serenaded by Breasted as he strummed his guitar and twanged out the ersatz epic."

Cartoon by James T. Berryman, *The Campaign of '48 in Star Cartoons, Washington Evening Star-News*, 1948.

The song began:

Oh, listen to the speeches that baffle, beef and bore
As he waffles through the woodlands, and slides
along the shore
He's the politician who's touched by one and all
He's the demon driver of the Ruthless Cannonball

"The Kennedys took the saga in good spirit," Witcover wrote, "applauding at the end. 'The Ruthless Cannonball' became the press theme song for the Kennedy campaign," Witcover said.[477]

NOSTALGIA TRIP

How reporters covered whistle-stopping politicians changed and evolved along with the growth and popularity of campaign train tours.

David Hoffman, a White House correspondent for the *Washington Post*, remembered his first whistle-stop train tour. In 1984, he covered President Ronald Reagan's visit to five Ohio cities aboard the thirteen-car "Heartland Special." Hoffman and dozens of other reporters were flown by jet from Washington to the Buckeye State and then bused to a train depot.[478]

He noted that Reagan's campaign staff did its best to re-create, for a few hours, President Truman's famous free-wheeling, "give-'em-hell" style of campaigning. The staff went as far as to arrange for the president to ride the "Ferdinand Magellan," the luxuriously appointed railroad car used by Truman in 1948, when he whistle-stopped thousands of miles across the country in his successful uphill battle against Thomas Dewey.

A Herblock Cartoon, © The Herb Block Foundation, used under license.

The White House was very interested in carrying out the Truman theme, according to Hoffman. "At one point, there was a Walter Mondale placard held up by somebody along the way about what a great candidate [Mondale] was. Suddenly, in our part of the train, the whole PA system came alive, and you hear Reagan's voice saying 'The hell he is!' I believe to this day that that was deliberate. They were waiting for that moment for Reagan to say 'hell' so he could sound like Harry Truman."[479]

But Reagan's train was nothing like Truman's. Reagan's vintage private car was pulled by sleek diesel engines and equipped with sophisticated communications equipment, which the president used to call the crew of the space shuttle *Challenger* circling the earth hundreds of miles overhead.

The only time the traveling press corps saw the president was from a great distance. After the event, they were flown back to Washington.[480]

Hoffman said that Reagan's "Heartland Special" was "one of the most cleverly constructed and sophisticated political backdrops. But it was quite clear that this was no Harry Truman train. It was nothing like the time when trains were used for genuine campaigning."[481]

After riding in Reagan's "Heartland Special," Hoffman reflected on the life of reporters who covered more-modern electioneering politicians: "Most of the time we fly on an airplane, get bused to a speech site, hear the [candidate] speak, file the story, get back on the bus, then get back on the plane and go to the next site. You repeat that a hundred times."

But even though the press corps enjoyed the nostalgia and change of pace of a modern whistle-stop train, Hoffman observed, "I don't think anybody lost sight of why they were

President Ronald Reagan gives the thumbs-up sign on October 12, 1984, as he stands aboard the "Heartland Special," which is leaving Dayton, Ohio, for a two-hundred-mile trip through the western part of the state. Reagan traveled on the "Ferdinand Magellan," the same railroad car that was used by presidents Franklin D. Roosevelt and Harry S. Truman on their campaign train tours. (Photo by Al Behrman for the Associated Press, used under license.)

there. Nobody got so wrapped up in it that they thought it was 1948."[482]

Not all reporters were sad to see a decline in the use of whistle-stop trains on the campaign trail.

"Gone, too, are the unpredictable delays that shunt even campaign specials onto sidings, the teeth-rattling roadbeds that make writing or even reading impossible, the soot-smeared shirts with no laundry in sight, the days on end without a bath," *Los Angeles Times* reporter Don Irwin observed.[483]

THE BOYS ON THE BUS

On some campaign trails, buses helped provide a transition between trains and planes.[484]

Timothy Crouse's seminal work, *The Boys on the Bus*, provided a behind-the-scenes look at how journalists covered the 1972 presidential election.[485]

In 2020, the National Press Club sponsored "*The Boys on the Bus*—12 Elections Later," a reunion of several reporters who reminisced about the problems they encountered covering presidential candidates—and how the journalists overcame those challenges.[486]

Thomas Dewey may have been the first presidential contender to campaign by bus.[487] What was first a novelty became fairly common over time.

But the buses could be controversial. Take, for example, Texas governor W. Lee O'Daniel, a Democrat, who had a new campaign bus in his 1940 reelection campaign.

"What the Governor will have to say about his new campaign bus is awaited with eagerness," the Associated Press explained. "His political enemies claim the bus must have cost approximately $15,000 [more than $327,000 in 2023 dollars] and have criticized O'Daniel for assertedly accepting it as a gift from friends."[488]

Campaign buses, like their railroad counterparts, often had names.

In his 2000 run for the White House, Republican John McCain called his bus the "Straight Talk Express." One newspaper said the bus was "the natural heir to the 'Ferdinand Magellan,' the armor-plated train car Harry Truman utilized during his 1948 whistle-stop presidential campaign. . . .

"The Straight Talk Express is actually the lead bus in a

three-bus caravan," the *Cincinnati Post* reported. "It is specially equipped with a swiveling Captain's Chair where McCain plants himself after a campaign stop and takes a never-ending succession of questions from traveling reporters until the next destination is reached."[489]

One gubernatorial candidate may have had the best of both worlds when he turned his campaign bus into a replica of a whistle-stop campaign train. (See page 46.)

Like campaign trains, campaign buses could be prone to accidents. Vice President Dan Quayle found that out the hard way when a full-sized bus in his motorcade collided with a small school bus. Three high school students and the school bus driver suffered cuts and bruises.

Quayle was not on the bus when the accident happened, but his mother and aunt were.[490]

As technology slowly began to change the way politicians connected with voters, reporters had to adjust to a new way of covering candidates and deal with a new set of challenges and obstacles.

Reflecting on the change he had seen over the course of a fifty-year career in political journalism, Jules Witcover wrote in his 2005 book, *The Making of an Ink-Stained Wretch,* that "on the positive side, the mechanics of the job had in many ways become easier. Writing and filing by computer was faster and more efficient than pounding out stories on a portable Olivetti on the back of a bouncing bus, then dictating or hunting down the nearest Western Union office—if one existed.

"Getting off a bus or train and racing house to house looking for a phone, pleading to a startled housewife for the use of her line, may sound quaint now," he admitted. "But it was a necessary if frenetic and undependable way of getting the story to your paper. Misspelled names in print were frequent despite our laboriously spelling them out to harassed dictationists at the home office. . . .

"The tape recorder, which was just coming into general use by reporters when I started, was a great boon for accuracy in quoting interviewees and speechifying candidates."

But that new technology came with a price.

It turned "us into traveling stenographers. . . . [We had] to spend [more] time debating over a word or two on a scratchy tape when it would have been more fruitfully spent analyzing the significance of what had been said," Witcover pointed out.

"And the tape recorder often had an intimidating effect on candidates and other politicians [I] interviewed. It could make them more wary of what they said than they had been in the days when they were confronted only by pencil and pad."[491]

CHAPTER 6

The Sincerest Form of Flattery

"Fifteen thousand people were waiting in a light rain to meet the Surprise Party candidate [comedian Gracie Allen] when our train arrived in Omaha."[492]

—George Burns, *Gracie: A Love Story*

Campaign trains were so effective that others imitated them for their own promotional, commercial, political, or other purposes in the US and around the world. All the trains had one goal in common, however: to use the railroads and be seen by as many people as possible, whether it was for causes, businesses, industries, products, or politics.

PRETTY CORNY

To help celebrate and promote the region's success in raising corn in 1889, the business community of Sioux City, Iowa, sponsored the "Corn Palace Train," which toured the Eastern Seaboard.

"The corn-bedecked train left Sioux City in the spring of 1889, carrying 135 goodwill passengers. A band accompanied the party and played rousing tunes at the stops along the way," the *Annals of Iowa* recounted in an article.[493]

The train stopped at Washington, DC, so its passengers could attend the inauguration of President Benjamin Harrison. After the inauguration, the president and his cabinet boarded to inspect the train.

The *New York Times,* which covered the eastern tour, said, "Everything used in the decorations except the nails is the product of Iowa cornfields, and the whole train is a marvel of beauty."[494]

A RELIGIOUS EXPERIENCE

For communities in which there were no churches, the Catholic Church went the extra mile to bring a house of worship closer to them. That was the thinking in 1912, when a Catholic church on wheels—a railcar that had been converted into a small chapel—traveled through several western states.

The car—dubbed the "St. Peter"—was one of several built by the Catholic Church Extension Society and sent to sparsely settled areas "to give the people who seldom [had] an opportunity of attending mass and receiving the spiritual benefits of the church an opportunity to do so," according to one news report.

The chapel was "a complete church and residence on wheels" and was "equipped with every appointment found in a big church. Mass is held daily, except when the car is in motion or not in actual operation."[495]

PRECIOUS CARGO

The Liberty Bell—yes, *the* Liberty Bell in Philadelphia—went on a cross-country whistle-stop trip to the Panama-Pacific International Exposition in San Francisco in 1915.

The *1859 Oregon's Magazine* noted that "the Liberty Bell Special was a custom-designed, seven-car Pullman train. Its sixth car, built with heavy-duty shock absorbers, carried the cracked bell, which hung from heavy oak beams, under a copper canopy. At night, a generator lit the bell so people could see it as its train rushed through the dark."[496]

This was not the bell's first trip, Fred Klein wrote in an article on the website TrainWeb.org:

> In 1885 it travelled by rail to the Independence Exposition in New Orleans. Then, in 1893 it went to the Columbian Exposition at Chicago. Two years later the people in Atlanta examined the bell at the Cotton States Exposition. The bell attracted huge crowds wherever it went. Additional cracking occurred and pieces were chipped away by souvenir hunters. In January 1902, the city of Charleston, South Carolina, was to be the host for the South Carolina Inter-State and West Indian Exposition. That 1902 trip had a smaller train than the 1915 train, with two baggage cars, two Pullman-owned

> cars, and a flat car on the rear. A three-foot high nickel-plated guardrail was installed around the edge. The level of the floor on which the bell and its frame sat was the same as the rear platform of the observation car that it followed.

Because of worries about future cracking and souvenir hunters, the bell did not travel from Philadelphia again.[497]

The Liberty Bell was not the only symbol to go on a train tour. So did the Olympic torch.

The Union Pacific 1996 "Olympic Torch Relay" train consisted of two custom-painted Union Pacific locomotives and a nineteen-car passenger train. Over the course of two months, the train carried the Olympic flame in a specially designed "cauldron car" for more than thirty-five hundred miles across long stretches of the United States, including Arizona, Nevada, California, Utah, Wyoming, Colorado, Oklahoma, Missouri, Minnesota, Wisconsin, and Illinois.[498]

The torch train made a big impression on those who saw it.

"The last time people gathered here was when President Taft stopped in the same place," said Randy Roeseler of the Watertown (Wisconsin) Historical Society.[499]

Four years later, the torch made a similar whistle-stop-style train trip in Australia on its way to the 2000 Olympic Games in Sydney. The flame completed a thirty-hour trip across the outback aboard Australia's transcontinental train, the "Indian Pacific," the Associated Press reported.

"The flame, housed in its own railcar, left the remote Western Australian gold mining town of Kalgoorlie and made a whistle-stop tour of 11 tiny towns," according to the news organization.[500]

A WINNING THEME

Campaign-train-related themes have popped up in unexpected ways and places over the years, including movies, books, and advertisements.

In 1941, *Citizen Kane*, regarded by many as the greatest movie of all time, featured brief scenes in which the title character is seen on the back of a campaign train. In a sequence from a *News on the March* newsreel scene, actor Thomas A. Curran, portraying President Theodore Roosevelt, stands on the rear platform of a train as Charles Foster Kane, played by Orson Welles, looks on.[501]

It is worth remembering that towns with limited train service are what inspired the term *whistle-stop* in the first place. In 1946, a film noir called *Whistle Stop*, starring Ava Gardner and George Raft, was shown in theaters across the country. The movie was based on a book by the same name that was published in 1941. The title referred to a small town where the plot unfolds, not to a campaign train.[502]

Campaign-train-related scenes were featured on several covers of *New Yorker* magazine in the 1940s and 1950s. The drawings depict imaginary scenarios from whistle-stop tours, such as a politician accepting a giant watermelon from a supporter (see page 83),[503] a doctor examining the throat of a politician as concerned staff members look on (see page 63),[504] and a team of writers working on a candidate's next speech (see page 98).[505] Another cover shows people gathered at a rural depot waiting for a campaign train to arrive. A banner reading "Welcome to our next president" hangs over the tracks, tethered between a telephone pole and the depot chimney.[506]

A cartoon on the cover of *Newsweek* magazine in 1952 accompanied an article about President Truman whistle-stopping across the country on behalf of Democratic presidential candidate Adlai Stevenson. Over the caption "The Last Whistle Stop," the caricature shows Truman about to jump off a moving train with a cane in one hand and a bag in the other.[507]

Herb Block (a.k.a. Herblock), one of the best-known political cartoonists of all time,[508] drew several campaign-train-related cartoons, many of which are included in this book.

In the 1954 film *Suddenly,* Frank Sinatra starred as an assassin hired to kill a whistle-stopping president whose train was scheduled to stop in a small California town.[509]

In 2019, the final scene of CBS's popular TV series *Madam Secretary* featured the lead character, the US president, standing with her husband on the rear platform of a campaign train as it left a small-town depot. Deadline's Ted Johnson noted, "That the show ended onboard a whistlestop tour, a remnant of a bygone and simpler era, was an apt way to wrap the series. The show's hopeful tone and neatly wrapped scenarios often were an alternate political universe to the cynical and polarized Trump years."[510]

UPLIFTING ADS

Advertisers have been putting their products in make-believe situations for decades, encouraging consumers to imagine what it would be like to use cars, clothes, and other merchandise in fantasy scenarios.

Cream of Wheat piggybacked on a campaign train theme in a 1904 magazine ad. The advertisement portrayed a Black chef, who was the symbol of the company, standing on the back platform of a railroad car and delivering a campaign-style speech about the cereal to a crowd of people gathered below.

A Herblock Cartoon, © The Herb Block Foundation, used under license.

A 1956 magazine ad for Maidenform may have been the first use of a campaign train theme to sell women's underwear. It was part of a series of ads that ran in the 1950s and 1960s showing women wearing the company's products in various extraordinary settings.

This particular black-and-white ad featured a photograph of a model wearing a bra and gesturing from the rear platform of a railcar. A sign-toting supporter carries a placard that says, "We like Maidenform."[511]

Under the photo, a headline proclaims, "I dreamed I went whistle-stopping in my Maidenform bra." Beneath the headline, the copy plays off the theme of politics and trains: "I'm a sure winner because I'm on the right track! My platform: a vote for me is a vote for Maidenform. No wonder I'm the people's choice for the figure of the year!" The ad went on to describe the benefits of wearing the product.[512]

THE RIGHT FIGHT

As part of a decades-long campaign to guarantee that all women had the right to vote, a group of determined women launched a groundbreaking and controversial national railroad tour in 1916. In addition to advocating for women's suffrage, the organizers sought to ensure the election of a national political candidate who supported their cause.[513]

As described on page 130, the women were not always welcomed in the cities where the train stopped.

In that presidential election year, Republican Charles Evans Hughes was pitted against Democrat Woodrow Wilson. Hughes supported the suffrage movement,[514] while Wilson initially did not.[515]

To help back Hughes's race for the White House, take advantage of his support for women's suffrage, and also plead their case directly to the public, the National Hughes Alliance Women's Committee planned and orchestrated the "Women's Campaign Special." The train was organized by committee chair Frances A. Kellor, who believed that smart, educated women could use their knowledge and skills to tackle pressing social issues.

The tour was important for several reasons. For its time, it was a unique way for women to take part in a political campaign and put to rest the notion that politics was "too dirty" for the fairer sex.[516] It also broke new ground by having a political party back women in such a prominent manner.

In addition to staging rallies at train stations, the "Hughesettes" used the train as a jumping-off point to deliver speeches at venues in adjacent cities and towns. The tour racked up some impressive numbers: the Hughesettes spoke in twenty-eight states, traveled more than eleven thousand miles, and made more than two thousand speeches. More than six hundred thousand people met the train during the course of its round-trip journey around the country.

The "Women's Campaign Special" created a stir due to a smear campaign by detractors that accused the women of being "the idle rich."[517] In an effort to discredit the train tour, the Woodrow Wilson Independent League of Washington took out ads and distributed flyers calling the tour the "Women's Billionaire Train" and the "Golden Special." The labels were references to the women's husbands and were designed to increase public support for Wilson.

The copy pointed out that, in contrast to the Hughes train, "Our Wilson campaign is being conducted by volunteer workers and financed by the one-dollar voluntary contributions of the plain people of the state of Washington." It claimed that "we are for Woodrow Wilson because he places humanity and human rights above prosperity and privilege."[518]

In addition to being met with hostility on some occasions, the train faced other significant hurdles, including a media that did not initially treat the rail tour as legitimate political news, a Republican Party that did not care about women voters, and a train route that often avoided nonsuffrage states. On top of that, the Democratic Party encouraged its women leaders to publicly attack the train and its organizers, and many suffragists did not want to take sides.

The women behind the campaign special were able to overcome these obstacles, according to Kellor, and "accomplished some notable things for the national political life for women." They included opening "a national political door to independence, self-respect, interest, resourcefulness, purpose and capacity in women. The train meant for many women a real opportunity to serve their country by service, ideals, and contributions."

"The train was also a real service to men. It gave them a new point of view regarding women's powers of organization, resourcefulness, and ability to do teamwork," she observed.[519]

Although Hughes lost the election, Wilson eventually came out in support of women's right to vote, which became the law of the land four years after the campaign train tour.

PRESCRIPTION FOR SUCCESS

In 1936, as the country was recovering from the Great Depression, the Rexall drugstore chain faced two challenges: how to make it easy and affordable for druggists across the

ARE THE WOMEN OF WASHINGTON GOING TO PERMIT THE PLUTOCRATS OF THE EAST TO DICTATE TO THEM HOW THEY SHALL VOTE?
Read WHO are financing the

Women's Billionaire Train

The Women's Hughes Alliance is Backed Financially by

MRS. MARY HARRIMAN RUMSEY, *heiress to Harriman millions, Treasurer.*
MRS. ROBERT BACON, *whose husband left J. P. Morgan & Co. to be Roosevelt's Assistant Secretary of State.*
MRS. BERNARD RIDDER, *wife of the editor of the New York "Staat Zeitung," leader of the German propaganda against President Wilson.*
MRS. CROCKER, wife of the California mining and railroad millionaire.

Following are on the

Billionaire Train Fund Committee

MRS. DANIEL GUGGENHEIM, *of the Smelter Trust Family.*
MRS. CORNELIUS VANDERBILT, *representing inherited millions.*
MRS. HARRY PAYNE WITNEY, *daughter of the late Cornelius Vanderbilt.*
MISS MAUDE WETMORE, *of the wealthy Rhode Island family.*
ALICE ROOSEVELT LONGWORTH, *whose husband inherited a fortune.*

In Charge Billionaire Train

MRS. STOTSBURY, *whose husband is the Philadelphia partner of Morgan & Co.*
MRS. PHOEBE HEARST, *whose son, W. R. Hearst, owns millions in mines and lands in Mexico, an area equal to one-half the State of Washington.*
MRS. JOHN HAYS HAMMOND, *wife of the millionaire mining man.*

THE HUGHES CAMPAIGN *is being financed by*

the Greatest Fortunes in America

In 1906 Hughes sworn statement showed that his campaign for Governor was financed by J. P. Morgan, John D. Rockefeller, Andrew Carnegie, Charles M. Schwab, John W. Gates, W. E. Corey, W. Nelson Cromwell, B. M. Duke and others.

OUR WILSON CAMPAIGN IS BEING CONDUCTED BY VOLUNTEER WORKERS AND FINANCED BY THE ONE DOLLAR VOLUNTARY CONTRIBUTIONS OF THE PLAIN PEOPLE OF THE STATE OF WASHINGTON.
YOUR CONTRIBUTION, HOWEVER SMALL, WILL HELP

The Woodrow Wilson Independent League

OF WASHINGTON **Women's Bureau**

227 Lyon Bldg., Seattle. Tel.: Elliott 4297

WE ARE FOR WOODROW WILSON BECAUSE HE **PLACES** HUMANITY AND HUMAN RIGHTS ABOVE PROPERTY AND **PRIVILEGE.**

50

This poster criticizing the 1916 Women's Campaign Train for Hughes was produced by the Woodrow Wilson Independent League of Washington state. ("Women's Billionaire Train" poster, 1916, the Woodrow Wilson Independent League of Washington, Women's Bureau, Library of Congress, Manuscript Division, Papers of Thomas J. Walsh, Boxes 166–176, Democratic Campaigns.)

country who owned or worked in Rexall stores to attend the company's first national convention in six years, and how to inform the public about the benefits of shopping at Rexall. The answer was to tackle both problems with the same solution: take the company to the druggists and the public in a nationwide whistle-stop campaign train tour.

The "Rexall Train" was a coast-to-coast convention on rails, complete with exhibits and classrooms that local Rexall druggists who were delegates to the convention could visit when it rolled into their town. It doubled as a PR machine on wheels, delivering news and information about the company directly to consumers at train stations across the country.

The onboard displays and exhibits included product demonstrations and beauty tips, a model drugstore featuring a fully functioning soda fountain, a scale model of the parent company's eighteen-thousand-square-foot research department, and the chain store's latest brands of medicines, vitamins, pharmaceuticals, and other products.

Many of the train's nineteen air-conditioned cars were named for the company's newest products and decorated with the name and corporate colors of the chain drugstore. The "Rexall Train" covered twenty-nine thousand miles in eight months and visited forty-seven of the forty-eight existing states and parts of Canada.

About ten thousand company delegates and twenty thousand special guests attended the convention on wheels. The train made 262 stops and hosted almost 2.4 million visitors.

Leaving no promotional stone unturned, after the nationwide tour was complete, the company produced a children's board game based on the "Rexall Train" that was played with "miniature locomotive pieces."[520]

LAUGH TRACKS

Getting laughs was an important goal of a campaign train tour by a famous entertainer who pretended to run for president in 1940. With the country recovering from the Great Depression and World War II already raging in Europe, Americans needed all the levity and humor they could find.

In May of that year, Gracie Allen, part of the comedy act Burns and Allen, conducted a weeklong parody of a traditional whistle-stop campaign on a train provided by the Union Pacific Railroad, the "Gracie Allen Special Train."

Gracie ran as a candidate of the Surprise Party. The origin of the party's name was as much a joke as the rest of the campaign. She said that her mother was a Democrat, her father was a Republican, and she was born a Surprise.[521]

The publicity stunt was an integral part of Gracie's faux presidential campaign, which had started months earlier as a gag on the weekly *Burns and Allen* radio show. Her campaign slogan was "Down with common sense—vote for Gracie."[522]

The joke slowly took on a life of its own and blossomed into plans for a train tour in which Gracie would deliver a series of speeches at railroad stations and other venues between California and Nebraska. There was just one problem: Gracie did not want to do it, because she disliked making speeches. She finally relented after members of her family and everyone on the show's writing team agreed to accompany her on the trip.[523]

At the invitation of Eleanor Roosevelt, Gracie traveled to Washington, DC, to announce her candidacy and the train tour in a speech at the Women's National Press Club. The fictional Surprise Party had its own mascot (Laura the kangaroo) and motto ("It's in the bag").[524]

Like real candidates of today, Allen had a book (*How to Become President*), which was prepared by the Gracie Allen Self-Delusion Institute.[525] Her political fortunes were bolstered by a series of skits and jokes about the campaign that millions of people across the country heard on her radio show.[526]

She also touted her candidacy in guest appearances on other popular radio programs of the day, including *The Jack Benny Program* and *Texaco Star Theater*.[527]

Gracie even had an official campaign song called "Vote for Gracie." The lyrics included this line: "Even big politicians don't know what to do. Gracie doesn't know, either. But neither do you. So, vote for Gracie to win the presidential racie. That's right, you can't go wrong. Vote for Gracie, keep voting all day long!"[528]

The highlight of her satirical run for 1600 Pennsylvania Avenue was the whistle-stop campaign tour that began in Los Angeles and ended in Omaha, where fifteen thousand people greeted the train at the railroad station.[529]

But Gracie got cold feet again just before the train arrived at its first stop in Riverside, California. Although she was nervous and wanted to cancel the trip altogether, she agreed to go ahead with the first appearance to see how it would go. Gracie was greeted at the station by an enthusiastic and appreciative crowd of more than three thousand people.

She did so well that she agreed to complete the tour. As the trip progressed, her confidence appeared to improve, and she spoke forcefully and convincingly.[530]

According to Gracie's husband and comedy partner, George Burns, "She became a presidential candidate. . . . I was incredibly proud of her. It was amazing to me that she could do this. To me, she was always a fragile little girl who might fall over if the wind blew too hard.

"I found it hard to believe that she could control large crowds, but she was so good at campaigning that she probably could have become President—if it hadn't been for [Franklin] Roosevelt and [Wendell] Willkie."[531]

The train made thirty-four stops between California and Nebraska; all along the way Allen was met at train stations by bands and appreciative crowds. An estimated three hundred thousand people greeted the train, encouraged to do so as schools closed for the occasion and department stores held special sales in her honor.[532]

Just like those of real whistle-stopping politicians, Gracie's train was often welcomed by state and local public officials. She was presented with gifts on the campaign trail, including fresh doughnuts; boxes of oranges; coins, a trout, a lamb, and a pig; and handmade trophies, rugs, and blankets. At one stop she was given a neutered skunk, which was supposed to symbolize the other candidates.[533]

In Omaha she was nominated unanimously for president (she was the only candidate on the ballot) by a mock convention of eight thousand "delegates" that was held as part of the city's celebration of Golden Spike Days and sponsored by the city and Union Pacific Railroad. After her acceptance speech, she was carried away triumphantly in a sedan chair on the shoulders of twenty bearded supporters of the Surprise Party.[534]

She did not want to have a vice-presidential running mate because she did not want any vice on her ticket.[535]

Spoiler alert: Gracie Allen did not win the White House that year. But she did receive several thousand write-in votes and the endorsement of Harvard University. The Surprise Party candidate used the proceeds from sales of her book to help pay off the campaign's meager debts—about $16.75.[536]

HOORAY FOR HOLLYWOOD

To raise money to fight World War II and lift the country's spirits, members of the film industry banded together to take part in the "Hollywood Victory Caravan" train tour. In April and May 1942, the caravan transported dozens of big-name celebrities, who staged more than three hundred variety-style shows in fourteen cities. The stars often paraded down the street from the railroad station to the hotel where they would be staying or performing. The list of traveling movie stars included Bob Hope, Cary Grant, James Cagney, Laurel and Hardy, Humphrey Bogart, Bing Crosby, Bert Lahr, Pat O'Brien, and Barbara Stanwyck.

"The caravan is the most spectacular thing Hollywood has ever sent on tour," the Associated Press reported.[537]

GOOD MORNING AMERICA

In 2008, ABC's *Good Morning America* launched a "50 States in 50 Days" train tour that led up to that year's presidential election. The two-month trip examined the political and election year landscape in each state.

The "GMA whistle-stop tour" was an 874-foot traveling broadcast studio that consisted of three locomotives and eight railcars, including two historic antique passenger cars. A video produced by the network gave a behind-the-scenes look at preparation for the trip.[538]

TRACK SAFETY

In 1986, the "Cajun Crescent" traveled across central Louisiana in a whistle-stop campaign to help educate the public about railroad-crossing safety and encourage enforcement of laws governing motor-vehicle operation on railroad crossings.

The train traveled six hundred miles over a four-day period. Passengers included lawmakers, VIPs, and federal and state officials.[539]

HOMECOMING

To increase tourism in Tennessee, the "Homecoming '86 Special" took business leaders, celebrities, and politicians across the length of the state over the course of five days.

The whistle-stop train stopped at nineteen railroad stations, and thousands of people lined the route to wave as it sped by. The ten-car train included four cars with educational displays about railroad and Tennessee history.[540]

RETURNING THE FAVOR

To thank Americans for food they sent to France and other European countries via the first "Friendship Train" after World War II, the French people sent a "Merci Train" to the United States. It arrived on a French cargo ship in New York Harbor on February 3, 1949.[541]

Also known as the "French Gratitude Train," it was composed of forty-nine boxcars filled with tens of thousands of thank-you gifts, which included dolls, clothes, and furniture donated by French citizens.

One car was sent to the capital of each state then in existence. The forty-ninth car was shared by Hawaii and the District of Columbia. Parades and ceremonies were held in almost every state to welcome its assigned boxcar. In New York City alone, more than two hundred thousand people attended a welcoming reception for the Empire State's portion of the "Merci Train."[542]

TAKING HISTORY TO THE PEOPLE

Also in the aftermath of World War II, the US government sponsored the "Freedom Train," which displayed documents from the National Archives and the Library of Congress and other museums. The items included Thomas Jefferson's draft of the Declaration of Independence, George Washington's handwritten notes on the Constitution, the Gettysburg Address, and the Emancipation Proclamation.[543]

The purpose of the traveling exhibit, according to organizers, was to "help sell America to Americans" and prevent people from taking their country for granted.

The project was the brainchild of William Coblenz, who worked in the Public Information division of the US Department of Justice. He often spent his lunch hour at nearby museums and thought that a train tour would be an effective way to enable Americans who could not make it to the nation's capital to see many of the country's important historical documents.

More than 3.5 million people toured the train when it visited 326 towns and cities in forty-eight states. The traveling exhibit racked up 37,160 miles between September 1947 and January 1949.

A song touting the train, democracy, and the American form of government was penned by famed songwriter Irving Berlin. "The Freedom Train" was sung by Bing Crosby, one of the best-known entertainers of the day, and the popular Andrews Sisters.

The train had its share of controversy. At a time in American history when racial segregation was still practiced, two communities in the South refused to allow Black people and white people to board the train together to see the exhibits. In some cities they had to stand in separate lines or there were different viewing times for each race to ensure that they did not mingle. When officials in Birmingham, Alabama, and Memphis, Tennessee, prohibited Black people from boarding the train at all, organizers ordered the "Freedom Train" to bypass their communities.

In 1949, New York State launched its own version of the "Freedom Train" that visited 159 communities and was seen by almost one million people. The train consisted of six blue-and-gold cars and carried eighty-nine original documents reflecting various aspects of the state's history.

Eighty-three exhibits were enclosed in their own shatterproof glass displays that were arranged so that large groups of adults and schoolchildren could move through the car and stop for lessons at each of the display cases.[544]

FREEDOM AND FRIENDSHIP

In 1947 in Harrisburg, Pennsylvania, a US "Freedom Train" crossed paths with a "Friendship Train" that was traveling across the country to collect food and medicine for Europeans trying to recover from the ravages of World War II.[545]

The two trains were parked side by side at a train station in the capital of the Keystone State for twelve hours, and a special ceremony was staged to mark the occasion. As reported by one newspaper, "Cheers went up from hundreds in the Pennsylvania Railroad Station as the first cars of the famed Friendship Train nosed into the station to stand side-by-side with the train carrying the documents of this Nation's heritage."[546]

The "Friendship Train" was proposed by journalist and

broadcaster Drew Pearson, who, when he was reporting from Europe, saw communists being thanked for their contributions of food to Europeans. "The columnist loathed the thought of Communism in Europe. He believed that the United States could surpass the Communists in sending food to the desperate, hungry Europeans. Announcing his idea of sending food across the Atlantic in his broadcasts and columns on October 11, 1947, Pearson asked Americans to donate food from their homes, kitchens, gardens, and fields," according to the Friendship Train's website.[547]

The "Friendship Train" was so popular that it was divided into three parts to collect all the donations from across the country. The final haul totaled 270 boxcars, which was worth $40 million, or more than $548 million in 2023 dollars.

Some states, such as Oklahoma and Nebraska, launched their own versions of the train, which collected and sent grain and other items to Europe.[548]

"Freedom Trains" made a comeback in the 1970s.

To help mark the two hundredth anniversary of the founding of the United States, the "American Freedom Train" was created to celebrate the documents, events, and people that influenced the creation of the country. The twenty-six-car train displayed five hundred items from museums around the country, from George Washington's copy of the Constitution to other American treasures, including the dress Judy Garland wore in *The Wizard of Oz*, Martin Luther King Jr.'s pulpit and robes, samples of the rocks that astronauts brought back from the moon, and a stovepipe hat that belonged to President Abraham Lincoln.

Preparations for the project included a precursor train called the "Preamble Express," which in June 1974 scouted potential routes. In December 1974, once the plans and routes were in place, President Gerald Ford stood on the back platform of the

"Preamble Express" at a railroad station in Alexandria, Virginia, to inaugurate the "American Freedom Train."

Between 1975 and 1976, the train—featuring three restored steam locomotives and ten exhibition cars—traveled more than twenty-five thousand miles, stopped in more than 130 cities, and was visited by more than seven million people.[549]

There have been other trains since then that have taken various aspects of US history directly to the people via trains.

In 2005, the Indiana Historical Society sponsored a Lincoln history train that toured northern and southern parts of the state with a collection of Lincoln photographs and other artifacts.

The exhibits were housed in three refurbished sixty-five-foot Amtrak train cars. Activities on the train included photos, videos, and exhibits.[550]

Two years later, the cars were repurposed to help educate Hoosiers about the history of their state during the Civil War.[551]

The interactive exhibits included tents set up outside the train where visitors could participate in hands-on activities, like making regimental flags, and could study maps and photos.

BELL CURVE

Supporters of statehood for the District of Columbia traveled from the nation's capital to Philadelphia in July 1987 on the "Liberty Bell Express."

"We remind the American people that as we celebrate the 200th anniversary of the signing of the Constitution, it's time to mend the crack in the Liberty Bell," said Walter Fauntroy, the district's nonvoting member of Congress. He said the crack symbolized the fact that DC taxpayers had no voting representation in the House or Senate.

The campaign train made stops in Baltimore and Delaware to get the backing of local politicians. Organizers were disappointed when Maryland governor William Donald Schaefer failed to endorse the statehood initiative because of strong opposition from lawmakers in two Maryland counties.[552]

Almost nine hundred people paid forty-four dollars each to ride the train that ferried members of the DC Council and other politicians to the City of Brotherly Love.[553] Once there, the statehood advocates released balloons and, as reported by the *Washington Post*, "dumped symbolic crates into the Delaware River to recall the 1773 Boston Tea Party protest of British taxes."[554]

BY INVITATION ONLY

In 2017, the Cornhusker State sponsored the "Nebraska 150 Express" to help celebrate the 150th anniversary of its statehood. The train, powered by a vintage 1950s Union Pacific locomotive, made a series of ninety-minute visits across Nebraska over the course of three days.[555]

The "Nebraska 150 Express" provided the opportunity for communities across Nebraska to celebrate the state's sesquicentennial, according to Nebraska governor Peter Ricketts. "I appreciate Union Pacific, a company that has had such an important and positive impact on Nebraska, taking such a vested interest in our state's celebration of its great history," Ricketts stated in a press release.[556]

Members of the public who wanted to ride or tour the "Nebraska 150 Express" were out of luck, however. It was an event to which only "a select group of Nebraska native celebrities and notable figures" were invited, the press release said.[557]

"To ensure the trip remains on schedule and the tour reaches as many Nebraskans as possible, public train tours and tickets are not available," it noted.[558]

The VIP guests were scheduled to disembark along the route to sign autographs, take pictures, and have their pictures taken with people who had come to greet the "Express."[559]

HO HO HO!

Every year since 1943, Santa Claus has taken a regional whistle-stop tour to deliver toys to children in two states. In 2017, the "Santa Train" made fourteen stops along a 110-mile route between Shelbyville, in north-central Kentucky, and Kingsport, Tennessee.

The train was first started by merchants in Kingsport to express their appreciation to customers in the region. The trip is sponsored by the CSX railroad company, the Kingsport Chamber, and other regional businesses and organizations.[560]

"We don't throw anything but soft fur toys off the back [of the train]," said volunteer Don Royston. "We send trucks up along the way. We have three 18-foot trucks that leapfrog down the train route, [then] back up to the crowds to distribute toys and gifts, fresh fruit—apples and oranges—that help everyone in these tough times we're having."

Amy McColl of the Kingsport Chamber pointed out that decades after the original train trip, "families continue to come out. As their families grow, it becomes part of a tradition for them. You will see grandfathers, fathers, mothers, grandchildren—sometimes three generations all have different memories of their experiences with the Santa Train. When it becomes the most magical is when you focus on that experience of Santa, seeing the celebrity rider and seeing the train come through your hometown."

In 2017, the Santa train delivered seventeen tons of food and toys along the 110-mile route.[561]

ROBERT REDFORD

Other corporations and organizations that have mimicked campaign trains in their marketing or promotional activities include General Motors, Ringling Bros. Circus, and railroad companies.

A train tour was even used as a publicity stunt in Florida to promote *The Candidate*, a movie starring Robert Redford. The 1972 film was about a successful campaign for the United States Senate. Redford made the campaign-train-style trip from Jacksonville, Florida, to Miami to promote the film. He was accompanied on the back platform of the train by Jeremy Larner, who wrote the movie script and was a former speechwriter for a real presidential candidate—US senator Eugene McCarthy.[562]

"I am not a candidate," Redford announced at the West Palm Beach train station. "I'm just a guy who made a film about a candidate, so please, however you may vote, don't vote for me.

"The truth is, I am not qualified to run for office, I am not competent. I have no experience. I have no program."[563]

NONSTARTERS

Sometimes, despite interest in staging a cause-related whistle-stop train tour, organizers lacked the resources to turn ambitious plans into reality.

That was the case when, in 1986, country music icon Johnny Cash wanted to take his version of a "Freedom Train" on a month-long whistle-stop tour from Memphis to Baltimore. The train would honor Vietnam veterans and call national attention to service members missing in action. The trip, which had been scheduled for the spring of 1987, was canceled when backers were unable to raise enough money for the patriotic project.

That same year another country and western singer, Merle Haggard, tried to organize a last-minute whistle-stop train tour from his hometown of Bakersfield, California, to a scheduled Farm Aid concert in Champaign, Illinois.

Dubbed "The American," the train would have sixteen cars and four locomotives. It was going to make thirty-nine stops in eight states and carry other well-known musicians, including Willie Nelson, Tammy Wynette, and Arlo Guthrie. The star-studded train tour would have helped publicize the plight of American farmers as it made its way to the fundraising event.[564]

But Haggard faced several challenges in securing a train. That's when he called on his longtime friend President Ronald Reagan for assistance. The White House immediately stepped in and smoothed things out. It looked like the trip was going to happen after all.[565]

But like Cash, Haggard was forced to cancel the tour because of funding problems. He fell $250,000 short of the $606,000 that was needed to rent the train from Amtrak. Although his attempts to reschedule the trip were unsuccessful, the singer wound up being in debt to Amtrak to the tune of $47,000.[566]

THESE CANDIDATES WERE REAL CHARACTERS

Winnie the Pooh tried to give human candidates a run for their money when the bear ran for president in the 1960s, '70s, and '80s.

In his second try for national office, in 1972, the furry

politician launched a drive for the White House with a ticker-tape parade down Disneyland's Main Street, U.S.A. This was followed by a two-week whistle-stop campaign train trip across the United States. Pooh was accompanied by his trusted political advisors, Tigger and Eeyore. The entourage stayed in a sleeper car at the back of the train and performed for crowds in a converted baggage car that had been turned into a stage.

The "political" journey was sponsored by Sears (which owned the rights to the character), Disney, and Amtrak. The route took the train from Los Angeles to Washington, DC, and back, then made a round trip up the coast to Seattle.

Although the whistle-stop campaign was a parody, it did generate genuine enthusiasm. At a small depot in New Mexico, about two thousand people came out at 1:30 a.m. in snow flurries, hoping to catch sight of the train as it passed.

Although the train was not scheduled to visit that community, it stopped long enough for Pooh and friends to do an impromptu show for the unexpected but appreciative crowd.[567]

Not to be outdone, to celebrate his fiftieth birthday in 1978, Mickey Mouse went on a cross-country whistle-stop campaign train tour organized by Walt Disney Productions.

The trip started out from Los Angeles, where a thousand people came to the station in Pasadena to see the mouse off.

The "Mickey Mouse Special" was a regularly scheduled Amtrak train for part of the journey, with a private car attached to the back.

"At each stop," the Associated Press reported, "a local band plays the Mickey Mouse theme song and Mickey, less than five feet tall, bounces out to pat children on their heads and shake their hands. He puts white gloves up to his mouth as if to say, 'All this for me?'"[568]

About a thousand people turned out in Albuquerque, New Mexico, to meet Mickey Mouse on November 14, 1978, as he celebrated his fiftieth birthday with a national train tour. The trip is an example of how others have mimicked whistle-stop campaigns for nonpolitical purposes. (Photo by John Holmes for the Associated Press, used under license.)

GOING WHERE THE VOTES ARE

In 1953, West Germany chancellor Konrad Adenauer campaigned by train in a bid for reelection.

The Associated Press said that the seventy-seven-year-old politician was "making his political opponents squirm with some campaign methods borrowed from the United States.

"Taking a leaf from American presidential candidates, the Chancellor is crisscrossing the nation on a 'whistle-stop' tour to let millions of German voters see and hear him," the wire service reported.

Adenauer traveled in a bright-red train "replete with all the trimmings of a U.S. presidential special—press agents, harried advisers, a radio telephone, bodyguards and a separate car for reporters."[569]

"He won by a landslide and concluded that the American Presidential campaign could be transplanted intact to West Germany," one newspaper explained.[570]

The whistle-stopping politician made "the same speech over and over again," the Associated Press reported. "And he speaks at such length—the average is an hour and a half—that his audience invariably becomes restive.

"It's not fair to my audiences to make short speeches," Adenauer commented. "They come long distances to hear me speak and I don't want to disappoint them."[571]

Twelve years later, another West German politician, Chancellor Ludwig Erhard, campaigned by train as well.[572]

In 1965, Canadian prime minister John Diefenbaker, "growling that there aren't many voters at 12,000 feet, made impressive use of the campaign train and the whistle-stopping technique which he knew so well," *The Gazette* reported. (He also did a campaign train tour in 1963.)[573]

The two-and-a-half-day vote-getting expedition involved four rallies.[574]

In 2008, Canada's Green Party leader Elizabeth May was the first politician since Diefenbaker to conduct such an extensive tour of the country.

"There's a certain benefit in actually being able to reach places their leaders don't reach and haven't reached since the last great cross-country whistle-stop tour," she observed.

May said that campaigning by train was "far more environmentally friendly than the emission-spewing jets used by her political rivals, allowing her campaign to have the lowest carbon footprint of any major party."[575]

In 2009, German chancellor Angela Merkel went on a 370-mile whistle-stop campaign trip aboard the same train that one of her predecessors—Konrad Adenauer—traveled on six decades earlier, during his train tour.

"The conservative leader described her ride in a glass-topped coach as a 'trip towards the future of Germany' and 'in memory of the roots' that shaped the country," one newspaper wrote.[576]

KHRUSHCHEV'S AMERICAN TOUR

One of the most unusual whistle-stop train tours in US history was taken by a leader of the Soviet Union.

In September 1959, Soviet leader Nikita Khrushchev made a well-publicized train trip between Los Angeles and San Francisco, with a campaign-style stopover in Santa Barbara.

"The long orange and red train was loaded with sullen, furtive Soviet security men and nervous-looking American security men. Up ahead, Army helicopters hovered protectively over the track. Alongside, police cars raced along parallel highways," according to a news outlet.

In Santa Barbara, the Soviet leader left the train to meet with people at the railroad station. The Associated Press reported that "he emerged smiling, waving, clasping his hands over his head. . . . He shook hands with the people."[577]

A TRENCH-COATED TRUDEAU

In 1974, Canadian prime minister Pierre Trudeau went on a campaign train tour. At each stop, the format was roughly the same, *The Gazette*'s George Radwanski reported.

"The train pulls into the station, and a trench-coated Trudeau appears on the broad rear platform of his private railway car, flanked by his wife and local Liberal [Party] officials. He delivers a brief, fighting speech with the aid of a powerful amplifying system and then wades into the crowd to shake hands and sign autographs," Radwanski wrote.

"Trudeau's whistle-stop appearances have been going over well largely because his new campaign style and the setting here blend so well together. The arm-waving, blazing-eyed, staccato voice delivery is a bit too hard for the close confines of a meeting hall, but it seems entirely appropriate at a brief outside rally at a train station.

"The idea originated with a staffer in the prime minister's office who drew up an elaborate blueprint for conducting the entire campaign from a train. This was rejected for a variety of reasons, including the feeling that a whole campaign of a slow-moving train would have made Trudeau seem far too leisurely about the whole thing," Radwanski said.

"But using a train in the Maritimes enables the prime minister to reach far more [people] in less time than he could by plane and motorcade; it conveys the image of a fighting leader waging a tough, old-fashioned campaign; and it provides enough of a novelty to capture the attention of the media," he observed.[578]

NIXON, CARTER, AND SADAT

Two American whistle-stopping politicians went on separate campaign train tours with then-president Anwar Sadat of Egypt.

Months before he resigned because of the Watergate scandal, Republican president Richard Nixon accompanied Sadat in what United Press International called "a Mideast version of a whistle-stop tour" that gave "thousands of Egyptians another chance to honor [Nixon's] peacekeeping efforts."[579]

About 3.5 million Egyptians turned out to see Nixon and Sadat along the train's 150-mile route.[580]

Nixon later recalled that crowds "jammed the entire route on our three-hour train ride from Cairo to Alexandria as Sadat and I stood waving from an open coach. It was hot and dusty, and the swelling in my leg grew painful from standing so long. But I realized that Sadat felt it was important for as many people as possible to see us together. It was a way of confirming the new Egyptian-American relationship."[581]

Four years later, Jimmy Carter, who conducted a campaign train tour in his successful run for the White House in 1976, went to Egypt to accompany Sadat on another whistle-stop train tour.[582]

In 1992, Pakistani opposition leader Benazir Bhutto conducted a cross-country train campaign as part of her successful efforts to oust the Nawaz Sharif government.[583]

The next year, Nawaz Sharif used the same whistle-stopping tactic as part of his comeback campaign.[584]

WHISTLE-STOPPING ROYALTY

Members of the British royal family are no strangers to campaign trains.

In 1951, Princess Elizabeth and Prince Philip traveled Canada by train from Ottawa to Toronto, making several stops along the way in their ten-car royal train. Later that year, after her coronation, Queen Elizabeth and Prince Philip toured Ontario, Canada, on a whistle-stop train tour. Just like campaign train tours in the US, similar tours overseas could be subject to delays, problems, or other issues.

In 1954, "a jammed stop signal on a single-line track . . . held up Queen Elizabeth's special train miles from any settlement in the rolling New Zealand hinterland," Reuters wrote.

There was a second delay when the engineer dropped his hand signal used for clearing the track ahead. "This time, hundreds of New Zealanders on the scene cheered the Queen and the Duke of Edinburgh as railroad men hunted for the signal. It was found within two minutes and the tour proceeded," Reuters said.

"Thousands of cheering villagers lined the track as the royal train cut across the countryside followed by cars racing along parallel highways. Movie cameras whirred and spectators shouted welcomes as they sighted the royal couple on the rear platform of the red-and-white train."[585]

A newspaper observed that the royal couple's 150-mile whistle-stop tour through Canada in 1973 "had something of the air of an American election campaign as the Queen and Prince Philip waved from the balcony of the rear carriage to crowds lining the track at every town and village."

Security was understandably tight.

"A 'decoy' train preceded the royal train by half an hour. Burnished to resemble the train carrying the Queen and Prince Philip, it had the word 'Elizabeth' on its side to confuse any would-be demonstrators," the *Daily Telegraph* observed.[586]

Of all the campaign train tours conducted outside the United States, the 1947 royal train tour in South Africa was perhaps the longest and generated the most news coverage. The 4,920-mile tour of more than four hundred cities was made on a train that was a third of a mile long and described as a "palace on wheels."

In addition to members of the royal family—King George VI, Queen Elizabeth, Princess Elizabeth (the future Queen Elizabeth II), and Princess Margaret—the "White Train" carried members of the royal staff, including footmen, valets, secretaries, flower arrangers, hairdressers, and others.[587]

"The royal family travelled ceaselessly, from February to

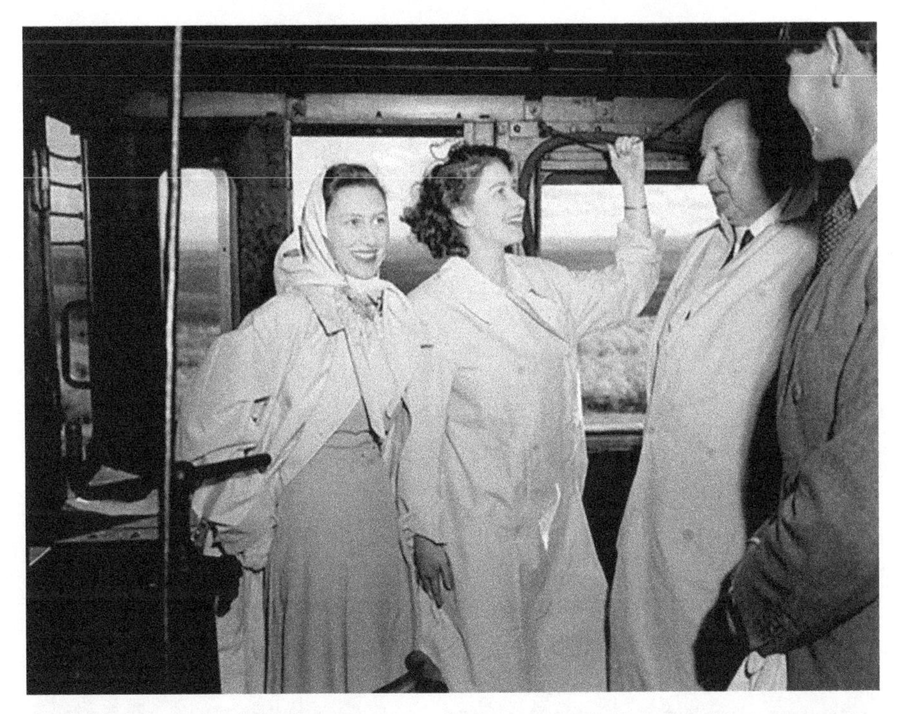

Princess Margaret (left) looks on as Princess Elizabeth (center) takes a hands-on approach to the British royal family's 1947 whistle-stop tour of South Africa. The future queen of England sounds the whistle as the royal train approaches Swellendam, one of the oldest towns in South Africa. (Transnet Heritage Library Photo Collection, used by permission.)

April, on a specially commissioned, white-and-gold train, meeting thousands of people at every stop along the way," according to *The Last Hurrah: The 1947 Royal Tour of Southern Africa and the End of Empire* by Graham Viney, a book about the three-month journey.

"The tour was a show of imperial solidarity and a recognition of South Africa's contributions to the Allied cause during the Second World War," it explained.

"Magnificently modern, the 'White Train' was an impressive and beautiful sight, sweeping through the ochre-colored plains," as James Cameron of the *Daily Express* put it, "like an ivory arrow."

A member of the press corps covering the 1947 royal train tour in South Africa. Reporters were not on the same train as the royal family. Instead, they traveled and worked on a pilot train that preceded the royals' train by thirty minutes. (Transnet Heritage Library Photo Collection, used by permission.)

Reporters aboard a second train were housed and fed in comfort, Viney observed. They "could use a high-speed Morse transmitter to telegraph their reports directly from the train . . . and there was a darkroom for processing film," he noted.

A third train, dubbed the "Ghost Train," carried spare parts.[588]

In 2010, Prince Charles—who became King Charles III in 2022—traveled on a biofuel-powered royal train, taking his message about climate change across the UK.

Before boarding the train, he said, "What I hope to get across, to as many people as possible, is that however awful a predicament we face with climate change and the unsustainable use of the natural resources that keep us all alive, we aren't going to get anywhere by telling everyone what they need to stop doing. There's been quite enough of that in recent years, and we all know what the reaction is.

"So this week is going to be about the things that we can all start doing for our own benefit, for the benefit of everyone who shares this planet with us, and for the benefit of our children and their children, too," Charles concluded.[589]

APPENDIX

Keeping Track

These politicians and their surrogates used trains to reach voters at railroad depots and make trackside speeches as verified by newspaper stories and other accounts. The list does not document all their train tours, their routes, or all the years in which they campaigned by train. For updates or more information, visit WhistleStopPolitics.com.

Politician	*Year*	*Office Held or Sought*
1830s		
William Henry Harrison	1836	President[590]
1850s		
Stephen Douglas	1858	US Senate/Illinois[591]
Abraham Lincoln	1858	US Senate/Illinois[592]
1860s		
Andrew Johnson	1866	President[593]
Ulysses S. Grant	1868	President[594]

1870s

Horace Greeley	1872	President[595]
John Dix	1874	Governor/New York[596]
Rutherford B. Hayes	1877	President[597]

1880s

James A. Garfield	1880	President[598]
Benjamin Butler	1884	President[599]
James Blaine	1884	President[600]
John Logan	1884	Vice President[601]
Grover Cleveland	1884	President[602]

1890s

Benjamin Harrison	1891	President[603]
Adlai Stevenson	1892	Vice President[604]
William McKinley	1892	In Support of Benjamin Harrison[605]
William Jennings Bryan	1896	President[606]
William Goebel	1899	Governor/Kentucky[607]

1900s

Theodore Roosevelt	1900	Vice President[608]
Chauncey Depew	1900	In Support of Theodore Roosevelt[609]
John G. Woolley	1900	President/Prohibition Party[610]
Alton B. Parker	1904	President[611]
Henry Davis	1904	Vice President[612]
Charles Fairbanks	1904	Vice President[613]
Eugene Debs	1908	President[614]
John Kern	1908	Vice President[615]

James Sherman	1908	Vice President[616]
Samuel Gompers	1908	In Support of William Jennings Bryan[617]
William Howard Taft	1908	President[618]

1910s

Henry Stimson	1910	Governor/New York[619]
Hiram Johnson	1912	Vice President[620]
Lawrence Y. Sherman	1912	US Senate/Illinois[621]
Frank Reid	1912	State Attorney General/Illinois[622]
Woodrow Wilson	1912	President[623]
Augustus Owsley Stanley	1915	Governor/Kentucky[624]
Edwin P. Morrow	1915	Governor/Kentucky[625]
Charles Evans Hughes	1916	President[626]
Women for Hughes	1916	In Support of Charles Evans Hughes[627]

1920s

James M. Cox	1920	President[628]
Franklin D. Roosevelt	1920	Vice President[629]
Leonard Wood	1920	President[630]
Warren Harding	1920	President[631]
Charles Dawes	1924	Vice President[632]
John W. Davis	1924	President[633]
Theodore Roosevelt Jr.	1924	Governor/New York[634]
Alfred E. Smith	1928	President[635]
Albert Ottinger	1928	Governor/New York[636]
Herbert Hoover	1928	President[637]
Charles Curtis	1928	Vice President[638]

1930s

John Nance Garner	1932	Vice President[639]
Alf Landon	1936	President[640]
Frank Knox	1936	Vice President[641]
Elmer Benson	1936	Governor/Minnesota[642]

1940s

Wendell Willkie	1940	President[643]
John Bricker	1944	Vice President[644]
Harry S. Truman	1944	Vice President[645]
Thomas Dewey	1948	President[646]
Earl Warren	1948	Vice President[647]
Strom Thurmond	1948	President/Dixiecrats[648]

1950s

Adlai Stevenson II	1952	President[649]
William Fulbright	1952	Stand-In for Adlai Stevenson II[650]
Dwight Eisenhower	1952	President[651]
Richard Nixon	1952	Vice President[652]
Estes Kefauver	1956	Vice President[653]
Claude Wickard	1956	US Senate/Indiana[654]
Clement Miller	1958	Congress/California[655]
Joseph W. Barr	1958	Congress/Indiana[656]
Robert A. O'Neal	1958	Sheriff/Indiana[657]
Phillip L. Bayt	1958	Mayor/Indiana[658]

1960s

John F. Kennedy	1960	President[659]
Lyndon B. Johnson	1960	Vice President[660]

Henry Cabot Lodge Jr.	1960	Vice President[661]
John Connally	1962	Governor/Texas[662]
Lady Bird Johnson	1964	In Support of Lyndon B. Johnson[663]
Hubert Humphrey	1964	Vice President[664]
Barry Goldwater	1964	President[665]
William E. Miller	1964	Vice President[666]
Pierre Salinger	1964	US Senate/California[667]
William Scranton	1964	President[668]
Joe Tydings	1964	US Senate/Maryland[669]
Carlton Sickles	1964	Congress/Maryland[670]
Royce Hanson	1964	Congress/Maryland[671]
Democratic Candidates	1964	Various Offices/Oklahoma[672]
Vance Hartke	1964	US Senate/Indiana[673]
Philip H. Hoff	1966	Governor/Vermont[674]
Roger D. Branigin	1966	Congress/Indiana[675]
Karl Rolvaag	1966	Governor/Minnesota[676]
Charles Percy	1966	US Senate/Illinois[677]
Dick Tuck	1966	State Senate/California[678]
Edmund G. "Pat" Brown	1966	Governor/California[679]
Fred Harris	1966	US Senate/Oklahoma[680]
Preston Moore	1966	Governor/Oklahoma[681]
Warren W. Wilentz	1966	US Senate/New Jersey[682]
Robert Kennedy	1968	President[683]
Winthrop Rockefeller	1968	Governor/Arkansas[684]
Gaylord Nelson	1968	US Senate/Wisconsin[685]
Republican Party	1968	Various Offices/South Dakota[686]

Bronson La Follette	1968	State Attorney General/ Wisconsin[687]
Glenn Cunningham	1968	Congress/Nebraska[688]
William Clark	1968	US Senate/Illinois[689]
Eugene McCarthy	1968	President[690]
Republican Party	1968	Stop McGovern Campaign[691]

1970s

John Tunney	1970	US Senate/California[692]
Milton Shapp	1970	Governor/Pennsylvania[693]
George McGovern	1972	President[694]
Edmund Muskie	1972	President[695]
Ben Barnes	1972	Governor/Texas[696]
Howard Baker	1972	US Senate/Tennessee[697]
Richard Lugar	1974	US Senate/Indiana[698]
James McNulty	1975	County Commissioner/ Pennsylvania[699]
Gerald Ford	1976	President[700]
Jimmy Carter	1976	President[701]
Walter Mondale	1976	Vice President[702]
Bill Brock	1976	US Senate/Tennessee[703]
John Heinz	1976	US Senate/Pennsylvania[704]
Andrew Miller	1977	Governor/Virginia[705]
Ken Maddy	1978	Governor/California[706]
Hugh Carey	1978	Governor/New York[707]
Jack Eckerd	1978	Governor/Florida[708]
Paula Hawkins	1978	Lieutenant Governor/Florida[709]

1980s

John Anderson	1980	President[710]

Bill Clements	1982	Governor/Texas[711]
Chuck Robb	1982	Governor/Virginia[712]
Gerald Baliles	1982	Attorney General/Virginia[713]
Reubin Askew	1983	President[714]
Mickey Edwards	1984	Congress/Oklahoma[715]
Gary Hart	1984	President[716]
Julie Belaga	1985	Governor/Connecticut[717]
Tom Bradley	1986	Governor/California[718]
John McCain	1986	US Senate/Arizona[719]
Jim Broyhill	1986	US Senate/North Carolina[720]
William Donald Schaefer	1986	Governor/Maryland[721]
Fob James	1986	Governor/Alabama[722]
Harvey Sloane	1986	Mayoral Inauguration Tour/Kentucky[723]
Billy Tauzin	1987	Governor/Louisiana[724]
Marshall Coleman	1988	Governor/Virginia[725]
Michael Dukakis	1988	President[726]
Jesse Jackson	1988	President[727]
Paul Simon	1988	President[728]
David Durenberger	1988	US Senate/Minnesota[729]
Jim Martin	1988	Governor/North Carolina[730]
Wayne Dowdy	1988	US Senate/Mississippi[731]

1990s

William Donald Schaefer	1990	Governor/Maryland[732]
Tommy Thompson	1990	Governor/Wisconsin[733]
Jean Lloyd-Jones	1990	State Senate/Iowa[734]
Clayton Williams	1990	Governor/Texas[735]
Bruce King	1990	Governor/New Mexico[736]
Bill Richardson	1990	Congress/New Mexico[737]

Jeff Bingaman	1990	US Senate/New Mexico[738]
Casey Luna	1990	Lieutenant Governor/ New Mexico[739]
Dianne Feinstein	1990	Governor/California[740]
Edward Rendell	1991	Mayor/Philadelphia[741]
George H. W. Bush	1992	President[742]
Dan Quayle	1992	Vice President[743]
Howard Dean	1992	Governor/Vermont[744]
Mary Sue Terry	1993	Governor/Virginia[745]
Donald S. Beyer	1993	Lieutenant Governor/ Virginia[746]
William D. Dolan III	1993	Attorney General/Virginia[747]
George Allen	1993	Governor/Virginia[748]
William Weld	1994	Governor/Massachusetts[749]
Paul Cellucci	1994	Lieutenant Governor/ Massachusetts[750]
Mitt Romney	1994	US Senate/Massachusetts[751]
Joseph Malone	1994	State Treasurer/ Massachusetts[752]
Arne Carlson	1994	Governor/Minnesota[753]
Gary Revier	1994	Congress/Minnesota[754]
Robert Dole	1995	President[755]
Local Democratic Candidates	1995	Local Offices/Connecticut[756]
Bill Clinton	1996	President[757]
Mike Huckabee	1998	Governor/Arkansas[758]

2000s

George W. Bush	2000	President[759]
Dick Cheney	2000	Vice President[760]

Mel Carnahan	2000	US Senate/Missouri[761]
Wendell Bailey	2000	Lieutenant Governor/ Missouri[762]
Tom Osborne	2000	Congress/Nebraska[763]
George Pataki	2002	Governor/New York[764]
Rod Blagojevich	2003	Gubernatorial Inauguration Tour/Illinois[765]
Ernie Fletcher	2003	Governor/Kentucky[766]
John Kerry	2004	President[767]
John Edwards	2004	Vice President[768]
Greg Goode	2008	Congress/Indiana[769]
Barack Obama	2008	President[770]
Chet Culver	2009	Governor/Iowa[771]

2010s

Mary Fallin	2010	Governor/Oklahoma[772]
Brian Dubie	2010	Governor/Vermont[773]
David Young	2014	Congress/Iowa[774]
Chuck Grassley	2014	US Senate/Iowa[775]

2020s

Joe Biden	2020	President[776]
Peter Welch	2022	US Senate/Vermont[777]

NOTES

INTRODUCTION

1. Liz Carpenter, *Ruffles and Flourishes: The Warm and Tender Story of a Simple Girl Who Found Adventure in the White House* (New York: Doubleday, 1970), 144.
2. "CNN's Newsroom on the Rails: Reporting from a Train Across America," October 29, 2012, https://www.journalism.co.uk/news/cnn-newsroom-on-the-rails-reporting-from-a-train-across-america/s2/a550977/.
3. George McKee Elsey, *An Unplanned Life: A Memoir by George McKee Elsey* (Columbia: University of Missouri Press, 2005), 167.
4. Harry S. Truman, *Memoirs: Years of Trial and Hope* (Garden City, New York: Doubleday, 1956), 2:219.
5. George McGovern, letter to author, May 14, 1985.
6. Doris Kearns Goodwin, *Leadership in Turbulent Times* (New York: Simon & Schuster, 2018), 65.
7. Merriman Smith, "Whistle-Stop Tours Stir Old Memories," *Terre Haute Tribune*, September 27, 1964, 77, https://www.newspapers.com/article/the-terre-haute-tribune-ws-history-an/18933596/.
8. Sheritha Jones, "Back in the Day, April 27, 1968: Robert F. Kennedy Takes Whistle-Stop Tour Across Nebraska," *Omaha World-Herald*, April 27, 2023, https://omaha.com/news/local/history/back-in-the-day-april-27-1968-robert-f-kennedy-takes-whistle-stop-tour-across/article_31de7708-de02-11cd-9372-ef14411d9c1c.html.
9. George Herman, interview with author, June 27, 1985.
10. Don Phillips, "Richard M. Nixon: Rail Romantic," *Trains*, November 1971, 49–50.
11. Bob Withers, *The President Travels by Train: Politics and Pullmans* (Lynchburg, VA: TLC, 1996), 295.
12. Associated Press, "Carter Tries Whistlestops for a Pep-Up," *Omaha*

World-Herald, September 20, 1976, 18, https://www.newspapers.com/article/omaha-world-herald-1976-carter/123343256/.

13. Jim Wooten, letter to author, June 13, 1985.
14. Mike McCurry, email to author, June 23, 2022.
15. Mitch Weiss, "Clinton's Train Rolls On," Associated Press, August 27, 1996.
16. Annie Linskey, "Inside Joe Biden's Whistle-Stop Tour of Ohio and Pennsylvania," *Washington Post*, September 29, 2020, https://www.washingtonpost.com/politics/inside-joe-bidens-whistle-stop-tour-of-ohio-and-pennsylvania/2020/09/28/d2868f30-01f3-11eb-897d-3a6201d6643f_story.html.
17. Wilson Ring, "Welch Moves from House to Senate to Succeed Leahy in Vermont," Associated Press, November 8, 2022, https://apnews.com/article/vermont-senate-race-2022-midterm-elections-91c2cd6d4acac1291876cf5f50475515.
18. *New York Times*, "Aides Term Reagan's Train Tour One of Campaign's Best Days," quoted in Finlay Lewis, *Star-Tribune*, October 13, 1984, 3, https://www.newspapers.com/article/star-tribune-1984-reagan-ohio-o/20763145/.
19. United Press International, "George W. Bush Whistle Stop Train Tour," August 4, 2000, https://www.upi.com/News_Photos/view/upi/fe1b90da9b3e7cce20f03db3389dde38/George-W-Bush-whistle-stop-train-tour/.
20. "Bush, Cheney on Whistle-Stop Tour," *Philadelphia Inquirer*, August 5, 2000, https://www.newspapers.com/article/the-philadelphia-inquirer-2000-bush-an/19660470/.
21. Mary McGrory, interview with author, August 19, 1986.
22. "Collected Warner Pathe Newsreels of Truman and Eisenhower," https://www.youtube.com/watch?v=E0J_2wEkgIc.
23. Mildred Gordon and Gordon Gordon, *Murder Rides the Campaign Train* (New York: Bantam, 1956).
24. William Carroll, *Gracie Allen for President 1940: Vote with the Surprise Party* (San Marcos, CA: Coda Publications, 2000).
25. Catalina Camia, "Which Pol Does Jay Leno Skewer Most? Bill Clinton Top Joke Target," *USA Today*, February 4, 2014, https://www.usatoday.com/story/news/politics/onpolitics/2014/02/04/jay-leno-tonight-show-bill-clinton-jokes/81604460/.

26. "Quotes of the Week," *Boston Globe*, August 31, 1996, 11, https://www.newspapers.com/article/the-boston-globe-1996-jay-nelo-clinton/130299899/.
27. James Wilson, "Whistlestop Days Seem Gone Forever," *Los Angeles Times*, October 6, 1968, 93, https://www.newspapers.com/article/the-los-angeles-times-ws-history-and-a/20475611/.
28. Jack Bell, *The Splendid Misery: The Story of the Presidency and Power Politics at Close Range* (New York: Doubleday, 1960), 247.
29. James A. Farley, *Behind the Ballots: The Personal History of a Politician* (New York: Harcourt, Brace, 1938), 166.
30. Grace Tully, *F. D. R.: My Boss* (New York: Charles Scribner's Sons, 1949), 203–5.
31. Tully, 203–4.
32. "On Track Back Home," *New York Times*, July 21, 1984.
33. Mickey Edwards, "Edwards Express" Whistle-Stop Train Tour (remarks of Congressman Mickey Edwards, July 28, 1984), in author's collection.

CHAPTER 1: A SENTIMENTAL JOURNEY

34. Merle Miller, *Plain Speaking: An Oral Biography of Harry S. Truman* (New York: Penguin Group, 1974), 241.
35. Arthur Edson, "Operation Whistle-Stop" (presentation, Women's National Press Club, Washington, DC, October 21, 1964).
36. Herb Thompson, "The Last Whistle Stop Campaign," *The State*, October 1984, 1.
37. Phil Riesman, "The Lincoln Depot Museum in Peekskill Captures a Moment in History," *The Journal*, November 4, 2014.
38. Edward Gill, letter to author, July 15, 1985.
39. Tony Sauro, "RFK in Stockton: 40 Years Ago Today," *The Record*, May 30, 2008, https://www.recordnet.com/story/news/2008/05/30/rfk-in-stockton-40-years/63224648007/.
40. Sauro.
41. Sam Matthews, "Final Tracy Whistle Stop 50 Years Ago Today," *Tracy Press*, October 3, 2014, http://www.goldenstatenewspapers.com/tracy_press/our_town/sam_matthews/final-tracy-whistle-stop-years-ago-today/article_abaff356-4b4c-11e4-a557-3b0c662a37ff.html.

42. "February 21, 1804: World's First Steam Locomotive," San Bernardino History and Railroad Museum, accessed August 8, 2023, http://www.sbdepotmuseum.com/1800-1849/february-21-1804-worlds-first-steam-locomotive.html.
43. "U.S. Timeline: The 1820s," America's Best History, accessed August 8, 2023, https://americasbesthistory.com/abhtimeline1825m2.html.
44. Freeman H. Hubbard, *Encyclopedia of North American Railroading: 150 Years of Railroading in the United States and Canada* (New York: McGraw-Hill, 1981), 306.
45. "The Beginnings of American Railroads and Mapping," Library of Congress, accessed September 12, 2023, https://www.loc.gov/collections/railroad-maps-1828-to-1900/articles-and-essays/history-of-railroads-and-maps/the-beginnings-of-american-railroads-and-mapping/#:~:text=The%20first%20railroad%20charter%20in,opened%20before%20the%20year%20ended.
46. Withers, *The President Travels*, 1.
47. "Riding the Rails with U.S. Presidents," *USA Today*, January 19, 2017, https://www.usatoday.com/story/travel/destinations/2017/01/19/amtrak-president-trains/96778962/.
48. "The Beginnings of American Railroads and Mapping," Library of Congress, https://www.loc.gov/collections/railroad-maps-1828-to-1900/articles-and-essays/history-of-railroads-and-maps/the-beginnings-of-american-railroads-and-mapping/; "All Aboard: Making Tracks with the Presidential Trail," Benjamin Harrison Presidential Site, accessed August 8, 2023, http://www.presidentbenjaminharrison.org/learn/exhibits/past-exhibits/19-learn/exhibits/past-exhibits/62-all-aboard-making-tracks-with-the-presidential-train.
49. Wikipedia, s.v. "Rail Transportation in the United States," accessed August 8, 2023, https://en.m.wikipedia.org/wiki/Rail_transportation_in_the_United_States#History.
50. Neil A. Wynn, *The A to Z of the Roosevelt-Truman Era* (Lanham, MD: Rowman & Littlefield Publishing Group, 2009), 326.
51. William Safire, *The New Language of Politics: A Dictionary of Catchwords, Slogans, and Political Usage* (New York: Collier Books, 1968), 733.
52. Editorial, *Jackson Sun*, October 22, 1952.

53. Associated Press, "'Whistle-Stop' Statement by Taft Backfires," *Green Bay Press-Gazette*, June 19, 1948, https://www.newspapers.com/article/green-bay-press-gazette-ws-derogatory/19617752/.
54. Associated Press, "Resent Taft's Crack About Whistle-Stop," *Daily Tribune*, June 19, 1948, https://www.newspapers.com/article/the-daily-tribune-taft/120153420/.
55. Associated Press, "Democrats Make Political Hay of 'Whistle-Stop' Jab," *The Ogden Standard-Examiner*, June 10, 1948, 1.
56. "Truman Raps 2 Chairmen," *Omaha World-Herald*, June 15, 1948, 5, https://www.newspapers.com/image/882903857/?terms=truman%20raps%202%20chairmen&match=1.
57. Associated Press, "Truman Speaks in N.Y. Today," 1.
58. David Botti, "Presidential Candidates Crave the Spotlight: 200 Years Ago That Was Taboo," *New York Times*, November 3, 2019, https://www.nytimes.com/2019/11/03/video/presidential-candidates-campaigns.html.
59. Hubbard, *Encyclopedia*, 51.
60. Benjamin P. Thomas, *Abraham Lincoln: A Biography* (New York: Modern Library, 1952), 184.
61. Thomas, 148.
62. John W. Starr Jr., *Lincoln and the Railroads: A Biographical Study* (New York: Dodd, Mead, 1927), 136.
63. Larry Tagg, *The Unpopular Mr. Lincoln: The Story of America's Most Reviled President* (El Dorado Hills: Savas Beatie, 2009), 53.
64. Bruce Chadwick: *Lincoln for President: An Unlikely Candidate, an Audacious Strategy, and the Victory No One Saw Coming* (Naperville: Sourcebooks, 2009), 239.
65. Wikipedia, s.v. "Swing Around the Circle," accessed August 8, 2023, https://en.m.wikipedia.org/wiki/Swing_Around_the_Circle#:~:text=Swing%20Around%20the%20Circle%20is,Democrats)%20in%20the%20forthcoming%20midterm.
66. Ejler Jakobsson, "Whistle Stop," *Railroad Magazine*, August 1956, 20–21.
67. Withers, *The President Travels*, 37.
68. Withers, 37–38.
69. Keith Melder, "Bryan the Campaigner," *Bulletin of the United States National Museum* 241 (1965): 73.
70. "Held Up by the People," *Democrat and Chronicle*, April 8, 1905,

6, https://www.newspapers.com/article/democrat-and-chronicle-1905-teddy-roosev/123319582/.

71. *Public Papers of the Presidents of the United States*, National Archives, 584, https://www.govinfo.gov/app/collection/ppp.
72. International News Service, "Truman Plans to Launch Campaign in Mid-September," *Scrantonian Tribune*, August 15, 1948.
73. Truman, *Memoirs*, 210.
74. John C. Cutter, "President Embarks on 'Whistle-Stop' Tour," *Atlanta Constitution*, May 8, 1950, https://www.newspapers.com/article/the-atlanta-constitution-1950-truman/21154174/.
75. "Court Rejects Suit to Bar President's Whistle-Stop Tour," *Evening Star*, September 26, 1952.
76. Associated Press, "Whoa, Mr. President," *Johnson City Press*, September 25, 1952, https://www.newspapers.com/article/johnson-city-press-1952-truman-lawsuit/126978816/.
77. Independent News Service, "Taxpayer Asks Court Order to Keep President on Job," *Fort Worth Star-Telegram*, September 25, 1952, 11, https://www.newspapers.com/article/fort-worth-star-telegram-1952-truman-law/126978543/.
78. Associated Press, "Calls Truman Trip Debacle," *Daily Chronicle*, September 30, 1952, 1, https://www.newspapers.com/article/the-daily-chronicle-1952-truman-criticis/127031914.
79. Milton Coleman, "Mondale Aims Pitch at Party's Unfaithful," *Washington Post*, October 12, 1984, https://www.washingtonpost.com/archive/politics/1984/10/12/mondale-aims-pitch-at-partys-unfaithful/2ea2533c-4bc8-4a31-82dd-d1b32900757b/.
80. "All Aboard," *Akron Beacon Journal*, September 26, 1992, 27, https://www.newspapers.com/article/the-journal-news-1976-ford-illinois/19607679/.
81. Reuters, "Republicans Complain About Clinton Campaign Train Trip," October 28, 1996.
82. William Claiborne, "Dole Tells Rally He Will Not Write Off California, Despite Clinton's Lead," *Washington Post*, August 31, 1996, A15.
83. Michael F. Blake, *Go West Mr. President: Theodore Roosevelt's Great Loop Tour of 1903* (Helena, MT: TwoDot, 2020), 3.
84. Douglas Brinkley, *The Wilderness Warrior: Theodore Roosevelt and the Crusade for America* (New York: Harper Perennial, 2009), 502.

85. Blake, *Go West*, 3.
86. Francis M. Jordan, "Johnson Whistle-Stops in Old Campaign Tradition," *Courier-Post*, October 18, 1960, 12, https://www.newspapers.com/article/courier-post-ws-history-records/127468723/.
87. Meredith Hindley, "Lady Bird Special," *Humanities* 34, no. 3 (May/June 2013), https://www.neh.gov/humanities/2013/mayjune/feature/lady-bird-special.
88. Liz Carpenter, "Operation Whistle-Stop" (presentation, Women's National Press Club, Washington, DC, October 21, 1964).
89. Carpenter, *Ruffles and Flourishes*, 145.
90. Carpenter, "Operation Whistle-Stop."
91. "Campaigning for His First Elective Office," *Tampa Times*, April 14, 1996, 10, https://www.newspapers.com/article/the-tampa-times-1966-tuck-california/19691239/.
92. Steve Harvey, "When Baseball Becomes Oddball," *Los Angeles Times*, February 3, 1999, https://www.latimes.com/archives/la-xpm-1999-feb-03-me-4301-story.html.
93. Rosamond Stahl, "VIPs Used to Whistle-Stop at Willard," *Sandusky Register*, October 27, 1960, 19, https://www.newspapers.com/article/the-sandusky-register-ws-history-and-a/20778325/.
94. "Socialist Red Special," *Montana News*, July 23, 1908, 1, https://www.newspapers.com/article/montana-news-1908-debs-announcement/19147414/.
95. Associated Press, "Ford Trains Across Illinois," *Journal News*, October 17, 1976, 2, https://www.newspapers.com/article/the-journal-news-1976-ford-illinois/19607679/.
96. Mark Mayes, "Clinton's Train Keeps Rolling," *Lansing State Journal*, August 29, 1996, 1, https://www.newspapers.com/article/lansing-state-journal-1996-clinton-m/20249974/.
97. Associated Press, "Dole, in New Hampshire, Promises to Win This Time," *Democrat and Chronicle*, December 9, 1995, 5.
98. Frances Lewine, "Lady Bird Special Begins Trip South; Here Tomorrow," *Daily Times-News*, October 6, 1964.
99. "Mr. and Mrs. Thomas Dewey Aboard the Dewey Victory Special in Warrensburg, Missouri," Harry S. Truman Presidential Library & Museum, accessed August 22, 2023, https://www.trumanlibrary.gov/photograph-records/2006-350.
100. Richard Rodda, "Nixon Admits $16,100 Aid Fund, Campaigns

through Valley," *Sacramento Bee*, September 19, 1952, 1, https://www.newspapers.com/image/624325265/?match=1&clipping_id=133328602.

101. Robert A. Caro, *The Passage of Power: The Years of Lyndon Johnson* (New York: Alfred A. Knopf, 2012), 148.
102. Associated Press, "Adlai 'Ghost Train' in Near-Fatal Back-Up at Silver Spring," *Cumberland News*, November 1, 1952, https://www.newspapers.com/article/the-cumberland-news-1952-fulbright-s/20394585/.
103. Worth Bingham, "Nixon 'Special' to Visit 6 States," *Courier-Journal*, October 26, 1960, 2, https://www.newspapers.com/article/the-courier-journal-1960-nixon-pat-a/127780436/.
104. Bill Lambrecht, "Kerry to Edwards: Next Week, Meet Me in St. Louis," *St. Louis Post-Dispatch*, July 30, 2004, A1, https://www.newspapers.com/article/st-louis-post-dispatch-2004-kerry-and/19661113/.
105. Bob Kemper, "On Train Tour, Bush Courts Swing Voters," *Chicago Tribune*, August 10, 2000, 66, https://www.newspapers.com/article/chicago-tribune-2000-bush-california/20570005/.
106. "Joe Biden Express Rolls into Western Pennsylvania for Whistle-Stop Train Tour," *Tribune-Review*, September 30, 2020, https://triblive.com/local/westmoreland/joe-biden-express-rolls-into-western-pennsylvania-for-whistle-stop-train-tour/.
107. Associated Press, "Stevenson Rides 'Joe Smith' Special," AP Wirephoto, October 4, 1956.
108. Marvin L. Arrowsmith, "'Joe Smith' in Spotlight as Politicians' Darling," Associated Press, *Robesonian*, September 19, 1956, 11, https://www.newspapers.com/image/42041969/?match=1&clipping_id=127782171.
109. "Inside Washington—Barry Called Trigger Happy," *El Paso Herald-Post*, October 3, 1964, 4, https://www.newspapers.com/image/798214841/?match=1&clipping_id=127968351.
110. Jakobsson, "Whistle Stop," 26.
111. Michael F. Reilly and William J. Slocum, *Reilly of the White House* (New York: Simon & Schuster, 1947), 33.
112. Reilly and Slocum, 32–33.
113. Edward G. Lengel, "Franklin D. Roosevelt's Train Ferdinand

Magellan," The White House Historical Association, https://www.whitehousehistory.org/franklin-d-roosevelt-rsquo-s-train-ferdinand-magellan.

114. Hugh Scott, "Operation Whistle Stop! Lincoln Showed Eisenhower and Stevenson the Way," *Philadelphia Inquirer*, September 28, 1952, 153, https://www.newspapers.com/article/the-philadelphia-inquirer-1952-stevens/19905326/.
115. Robert J. Donovan, *Conflict and Crisis: The Presidency of Harry S. Truman* (New York: W. W. Norton, 1977), 395.
116. United Press International, "Campaigning by Train Staging a Comeback," *Tampa Tribune*, September 20, 1976, 7, https://www.newspapers.com/article/the-tampa-tribune-ws-history-and-analy/20476806/.
117. Jakobsson, "Whistle Stop," 26.
118. A. Merriman Smith, *Thank You, Mr. President: A White House Notebook* (New York: Harper & Brothers, 1946), 31–32.
119. "U.S. Car No. 1," National Park Service, accessed August 22, 2023, https://www.nps.gov/nr/travel/presidents/us_car_number_one.html.
120. "Reagan Rails Against Mondale During Ironic Whistle-Stop Tour," *Arizona Republic*, October 13, 1984, 21, https://www.newspapers.com/article/arizona-republic-1984-reagan-ohio/19551405/.
121. Withers, *The President Travels*, 18.
122. Withers, 100.
123. Withers, 98.
124. Hubbard, *Encyclopedia*, 52.
125. Jakobsson, "Whistle Stop," 17–18.
126. Jakobsson, 17–18.
127. Bell, *Splendid Misery*, 247–248.
128. Jody Powell, interview with author, circa 1986.
129. O. P. Newman, "W. Wilson Talks; Close Range Pleases Crowds in Michigan," *Detroit Evening Times*, Saturday, September 21, 1912, 11, https://www.newspapers.com/article/detroit-evening-times-1912-wilson-di/127030887/.
130. Sidney Shalett, "Those Campaign-Train Monkeyshines," *Saturday Evening Post*, September 20, 1952.
131. Robert Bendiner, *White House Fever: An Innocent's Guide to*

Principles and Practices, Respectable and Otherwise, Behind the Election of American Presidents (New York: Harcourt, Brace, 1960), 116.

132. James Reston, "Old Train Adds Glamour to Adlai's Tour," *Cincinnati Enquirer,* October 7, 1956, 116, https://www.newspapers.com/image/103545392/?match=1&clipping_id=127601121.
133. "The Presidency: If the People Choose," *Time,* March 12, 1956, https://content.time.com/time/subscriber/article/0,33009,861962-3,00.html.
134. W. H. Lawrence, *New York Times* News Service, "Democrats Make Campaign Plans," *Chattanooga Daily Times,* June 22, 1956, 14, https://www.newspapers.com/image/604282672/?match=1&clipping_id=137333077.
135. E. W. Kenworthy, "Campaign Special: TV or Train?" *New York Times Magazine,* April 29, 1956, 13.
136. Carpenter, *Ruffles and Flourishes,* 144.
137. ". . . and the Tarmac Takeoff," *Washington Post,* March 10, 1988.
138. Edward Segal, "Newfangled Campaigns Have Whistle Stops Too," *Washington Post,* March 26, 1988.
139. Associated Press, "Dukakis Invokes Truman's Name on Whistle-Stop Tour," *Springfield News-Leader,* August 20, 1988, 9, https://www.newspapers.com/article/the-springfield-news-leader-1988-dukak/18953680/.
140. Associated Press, "Dukakis Rejects Jackson Budget Request," *Democrat and Chronicle,* April 25, 1988, 3, https://www.newspapers.com/article/democrat-and-chronicle-1988-dukakis/20275369/.
141. Associated Press, "Jackson's 'Rainbow Express' Does Tour in New Hampshire," *Greenville News,* February 15, 1988, 7, https://www.newspapers.com/article/the-greenville-news-1988-jackson-new/20275600/.
142. "Officials Ride Train to Advocate Statehood," *Miami Herald,* July 13, 1987, 106, https://www.newspapers.com/article/the-miami-herald-liberty-bell-express-19/123806629/; United Press International, "D.C. Presses Statehood Bid," *Tyler Courier-Times,* July 12, 1987, 12, https://www.newspapers.com/image/587206174/?match=1&clipping_id=127897266; Tom Sherwood, "Liberty Train Hauls Statehood Banner," *Washington Post,* July 13, 1987, https://www.washingtonpost

.com/archive/local/1987/07/13/liberty-train-hauls-statehood-banner/be9d1bfb-c744-48e7-b1da-0cd03f8d1223/.

143. Douglas Birch, "Obscenities Halt Schaefer Tour in Its Tracks," *Evening Sun*, June 24, 1986, 33, https://www.newspapers.com/article/the-evening-sun-linthicum-1986-schaefer/63678321/.
144. "Reagan Rails Against Mondale," *Arizona Republic.*
145. Associated Press, "Reagan Follows Path of Truman—At Least on Train," *Argus-Leader,* October 12, 1984, 7, https://www.newspapers.com/article/argus-leader-1984-reagan-ohio-kk/20777474/.

CHAPTER 2: THE TRAVELING CIRCUS

146. Shalett, "Monkeyshines."
147. John M. Hilpert, *American Cyclone: Theodore Roosevelt and His 1900 Whistle-Stop Campaign* (Jackson: University Press of Mississippi, 2015), 65.
148. Alden Hatch, *Edith Bolling Wilson: First Lady Extraordinary* (New York: Dodd, Mead, 1961), 201–2.
149. Tully, *F. D. R.: My Boss*, 203.
150. Tully, 206.
151. "Campaign May Include Whistle-Stop Tours," *Rapid City Journal*, September 15, 1960, 42, https://www.newspapers.com/article/rapid-city-journal-1952-eisenhower-t/130763170/.
152. Lady Bird Johnson, *A White House Diary* (New York: Holt, Rinehart & Winston, 1970), 194.
153. Jan Jarboe Russell, *Lady Bird: A Biography of Mrs. Johnson* (New York: Scribner, 1999), 251.
154. Carpenter, *Ruffles and Flourishes*, 147–48.
155. Warren J. Sawall, letter to author, July 29, 1985.
156. Edward Segal, "The Revival of Whistlestop Campaigning," *Roll Call*, September 23, 1991, 59.
157. Gene Gibbons, "Clinton Train Trip 'Incredibly Complicated'—Expert," Reuters, August 26, 1996.
158. James Bennet, "Democrats to Borrow (and Add to) a Page," *New York Times*, August 25, 1996, 28, https://www.nytimes.com/1996/08/25/us/democrats-to-borrow-and-add-to-a-page.html.
159. Anne Farris, "In Clinton-Gore Sequel to '92, Thomason Is Back on Board," *Washington Post*, August 24, 1996, A10.

160. Farris, 24.
161. Hatch, *Edith*, 202.
162. Anne Terry White, *Eugene Debs: American Socialist* (New York: Lawrence Hill, 1974), 79.
163. Gordon Gordon, "Campaign Trains," *Railroad Magazine*, February 1953, 51.
164. Gordon, 51.
165. Ray Tucker, "Cost of Truman Campaign Estimated at $200,000," *North Adams Transcript*, October 25, 1952, 4, https://www.newspapers.com/image/545354422/?match=1&clipping_id=127786359.
166. Jesse Shaffer, "247-Mile Nixon Trip Costs GOP $100,000," *Cincinnati Enquirer*, October 23, 1968, 14, https://www.newspapers.com/article/the-cincinnati-enquirer-1968-nixon-c/19687303/.
167. Maurice Fliess, "Carter's Train Whistles Memories of Truman," *Austin American-Statesman*, September 19, 1976, 10.
168. "Clinton's Trip to Chicago an Expensive Train Ride," *Indianapolis Star*, August 29, 1996, 8.
169. Gene Gibbons, "Scenes on a Train: Clinton Chugs to Chicago," Reuters, August 26, 1996.
170. Bell, *Splendid Misery*, 248–50.
171. Richard H. Rovere, "Letter from a Campaign Train," *New Yorker*, October 16, 1948, 27.
172. Robert J. Donovan, "The Best in Campaign Fun: Whistle-Stopping," *Courier-Journal*, July 28, 1964, 6, https://www.newspapers.com/article/the-courier-journal-ws-history-and-ana/21209732/.
173. David McCullough, *Truman* (New York: Simon & Schuster, 1992), 656.
174. Timothy G. Smith, ed., *Merriman Smith's Book of Presidents: A White House Memoir* (New York: W. W. Norton, 1972), 155.
175. Tully, *F. D. R.: My Boss*, 206.
176. Smith, *Thank You, Mr. President*, 38.
177. Jakobsson, "Whistle Stop," 24.
178. "Dreyfus 'Train' to Leave Monday," *Stevens Point Journal*, July 21, 1978, 1.
179. "A Real Whistlestop," *The Chronicle*, September 19, 1984.
180. Meg Dennison, "Philbin Begins Tour of Vermont," Associated Press, July 16, 1992, 1.

181. Robert W. Merry, *President McKinley: Architect of the American Century* (New York: Simon & Schuster, 2017), 138.
182. Jakobsson, "Whistle Stop," 17.
183. Jakobsson, 17.
184. Withers, *The President Travels*, 131.
185. Lengel, "Franklin D. Roosevelt's Train."
186. Truman, *Memoirs*, 211.
187. Truman, 219.
188. McCullough, *Truman*, 699.
189. McCullough, 698.
190. McCullough, 699.
191. Miller, *Plain Speaking*, 249.
192. McCullough, *Truman*, 698.
193. Richard L. Gruenther and Robert H. Ferrell, eds., "The Eisenhower Campaign of 1952: The Letters of Homer Gruenther," *Nebraska History* 69 (1988), 30–39.
194. Ken Hechler, *Working with Truman: A Personal Memoir of the White House Years* (New York: G. P. Putnam's Sons, 1982), 251–52.
195. McGrory, interview with author.
196. Bendiner, *White House Fever*, 112.
197. Robert Cutler, *No Time for Rest* (New York: Little, Brown, 1965), 291.
198. Larry J. Sabato, "Richard Nixon's 'Secret Fund'—1952," *Washington Post*, 1998, https://www.washingtonpost.com/wp-srv/politics/special/clinton/frenzy/nixon.htm.
199. Richard Nixon, *Six Crises* (New York: Doubleday, 1962), 81–82.
200. Sabato, "Richard Nixon's 'Secret Fund.'"
201. Ron Fournier, "As Train Chugs Toward Chicago, Clinton Targets Family Abusers," Associated Press, August 27, 1996.
202. Merlo J. Pusey, *Charles Evans Hughes* (New York: MacMillan, 1951), 339.
203. Donald A. Ritchie, *Electing FDR: The New Deal Campaign of 1932* (Lawrence: University Press of Kansas, 2007), 140.
204. James Roosevelt and Sidney Shalett, *Affectionately, F.D.R.: A Son's Story of a Lonely Man* (New York: Harcourt, Brace, 1959), 230–31.
205. Mary Earhart Dillon, *Wendell Willkie: 1892–1944* (New York: J. B. Lippincott, 1952), 206.

206. Bendiner, *White House Fever*, 112.
207. Bess Furman, "Operation Whistle-Stop" (presentation, Women's National Press Club, Washington, DC, October 21, 1964).
208. David Pietrusza, *Roosevelt Sweeps Nation: FDR's 1936 Landslide and the Triumph of the Liberal Ideal* (New York: Diversion Books, 2022), 19, Kindle.
209. Betty Pryor, "Pat Nixon Will Stump for Votes with Husband," *Pittsburgh Press*, July 13, 1952, https://www.newspapers.com/image/141583396/?match=1&clipping_id=127619899.
210. Alvaretta S. Atkinson, "Pat Nixon Impresses by Her Charm and Sincerity," *Leader-Telegram*, October 16, 1952, 7, https://www.newspapers.com/article/leader-telegram-1952-nixon-wisconsin/21189182/.
211. Associated Press, "Johnson Sets 60-Speech Whistle-Stop Tour of South," *Tampa Tribune*, October 5, 1960, 4, https://www.newspapers.com/image/329701969/?match=1&clipping_id=131963448.
212. Reuters, "Chelsea Makes Political Debut on Clinton Train Trip," August 25, 1996.
213. Edith Bolling Wilson, *My Memoir* (New York: Bobbs-Merrill, 1938), 273–74.
214. "Woodrow Wilson Suffers a Stroke," History.com, November 16, 2009, https://www.history.com/this-day-in-history/woodrow-wilson-suffers-a-stroke.
215. Hatch, *Edith*, 206.
216. Howard Markel, "When a Secret President Ran the Country," *PBS NewsHour*, October 2, 2015, https://www.pbs.org/newshour/health/woodrow-wilson-stroke.
217. Paul F. Boller Jr., *Presidential Campaigns: From George Washington to George W. Bush* (New York: Oxford University Press, 1984), 238–39.
218. Richard J. Ellis, *Presidential Travel: The Journey from George Washington to George W. Bush* (Lawrence: University Press of Kansas, 2008), 209.
219. Ellis, 209.
220. Dillon, *Wendell Willkie*, 203–4.
221. Bruce Biossat, "Running Campaign Train Takes Lot of Military Planning, Work," *Daily Tribune*, September 20, 1952, 4.

222. Cutler, *No Time*, 280.
223. "Have Narrow Escape: President Roosevelt's Train Bruises People at Lake Mills, Wis.," *Leader-Telegram*, April 5, 1903, https://www.newspapers.com/image/239401391/?terms=While%20some%20were%20slightly%20bruised%20in%20the%20scramble%2C%20no%20one%20was%20seriously%20hurt%2C%22%20&match=1.
224. "Gov. Wilson's Train in Grave Danger," *Brooklyn Daily Eagle*, October 5, 1912, 2, https://www.newspapers.com/image/54474522/?terms=Big%20welcome%20in%20Omaha&match=1.
225. "Hughes Near Death from His Own Campaign Train When Motorcar Stalls," *Harrisburg Telegraph*, October 30, 1916, 5, https://www.newspapers.com/article/harrisburg-telegraph-1916-hughes-acc/20479019/.
226. "Engineer of Cox Special Leaps to Save Life," *Evening News*, October 20, 1920, 1, https://www.newspapers.com/article/the-evening-news-1920-cox-train-acci/19043443/.
227. "Cox's Special Wrecked Near Maricopa, Arizona," *University Daily Kansan*, September 24, 1920, 1, https://www.newspapers.com/article/university-daily-kansan-1920-cox-acciden/121626579/.
228. United Press, "Platform Falls, Stevenson Safe," *Philadelphia Inquirer*, October 28, 1952, 2, https://www.newspapers.com/article/the-philadelphia-inquirer-1952-stevens/19643066/.
229. Associated Press, "Stevenson Ghost Train Perils Shrieking Crowd," *Philadelphia Inquirer*, November 1, 1952, 6, https://www.newspapers.com/article/the-philadelphia-inquirer-1952-fulbrig/20394468/.
230. United Press Telephoto, October 31, 1952, https://www.newspapers.com/image/402626185/?terms=rushed%20toward%20the%20back%20platform%2C%20the%20train%20suddenly%20backed%20up%2C%20causing%20dozens%20of%20persons%20to%20scramble%20for%20safety.%20No%20one%20was%20hurt&match=1.
231. "Clark Campaign Train Halted by Fatal Crash," *Pantagraph*, August 13, 1968, https://www.newspapers.com/article/the-pantagraph-1968-illinois-clark-accid/19147386/.
232. "Stand Falls, Injures 12," *Tampa Bay Times*, August 29, 1996, 10, https://www.newspapers.com/article/tampa-bay-times-1996-clinton-people/20249761/.

233. Withers, *The President Travels*, 60–61.
234. Ray Ginger, *Eugene V. Debs: A Biography* (New York: Collier Books, 1949), 294–95.
235. Freeman H. Hubbard, "Political Stand-In," *Tracks*, October 1950, 9–11.
236. Bernard Asbell, *When F.D.R. Died* (New York: Holt, Rinehart and Winston, 1961), 102–3.
237. Miller, *Plain Speaking*, 174.
238. Gruenther and Ferrell, "Eisenhower Campaign of 1952," 34.
239. "Crowd Gathers for Whistle-Stop Talk, Settles for Whistle," *Marshfield News-Herald*, October 25, 1952, https://www.newspapers.com/article/marshfield-news-herald-1952-nixon-wi/21189131/.
240. Patrick Healy, "Edwards Sent to Kan. for Makeup Rally," *Boston Globe*, August 8, 2004, 102, https://www.newspapers.com/article/arizona-republic-2004-kerry-and-edwar/19661423/.
241. "Edwards Repays Loyal Kansans," *Democrat and Chronicle*, August 9, 2004, 10, https://www.newspapers.com/article/democrat-and-chronicle-2004-kerry-ad-e/19661065/.
242. Associated Press, "Publicity Makes Jackie Drop Pell's Tour Plan," *Green Bay Press-Gazette*, October 25, 1972, 37, https://www.newspapers.com/article/green-bay-press-gazette-1972-pell-rh/19616800/.
243. Mike Shanahan, "Anderson Cancels Train Tour," Associated Press, *Leader-Telegram*, August 28, 1980, 2, https://www.newspapers.com/article/leader-telegram-1980-anderson15/18981457/.
244. Associated Press, "Anderson Drops State Train Tour," *Manitowoc Herald-Times*, August 29, 1980, 1.
245. Associated Press, "Anderson Adopts Whistle-Stop Tactic," *Atlanta Constitution*, November 2, 1980, 6, https://www.newspapers.com/article/the-atlanta-constitution-1980-anderson/18983823/.
246. Jay Tunney, email to author, June 16, 2018.
247. Associated Press, "No Whistle-Stop Campaign," *Iowa City Press-Citizen*, October 6, 1982, 6, https://www.newspapers.com/article/iowa-city-press-citizen-1982-iowa-demo/20328454/.
248. Associated Press, "Secret Service Nixes Bush Train Ride," *Stevens Point Journal*, August 12, 1991, 7, https://www.newspapers.com/article/stevens-point-journal-1992-bush-secr/21121887/.

249. Adlai E. Stevenson III, letter to author, April 1, 1985.
250. Miller, *Plain Speaking*, 248.
251. Goodwin, *Leadership in Turbulent Times*, 90.
252. Raymond Brooks, "Cheering Throng Says 'Howdy, Mr. President,'" *Austin American-Statesman*, September 27, 1948, 1, https://www.newspapers.com/article/austin-american-statesman-1948-truman-lb/121494640/.
253. "President Endorses Johnson," *Austin American-Statesman*, September 27, 1948, 1, https://www.newspapers.com/article/austin-american-statesman-1948-truman-lb/121494640/.
254. Withers, *The President Travels*, 210.
255. Jane Dick, *Volunteers and the Making of Presidents* (New York: Dodd, Mead, 1980), 211–12.
256. Committee to Re-Elect Governor Brown, Itinerary for October 29, 1966.
257. Gary Hart, *Right from the Start: A Chronicle of the McGovern Campaign* (New York: Quadrangle, 1973), 187.
258. John Parish, "Baker Campaign Train to Make Area Stops," *Jackson Sun*, October 22, 1978, 5, https://www.newspapers.com/article/the-jackson-sun-1978-howard-baker-ro/131154405/.
259. Associated Press, "Baker Takes Car on Final Leg of State Tour," *Johnson City Press*, November 3, 1978, 14, https://www.newspapers.com/article/johnson-city-press-1978-howard-baker/131154619/.
260. Paul Nowell, "Martin Whistlestop Tour Rolls Across N.C.," Associated Press, October 24, 1988.
261. Monica Morgan, "Rosa Parks Travelling with President Bill Clinton's Whistle-Stop Presidential Campaign Tour, 1996," Photo, Civil Rights Digital Library, accessed August 10, 2023, https://crdl.usg.edu/record/loc_rosaparks_47457.
262. Gibbons, "Scenes on a Train."
263. William T. Pheiffer, letter to author, March 28, 1985.
264. Ellis, *Presidential Travel*, 211–12.
265. Associated Press, "Dewey Gets Rodeo Trophy," AP Photo, September 26, 1948.
266. "Elephant Greeting Taft in Northfield, Minnesota," September 26, 1908, George Grantham Bain Collection. Courtesy of the Library of Congress, Prints & Photographs Division, LC-USZ62-101136.

267. Associated Press, "From a Collector," AP Photo, February 18, 1972, https://www.newspapers.com/article/the-tampa-tribune-1972-muskie-flori/19613694/.
268. Associated Press, "Baby-Kissing Season Opens," AP Photo, August 26, 1936.
269. Associated Press, "New Hazard Crops Up for Nixon," *Marshfield News-Herald*, October 25, 1952, 5, https://www.newspapers.com/article/marshfield-news-herald-1952-nixon-wi/21189084/.
270. Acme, "Getting to Be a Habit," Acme Newspictures, September 23, 1936.
271. Acme, "President a Youngster to Henry," Acme Telephoto, May 8, 1950.
272. Associated Press, "She Likes Ike," AP Photo, September 19, 1952.
273. Associated Press, "War Hoops and Cowboy Hats Greet Roosevelt," AP Photo, September 19, 1932.
274. Withers, *The President Travels*, 63.
275. Andrew I. Paul, "A Bully Show: Theodore Roosevelt 1900 Campaign Tour Through Nebraska," *Nebraska History* (Fall 1992), 139.
276. Withers, *The President Travels*, 149.
277. Withers, 208.
278. United Press, "Peek-A-Boo Candidate," UP Photo, October 31, 1952.
279. John Bartlow Martin, *Adlai Stevenson of Illinois: The Life of Adlai E. Stevenson* (New York: Anchor Books, 1977), 673.
280. United Press, "Stevenson Gets Whistlestop Gift," *The Tribune*, November 1, 1952.
281. Mary McGrory, "Whistlestop: A Campaign Idyl," *Sunday Star*, October 21, 1956, A23.
282. Bob von Sternberg, "A Memorable Whistle-Stop Tour in '52," *Minneapolis Star Tribune*, April 12, 1994, 19, https://www.newspapers.com/image/192866220/?match=1&clipping_id=128667605.
283. Marshall B. Atkinson, "Rick Lake Gives Nixon Huge Swiss Cheese, Aides Baffled," *Daily Telegram*, October 25, 1952, https://www.newspapers.com/image/300558431/?terms=%20Gives%20Nixon%20Huge%20Swiss%20Cheese%2C%20Aides%20Baffled%2C&match=1.
284. Carpenter, *Ruffles and Flourishes*, 167.

285. "Bread Instead of Roses," *Asbury Park Press*, September 21, 1976, 38, https://www.newspapers.com/image/143849035/?match=1&clipping_id=130851745.

CHAPTER 3: TRACKSIDE SPEECHES

286. Ritchie, *Electing FDR*, 139.
287. Reston, "Old Train," 116.
288. "'Whistle-Stop' Comeback," *The Times*, July 21, 1960, https://www.newspapers.com/article/the-times-ws-1960-train-tours-by-ken/20781754/.
289. "Whistle-Stopping," *El Paso Herald-Post*, September 22, 1964, 16, https://www.newspapers.com/article/el-paso-herald-post-ws-history-and-ana/18949653/.
290. Thomas, *Abraham Lincoln*, 184.
291. "Harrison at Atlanta," *Chicago Tribune*, April 16, 1891, 1, https://www.newspapers.com/article/chicago-tribune-1891-harrison-cannon/123348165/.
292. Withers, *The President Travels*, 60.
293. Richard Strout, *Christian Science Monitor*, Western Union Press Message, August 26, 1936.
294. Walter Fitzmaurice, "Campaign Special," *Trains*, March 1947, 17.
295. "Memorandum to Advance Men Re: Train Advancing," October 15, 1960, Richard Nixon Presidential Library, accessed August 11, 2023, https://www.nixonlibrary.gov/sites/default/files/virtuallibrary/documents/whsfreturned/WHSF_Box_48/WHSF48-04.pdf.
296. "Memorandum."
297. Margaret Truman, *Harry S. Truman* (New York: William Morrow, 1973), 22–23.
298. Caro, *Passage of Power*, 145.
299. Associated Press, "Brown's Campaign Train Gets Ticket," *Lawton Constitution and Morning Press*, October 30, 1966, 33, https://www.newspapers.com/article/the-lawton-constitution-and-morning-pres/21242192.
300. Boller, *Presidential Campaigns*, 198.
301. "Big Bull Moose Roams over Familiar Ranges," *Lincoln Journal*

Star, September 7, 1912, 1, https://www.newspapers.com/article/lincoln-journal-star-1912-roosevelt/19262868/.

302. Richard L. Strout, interview with author, June 21, 1985.
303. Marquis Childs, *Witness to Power* (New York: McGraw-Hill, 1975), 22.
304. Bess Furman, *Washington By-Line: The Personal History of a Newspaperwoman* (New York: Alfred A. Knopf, 1949), 249–50.
305. Dillon, *Wendell Willkie*, 206–7.
306. David Pietrusza, *1948: Harry Truman's Improbable Victory and the Year That Transformed America's Role in the World* (New York: Diversion Books, 2011), 129–30, Kindle.
307. Pietrusza, 130.
308. Elsey, *An Unplanned Life*, 167–68.
309. Frank McNaughton and Walter Hehmeyer, *This Man Truman* (New York: McGraw-Hill, 1945), 179.
310. McNaughton and Hehmeyer, 179.
311. Wilson W. Wyatt Sr., *Whistle Stops: Adventures in Public Life* (Lexington: University Press of Kentucky, 1985), 106.
312. Alben W. Barkley, *That Reminds Me* (Garden City, NY: Doubleday, 1954), 139.
313. Edson, "Operation Whistle-Stop."
314. Cutler, *No Time*, 282.
315. Caro, *Passage of Power*, 146.
316. Edmund W. Starling and Thomas Sugrue, *Starling of the White House: The Story of the Man Whose Secret Service Detail Guarded Five Presidents from Woodrow Wilson to Franklin D. Roosevelt* (Chicago: People's Book Club, 1916), 300–302.
317. Bendiner, *White House Fever*, 112.
318. Carpenter, "Operation Whistle-Stop."
319. Newsweek Staff, "The Man in the Middle," December 17, 1995, Newsweek.com, accessed August 11, 2023, https://www.newsweek.com/man-middle-180460.
320. Hechler, *Working with Truman*, 99.
321. Smith, *Merriman Smith's Book of Presidents*, 149.
322. Robert J. Donovan, "Grassroots," *Courier-Journal*, July 28, 1964, 6, https://www.newspapers.com/article/the-courier-journal-ws-history-and-ana/21209732/.
323. Donovan, "Grassroots," 6.

324. Unidentified Reporter, "Operation Whistle-Stop" (presentation, Women's National Press Club, Washington, DC, October 21, 1964).
325. Nixon, *Six Crises*, 78.
326. Miller, *Plain Speaking*, 249.
327. Phillips, "Richard M. Nixon," 49–50.
328. Starling and Sugrue, *Starling of the White House*, 236.
329. Nixon, *Six Crises*, 78–80.
330. Jakobsson, "Whistle Stop," 22.
331. Associated Press, "General Snafu on Tour Train Disrupts Ike," *Rutland Daily Herald*, October 2, 1952, https://www.newspapers.com/image/533733535/?match=1&clipping_id=127836199.
332. Phillips, "Richard M. Nixon," 50.
333. Gordon, "Campaign Trains," 47.
334. Gordon, 48-49.
335. Herman, interview with author.
336. David S. Broder, "California's National Treasure," *Washington Post*, February 21, 1996, A19.
337. "Whistle-Stop Anniversary: LBJ Special's Culpeper Visit," *Culpeper Star-Exponent*, October 10, 1994, 1.
338. George Dixon, "The Flourishing Fraternities," *San Francisco Examiner*, November 9, 1960, 32, https://www.newspapers.com/image/458708199/?match=1&clipping_id=131739248.
339. Mary Stevens Jones, "What LBJ Did for Culpeper," *Culpeper Star-Exponent*, January 26, 1973.
340. Furman, "Operation Whistle-Stop."

CHAPTER 4: HECKLERS, PRANKSTERS, AND PROTESTERS

341. United Press International, "Barry Fans Heckle Pierre Train Tour," *Oakland Tribune*, August 30, 1964, 2, https://www.newspapers.com/article/oakland-tribune-1964-salinger-califo/21162749/.
342. James Gindlesperger, "Swing Around the Circle Tour Tragedy," *Johnstown*, December 15, 2021.
343. Withers, *The President Travels*, 31–34.
344. Ron Chernow, *Grant* (New York: Penguin Random House, 2017), 577–81, Kindle.
345. Erika Holst, "Springfield Snubbed a President," August 18,

2016, *Illinois Times*, accessed August 11, 2023, https://www.illinoistimes.com/springfield/springfield-snubbed-a-president/Content?oid=11452155.

346. "Past Campaigns Stirred by Song," *Rock Island Argus*, July 7, 1916, 8.
347. Hilpert, *American Cyclone*, 263, 295.
348. Hilpert, 247, 295.
349. "Tried It Again," *Indianapolis Journal*, September 28, 1900, 1–2, https://www.newspapers.com/image/167048224/?match=1&clipping_id=127839830.
350. Elizabeth Kolbert, "Unhappy Warrior," *New Yorker*, February 25, 2001, https://www.newyorker.com/magazine/2001/03/05/unhappy-warrior.
351. "How Bad Was the Great Depression? Gauging the Economic Impact," Federal Reserve Bank of St. Louis, accessed August 11, 2023, https://www.stlouisfed.org/en/the-great-depression/curriculum/economic-episodes-in-american-history-part-3.
352. Associated Press, "President Lauds G.O.P. Program," *Buffalo Evening News*, October 24, 1932, 12, https://www.newspapers.com/image/838907558/?match=1&clipping_id=131744092\New.
353. Starling and Sugrue, *Starling of the White House*, 299.
354. Glen Jeansonne, *Herbert Hoover: A Life* (New York: New American Library, 2016), 285, Kindle.
355. United Press, "Nevada Heckler Arouses Hoover," *Times-News*, November 9, 1932, https://www.newspapers.com/article/the-times-news-1932-hoover-heckler/120707183/.
356. International News Service, "Hoover Dares Elko Heckler to Step Up and Take Medicine," *Waterloo Daily Courier*, November 8, 1932, 2, https://www.newspapers.com/article/the-courier-1932-hoover-heckler/120706805/.
357. Associated Press, "Attack Watchman Guarding Track for Hoover's Train," *Kokomo Tribune*, November 8, 1932, 1, https://www.newspapers.com/article/the-kokomo-tribune-1932-hoover-guard/20118439/.
358. Associated Press, "Find Dynamite Near Track of Hoover Special," *Journal and Courier*, November 8, 1932, 1, https://www.newspapers.com/article/journal-and-courier-1932-hoover-dyna/19686748/.

359. Herbert G. Monroe, "President's Special," *Railroad Magazine*, November 1945, 17.
360. Dillon, *Wendell Willkie*, 215.
361. Bernard J. Losh, "Rear Platform Campaigns Not Always Successful," *Dayton Daily News*, September 28, 1952, 97, https://www.newspapers.com/image/401828397/?clipping_id=21238286&fcfToken=eyJhbGciOiJIUzI1NiIsInR5cCI6IkpXVCJ9.eyJmcmVlLXZpZXctaWQiOjQwMTgyODM5NywiaWF0IjoxNjg4OTA2MTA0LCJleHAiOjE2ODg5OTI1MDR9.wUwDvbkfj8M6L1H38tQ9ReSGIDNkfygKaD3k6N6_NWU.
362. Smith, *Thank You, Mr. President*, 90.
363. Tully, *F. D. R.: My Boss*, 205.
364. Monroe, "President's Special," 14–15.
365. Jakobsson, "Whistle Stop," 25–26.
366. Andrew Rosenthal, "High-Tech Whistle-Stops for Dukakis," *New York Times*, August 20, 1988, 7, https://www.nytimes.com/1988/08/20/us/high-tech-whistle-stops-for-dukakis.html.
367. Fitzmaurice, "Campaign Special," 22.
368. Truman, *Harry S. Truman*, 26–27.
369. Truman, 27.
370. "Bryan's 'Cross of Gold' Speech: Mesmerizing the Masses," History Matters, The U.S. Survey Course on the Web, George Mason University, https://historymatters.gmu.edu/d/5354/.
371. Sonia Kallick, "Speech Overwhelms Hearts, but Pocketbooks Voted," *Lemont Metropolitan*, July 1, 1993, 8, https://www.newspapers.com/image/699896455/?fcfToken=eyJhbGciOiJIUzI1NiIsInR5cCI6IkpXVCJ9.eyJmcmVlLXZpZXctaWQiOjY5OTg5NjQ1NSwiaWF0IjoxNjg4ODMyNjYyLCJleHAiOjE2ODg5MTkwNjJ9.p9OTc22Ak6L4ZpDrNJ9gSD7hl8YqaU_TMoBDcLQC-uE.
372. "Bryan Spots Pickpockets," *Kansas City Times*, September 13, 1896, 1, https://www.newspapers.com/image/649205183/?clipping_id=122924254&fcfToken=eyJhbGciOiJIUzI1NiIsInR5cCI6IkpXVCJ9.eyJmcmVlLXZpZXctaWQiOjY0.
373. Boller, *Presidential Campaigns*, 182.
374. Truman, *Harry S. Truman*, 26.
375. Martin, *Adlai Stevenson of Illinois*, 685.
376. Martin, 687.

377. Richard Nixon, *RN: The Memoirs of Richard Nixon* (New York: Simon & Schuster, 1978), 94.
378. Nixon, *Six Crises*, 87–88.
379. Nixon, *Six Crises*, 88.
380. United Press International, "Derailment Scare Hits Nixon Train," *Anniston Star*, October 28, 1960, 1.
381. United Press International, 1.
382. United Press International, "Tomatoes, Eggs Thrown at Nixon," *Shamokin News-Dispatch*, October 28, 1960, https://www.newspapers.com/article/shamokin-news-dispatch-1960-nixon-in/19877758/.
383. Associated Press, "Tomatoes Greet Dewey," AP Photo, October 14, 1948.
384. Associated Press, "Stevenson Cheered, Egg Thrown on Indiana Trip," *Anderson Herald*, October 23, 1952, 1, https://www.newspapers.com/article/anderson-herald-1952-stevenson-egg-prote/120652102/.
385. United Press, "Coed's Mother Says Stevenson Egg Fresh," *Columbus Ledger*, October 23, 1952, 18, https://www.newspapers.com/article/the-columbus-ledger-1952-stevenson-egg-p/120652434/.
386. *The Washington Post*, "'Bring-Us-Together' Girl Found Placard," quoted in *The Los Angeles Times*, January 21, 1969, 21, https://www.newspapers.com/image/383139806/?match=1&clipping_id=137330181.
387. Loye Miller, "Operation Whistle-Stop" (presentation, Women's National Press Club, Washington, DC, October 21, 1964).
388. Miller.
389. Wikipedia, s.v. "Dick Tuck," accessed August 14, 2023, https://en.m.wikipedia.org/wiki/Dick_Tuck.
390. David Wise, "GOP Agents Bounce 'Spy,'" Herald Tribune News Service, *Journal Herald*, September 30, 1964, 1.
391. Wise, 1.
392. Frances A. Kellor, *Women in the Campaign* (New Haven, CT: Yale Review, 1917; repr., New York: McConnell Press), https://elisabethfreeman.org/1916-hughes-womens-campaign-train/#gallery/9__357689335/129.
393. Carpenter, *Ruffles and Flourishes*, 162.
394. Carpenter, 162.

395. Carpenter, 163.
396. Carpenter, "Operation Whistle-Stop."
397. Carpenter, *Ruffles and Flourishes*, 165.
398. Matthews, "Final Tracy Whistle Stop."
399. Thurston Clarke, *The Last Campaign: Robert F. Kennedy and 82 Days That Inspired America* (New York: Henry Holt, 2008), 200.
400. Hunter S. Thompson, *Fear and Loathing on the Campaign Trail '72* (San Francisco: Straight Arrow Books, 1973), 106–7.
401. Ben Funk, "Hecklers at Whistle-Stop End Push Muskie Past Boiling Point," *Tampa Tribune*, February 20, 1972, 28.
402. The American Presidency Project, "Remarks During a Michigan Whistlestop Tour," UC Santa Barbara, accessed August 14, 2023, https://www.presidency.ucsb.edu/documents/remarks-during-michigan-whistlestop-tour.
403. Michael Kelly, "Political Memo: Those Chicken Georges and What They Mean," *New York Times*, September 30, 1992, https://www.nytimes.com/1992/09/30/us/the-1992-campaign-political-memo-those-chicken-georges-and-what-they-mean.html.
404. Reuters, "Clinton Buoyed by Whistle-Stop Tour," August 28, 1996.
405. Jill Zuckman, "Whistle-Stop in Missouri Town Raucous," *Chicago Tribune*, August 7, 2004, https://www.spokesman.com/stories/2004/aug/07/whistle-stop-in-missouri-town-raucous/.

CHAPTER 5: MEET THE PRESS

406. Smith, *Thank You, Mr. President*, 45.
407. Starr, *Lincoln and the Railroads*, 175.
408. Starr, 178–79.
409. Carroll Kilpatrick, "'Jet Campaigning' Efficient—But Dull," *Washington Post and Times-Herald*, September 16, 1956, E3.
410. Bruce Biossat, "Life Aboard Campaign Train Proves Hectic," Newspaper Enterprise Association, *Tallahassee Democrat*, October 6, 1952, 5, https://www.newspapers.com/image/244953414/?terms=the%20first%20stays%20the%20press%20car%20listens%20to%20the%20candidate%20spout%20over%20the%20.
411. Bell, *Splendid Misery*, 248.
412. Hobart Rowen, "Harry: A Stillness at Independence, and Hell on Rails," *Washington Post*, August 30, 1992.

413. Drew Pearson, "Campaign Train Song," Washington Merry-Go-Round, *Washington Post*, October 20, 1944, 8.
414. Jeremiah O'Leary, "Campaign Train Recalls Days of Yesteryear," *Washington Times*, October 15, 1984, 3A.
415. Melder, "Bryan the Campaigner," 73.
416. Smith, *Thank You, Mr. President*, 40–41.
417. Irwin Ross, *The Loneliest Campaign: The Truman Victory of 1948* (New York: New American Library, 1968), 190–91.
418. Ross, 192.
419. Alice Dunnigan, *Alone atop the Hill: The Autobiography of Alice Dunnigan, Pioneer of the National Black Press*, Carol McCabe Booker, ed. (Athens: University of Georgia Press, 2015), 122–23.
420. Bell, *Splendid Misery*, 246–47.
421. Herman, interview with author.
422. Herman.
423. Herman.
424. Carpenter, *Ruffles and Flourishes*, 161.
425. Carpenter, 161.
426. Bell, *Splendid Misery*, 249.
427. Bell, 249–50.
428. David M. Jordan, *FDR, Dewey, and the Election of 1944* (Bloomington: Indiana University Press, 2011), 229.
429. Charles M. Dean, "Dewey Battle," *Cincinnati Enquirer*, September 21, 1944, 4, https://www.newspapers.com/clippings/?query=The%20Governor%2C%20like%20most%20of%20the%20other%20passengers%2C%20agreed%20that%20the%20wreck%20was%20%27stupid.%22%20&user=4606739%3AEdwardsegal.
430. Pearson, "Campaign Train Song."
431. Photograph from Gardner Bridge, author's archives.
432. Smith, *Merriman Smith's Book of Presidents*, 147–48.
433. Frances Lewine, "Operation Whistle-Stop" (presentation, Women's National Press Club, Washington, DC, October 21, 1964).
434. Herman, interview with author.
435. Smith, *Thank You, Mr. President*, 41.
436. Smith, *Merriman Smith's Book of Presidents*, 157.
437. Robert Donovan, interview with author, July 17, 1985.
438. Shalett, "Monkeyshines."

439. Wikipedia, s.v. “Leo W. O’Brien,” accessed September 12, 2023, https://en.m.wikipedia.org/wiki/Leo_W._O%27Brien.
440. Stanley Weintraub, *Final Victory: FDR’s Extraordinary World War II Presidential Campaign* (New York: De Capo Press, 2012), 37–38.
441. Ben Cosgrove, “Behind the Picture: ‘Dewey Defeats Truman,’” Life.com, accessed August 14, 2023, https://www.life.com/history/dewey-defeats-truman-the-story-behind-a-classic-political-photo/.
442. McGovern Presidential Campaign, *Information for Press—Radio—TV: McGovern Campaign Special*, June 3, 1972.
443. Dewey-Warren 1948 Campaign, *Daily Travel Notes*, September 1–30, 1948, and October 1–16, 1948.
444. Bell, *Splendid Misery*, 248.
445. Jakobsson, “Whistle Stop,” 17.
446. Shalett, “Monkeyshines.”
447. Linda Lotridge Levin, *The Making of FDR: The Story of Stephen T. Early, America’s First Modern Press Secretary* (New York: Prometheus Books, 2008), 75.
448. Angelo, “Operation Whistle-Stop.”
449. Jakobsson, “Whistle Stop,” 20–21.
450. Miller, “Operation Whistle-Stop.”
451. Jules Witcover, *85 Days: The Last Campaign of Robert Kennedy* (New York: Quill, 1969), 161–62.
452. Biossat, “Life,” 5.
453. Carpenter, *Ruffles and Flourishes*, 159.
454. Don Irwin, “Campaign Train Chugs Toward Museumville,” *Los Angeles Times*, November 4, 1972, 19, https://www.newspapers.com/image/385899409/.
455. “ANP Correspondent on Presidential Special,” *St. Paul Recorder*, 1, https://www.newspapers.com/article/st-paul-recorder-dunnigan-truman-19/120221238/.
456. Dunnigan, *Alone atop the Hill*, 128–29.
457. Smith, *Merriman Smith’s Book of Presidents*, 148.
458. Bell, *Splendid Misery*, 248.
459. Edward Segal, “Press and Pols Together,” *Washington Journalism Review*, July/August 1988, 40.
460. Gardner Bridge, “Reporters on Campaign Trains Find It’s a Tiring Grind” *Buffalo News*, October 2, 1944, 9, https://www

.newspapers.com/article/the-buffalo-news-1944-garrdner-bridge-me/121044075/.

461. Smith, *Merriman Smith's Book of Presidents*, 181.
462. Richard L. Strout, "Covering Washington," *Unit Projects in Modern Literature*, October 15–31, 1935, 2–3.
463. Richard L. Strout, interview with author, circa 1986.
464. Gardner Bridge, "Reporter's Eye-View of Life Aboard a Campaign Train," Associated Press, *Owensboro Messenger*, October 6, 1944, 4.
465. McGrory, interview with author.
466. Richard L. Strout, "Memo on the Roosevelt Presidential Drought Trip," August 25–September 5, 1936.
467. Smith, *Thank You, Mr. President*, 41–42.
468. Carol Biliczky, "Campaigning from Trains Generates Century of Stories," *Akron Beacon Journal*, August 4, 2000, 29, https://www.newspapers.com/image/152299590/.
469. Donovan, interview with author.
470. Henry La Cossitt, "He Takes the President on Tour," *Saturday Evening Post*, June 16, 1951, 19.
471. Furman, "Operation Whistle-Stop."
472. Herman, interview with author.
473. Miller, "Operation Whistle-Stop."
474. Carpenter, "Operation Whistle-Stop."
475. Boller, *Presidential Campaigns*, 198–99.
476. Richard L. Strout, "The Journalistic Legacy of Tom Stokes" (presentation, Thomas L. Stokes Award Dinner, National Press Club, Washington, DC, May 5, 1959).
477. Witcover, *85 Days*, 162–63.
478. David Hoffman, interview with author, circa 1986.
479. Hoffman.
480. Hoffman.
481. Hoffman.
482. Hoffman.
483. Don Irwin of the Los Angeles Times News Service, "Campaign Trains Railroaded," *Florida Today*, November 6, 1972, 10a, https://www.newspapers.com/article/florida-today-ws-history-and-analysis/19614861/.
484. Wikipedia, s.v. "Campaign bus," accessed September 12, 2023, https://en.m.wikipedia.org/wiki/Campaign_bus.

485. Wikipedia, s.v. "*The Boys on the Bus*," accessed September 12, 2023, https://en.m.wikipedia.org/wiki/The_Boys_on_the_Bus.
486. The National Press Club, video: "*The Boys on the Bus*—12 Elections Later," Press.org, accessed September 12, 2023, https://www.press.org/newsroom/video-boys-bus-12-years-later.
487. Wikipedia, "Campaign bus."
488. Associated Press, "Texas Office Seekers Begin Stretch Sprint," *Fort Worth Star-Telegram*, July 15, 1940, 7, https://www.newspapers.com/article/fort-worth-star-telegram-1940-campaign/131200631/.
489. Bill Straub, "McCain Rolling into Town," *Cincinnati Post*, February 26, 2000, 10, https://www.newspapers.com/image/765442714/?match=1&clipping_id=131214932.
490. Pat Politano, "Campaign Bus Collides with School Bus," *Courier-News*, October 28, 1988, 6, https://www.newspapers.com/image/228901302/?clipping_id=131200823&fcfToken=eyJhbGciOiJIUzI1NiIsInR5cCI6IkpXVCJ9.eyJmcmVlLXZpZXctaWQiOjIyODkwMTMwMiwiaWF0IjoxNjkzODQzODk2LCJleHAiOjE2OTM5MzAyOTZ9.t8kHz5s8b0miDVXwiUEDqB3po6GfUEBDAOc024KUewo\.
491. Jules Witcover, *The Making of an Ink-Stained Wretch: Half a Century Pounding the Political Beat* (Baltimore: Johns Hopkins University Press, 2005), 325.

CHAPTER 6: THE SINCEREST FORM OF FLATTERY

492. George Burns, *Gracie: A Love Story* (New York: G. P. Putnam's Sons, 1988), 191.
493. Dorothy Schwieder and Patricia Swanson, "The Sioux City Corn Palaces," *Annals of Iowa* 41:8 (Spring 1973), 1209–27, https://doi.org/10.17077/0003-4827.11148.
494. Craig Kumerfield, "Sioux City Corn Palace Era Continues: Part 2," *Dell Rapids Tribune*, March 22, 2017, A3, https://www.newspapers.com/image/281942021/?clipping_id=19802244&fcfToken=eyJhbGciOiJIUzI1NiIsInR5cCI6IkpXVCJ9.eyJmcmVlLXZpZXctaWQiOjI4MTk0MjAyMSwiaWF0IjoxNjkwMDU5Mzg3LCJleHAiOjE2OTAxNDU3ODd9.kY5uKvaHYpYJzv-sGfQ-GKQM0BOOSgWNc8gBiMjcCiU.

495. "A Church on Wheels," *Whitefish Pilot*, September 26, 1912, 5, https://www.newspapers.com/article/the-whitefish-pilot-church-on-wheels-1/20043202/.
496. "When the Liberty Bell Came to Oregon," *1859 Oregon's Magazine*, July 12, 2019, https://1859oregonmagazine.com/think-oregon/history/when-the-liberty-bell-came-to-oregon/.
497. Fred Klein, "Liberty Bell Special 1915," TrainWeb.org, 2015, http://www.trainweb.org/fredatsf/liberty-bell.htm.
498. Atlanta Committee for the Olympic Games, "1996 Olympic Torch Relay at a Glance," *Washington Post*, accessed August 22, 2023, https://www.washingtonpost.com/wp-srv/sports/olympics/longterm/torches/relay.htm; "Atlanta 1996 Centennial Olympic Games Torch Relay Locomotives," Union Pacific, accessed August 15, 2023, https://www.up.com/heritage/fleet/commemorative/olympic-1996/index.htm.
499. Associated Press, "Torch Cheered on Way Across State," *Marshfield News-Herald*, June 3, 1996, 20, https://www.newspapers.com/article/marshfield-news-herald-olympic-torch-1/19658581/.
500. Associated Press, "Torch Completes Train Journey Across Outback," *Honolulu Star-Bulletin*, July 12, 2000, 29, https://www.newspapers.com/image/273597098/?clipping_id=19501095&fcfToken=eyJhbGciOiJIUzI1NiIsInR5cCI6IkpXVCJ9.eyJmcmVlLXZpZXctaWQiOjI3MzU5NzA5OCwiaWF0IjoxNjg4NDY5MTk2LCJleHAiOjE2ODg1NTU1OTZ9.G0DQlDlboymWmWrGL2QocwKcZuVAo8-P1pyxDWYCeuA.
501. "Thomas A. Curran as Teddy Roosevelt and Orson Welles as Charles Foster Kane in *Citizen Kane* 1941," Alamy.com, accessed September 12, 2023, https://www.alamy.com/thomas-a-curran-as-teddy-roosevelt-and-orson-welles-as-charles-foster-kane-in-citizen-kane-1941-director-orson-welles-screenplay-herman-j-mankiewicz-and-orson-welles-music-bernard-herrmann-mercury-productions-rko-radio-pictures-image348386158.html.
502. Wikipedia, s.v. "*Whistle Stop* (1946 film)," accessed September 12, 2023, https://en.wikipedia.org/wiki/Whistle_Stop_(1946_film).
503. *New Yorker*, August 14, 1948.
504. *New Yorker*, September 20, 1952.
505. *New Yorker*, September 21, 1940.

506. *New Yorker*, October 11, 1952.
507. "The Last Whistle Stop," *Newsweek*, November 10, 1952.
508. The Herb Block Foundation, accessed August 15, 2023, https://www.herbblockfoundation.org/.
509. Wikipedia, s.v. "*Suddenly* (1954 film)," accessed August 22, 2023, https://en.m.wikipedia.org/wiki/Suddenly_(1954_film).
510. Ted Johnson, "'Madam Secretary' Wraps with a Wedding and WhistleStop Goodbye," December 8, 2019, Yahoo.com, accessed August 15, 2023, https://www.yahoo.com/video/madam-secretary-wraps-wedding-whistlestop-050957665.html?guce_referrer=aHR0cHM6Ly93d3cuZ29vZ2xlLmNvbS8&guce_referrer_sig=AQAAAIuoei2TQR1yiqZKCk-DbMGlSXl16RstNYRRxINATcHgUj712NeJlevD78H6fe07QZZdRp-LlXI2kqtpLYH7kSNl5yCo00tcDdH2Sq7IBhbGXocXN6fTWwUiIUMKj6jTxJ9tKuJd5VYPLjIEXbkpJM07pN_SUYuEAsubpS-dVdis)&guccounter=2.
511. *Woman's Day*, October 1, 1956, 99.
512. *Woman's Day*, 99.
513. "1916 Hughes Women's Campaign Train," ElisabethFreeman.org, accessed August 15, 2023, https://elisabethfreeman.org/1916-hughes-womens-campaign-train/.
514. "Hughes Wants Woman's Suffrage Question Settled at Once," *Daily Journal*, August 1, 1916, https://www.coloradohistoricnewspapers.org/?a=d&d=DJT19160801.2.3&e=-------en-20--1--img-txIN%7ctxCO%7ctxTA--------0------.
515. "Suffragists Protest Woodrow Wilson's Opposition to Woman Suffrage, October 1916," Library of Congress, accessed September 12, 2023, https://www.loc.gov/resource/mnwp.276015.
516. "1916 Hughes Women's Campaign Train," ElisabethFreeman.org.
517. "1916 Hughes Women's Campaign Train."
518. "Women's Billionaire Train" poster, 1916, the Woodrow Wilson Independent League of Washington, Women's Bureau, Library of Congress Manuscript Division, Papers of Thomas J. Walsh, Boxes 166–176, Democratic Campaigns, Manuscript Division of the Library of Congress.
519. Kellor, "Women in the Campaign."
520. "Tonic for a Depressed Nation: The 1936 Rexall Train," CapnRexall.blogspot.com, accessed August 16, 2023, http://capnrexall.blogspot

.com/2017/09/the-1936-rexall-train-tonic-for.html; Wikipedia, s.v. "Rexall," https://en.wikipedia.org/wiki/Rexall; Adam Burns, "The Rexall Train," American-Rails.com, accessed August 16, 2023, https://www.american-rails.com/rexall.html#:~:text=The%20train%20went%20on%20a,its%20many%20hundreds%20of%20stops; "The Story of the Rexall Train of 1936," ThemeTrains.com, accessed August 16, 2023, https://www.themetrains.com/rexall-train-m-train-game.htm.

521. "Gracie for President 1940," *George Burns and Gracie Allen* (blog), April 2, 2009, georgegracie.wordpress.com/2009/04/02/gracie-for-president-1940/.
522. Carroll, *Gracie Allen for President 1940*, 7.
523. Burns, *Gracie*, 186–87.
524. Burns, 189.
525. Gracie Allen, *How to Become President* (New York: Duell, Sloan and Pearce, 1940).
526. Burns, *Gracie*, 185.
527. Burns, 186.
528. Burns, 190.
529. Burns, 191.
530. Burns, 189.
531. Burns, 192.
532. Carroll, *Gracie Allen for President*, 190.
533. Carroll, 12.
534. Carroll, 14.
535. Burns, *Gracie*, 191.
536. Burns, 192.
537. Associated Press, "Busy Bob Hope Leads New Hollywood Camp Caravan," *Tampa Tribune*, April 25, 1942, 12, https://www.newspapers.com/article/the-tampa-tribune-hollywood-victory-cara/21060907/.
538. ABC News, "Get Ready to Jump on the Whistle-Stop Train Sept. 15," September 9, 2008, https://abcnews.go.com/GMA/story?id=5750276&page=1.
539. Associated Press, "Whistlestop Train Trek Promotes Safety at Rail Crossings," August 24, 1986.
540. William E. Schmidt, "Tennessee Train Links Tourism and

Tradition," *New York Times*, May 23, 1986, https://www.nytimes.com/1986/05/23/us/tennessee-train-links-tourism-and-tradition.html.

541. William R. Conklin, "Washington Hails Gratitude Train," *New York Times*, February 3, 1949, 46.
542. "Merci Train," MerciTrain.org, accessed August 17, 2023, http://mercitrain.org/; Wikipedia, s.v. "Merci Train," accessed August 17, 2023, https://en.m.wikipedia.org/wiki/Merci_Train.
543. Ted Widmer, "Remembering the Freedom Train," *New Yorker*, November 26, 2017, https://www.newyorker.com/culture/culture-desk/remembering-the-freedom-train.
544. "The Story of the 1949–1950 New York State Freedom Train," ThemeTrains.com, accessed September 11, 2023, https://www.themetrains.com/new-york-state-freedom-train-main.htm; The Retronaut, "The Time America Put Its National Treasures on a Cross-Country Train," Mashable.com, July 4, 2015, https://mashable.com/archive/usa-freedom-train; "The Freedom Train," Genius, accessed August 17, 2023, https://genius.com/Bing-crosby-and-the-andrews-sisters-the-freedom-train-lyrics; "The Friendship Train of 1947," Friendship Train, accessed August 17, 2023, www.thefriendshiptrain1947.org.
545. Deb Kiner, "Freedom and Friendship Trains Met in Harrisburg in 1947, Vintage Photos," Penn Live, November 17, 2017, https://www.pennlive.com/life/2017/11/freedom_and_friendship_trains.html.
546. Kiner.
547. "The Friendship Train of 1947," Friendship Train.
548. "The Friendship Train of 1947."
549. Widmer, "Remembering the Freedom Train."
550. Earl Conn, "Lincoln History Train Coming to Muncie," *Star Press*, September 25, 2005, 37, https://www.newspapers.com/article/the-star-press-history-train-lincoln-200/124106072/.
551. Jake Ammeson, "Faces of the Civil War," *The Times* (Munster, Indiana), September 9, 2007, 61, https://www.newspapers.com/article/the-times-2007-history-train-indiana/124105874/.
552. United Press International, "D.C. Presses Statehood Bid," 12.
553. United Press International, 12.
554. Sherwood, "Liberty Train."
555. Jay Withrow, "U.P. Locomotive to Cross State to Help Celebrate

Nebraska's 150th Birthday," *Omaha World-Herald*, February 21, 2017.

556. Office of Nebraska Governor Pete Ricketts, "Gov. Ricketts, First Lady, and Union Pacific CEO Unveil 'Nebraska150 Express' Tour," press release, February 17, 2017, Union Pacific, https://www.up.com/media/releases/170217-nebraska-150-express.htm.
557. J. L. Schmidt, "Whistle-Stop Tour Will Highlight 150th Birthday," *Kearney Hub*, March 1, 2017, 4, https://www.newspapers.com/article/kearney-hub-2017-nebraska-150-express/130937314/.
558. Office of Nebraska Governor, "Gov. Ricketts."
559. Office of Nebraska Governor.
560. David McGee, "Santa Train Ready for 75th Journey," *Bristol Herald Courier*, November 17, 2017, A5, https://www.newspapers.com/image/965881335/?clipping_id=131080818.
561. McGee, A5.
562. Associated Press, "Redford Campaigns for His Own 'Candidate,'" *Tampa Bay Times*, July 11, 1972, 4, https://www.newspapers.com/article/tampa-bay-times-movie-promotion-1972/19808599/.
563. Harry Haun, "Whistle-Stopping with 'The Candidate,'" *Tennessean*, July 16, 1972, 168, https://www.newspapers.com/article/the-tennessean-movie-promotion-1972/19808388/.
564. Jim Lewis, "Cash to Lead '87 Patriotic Train," UPI Archives, November 26, 1986; William Trott, "Glimpses," UPI Archives, *Courier-Journal*, November 16, 1986, 2.
565. Richard Harrington, "The Chef and the Aid Train," *Washington Post*, September 7, 1985.
566. Jon Bream, "'It Never Has Been Fun' Being Merle Haggard," *Star Tribune*, April 6, 2016; Associated Press, "Whistle-Stop Blues," *Star Press*, September 15, 1985, 36, https://www.newspapers.com/article/the-star-press-merle-haggard-trip-can/20679289/; Robert Hilburn, "Singer Comes Up $250,000 Short: Merle Haggard's Tour for Relief Dropped," *Los Angeles Times*, September 15, 1985, https://www.newspapers.com/article/the-star-press-merle-haggard-trip-can/20679289/.
567. Mark Eades, "Do You Remember When Winnie the Pooh Ran for President?" *Orange County Register*, October 26, 2016, https://

www.ocregister.com/2016/10/26/do-you-remember-when-winnie-the-pooh-ran-for-president-at-disneyland/.

568. Associated Press, "Mickey Mouse Goes on Whistle-Stop Tour," *Central New Jersey Home News*, November 16, 1978, 17, https://www.newspapers.com/article/the-central-new-jersey-home-news-mickey/19555449/.
569. Associated Press, "Adenauer Adopts 'Whistle-Stop' Tours in Crucial Election Fight," *San Bernardino County Sun*, August 27, 1953, 21, https://www.newspapers.com/article/the-san-bernardino-county-sun-germany/18983878/.
570. Omer Anderson, "Adenauer Goes American-Style," *Herald and Review*, February 3, 1957, 4, https://www.newspapers.com/article/herald-and-review-germany-adenauer-1/20606205/.
571. Associated Press, "Adenauer Breaks Politicking Rules," *Hays Daily News*, September 13, 1957, https://www.newspapers.com/article/the-hays-daily-news-germany-adenauer/20606096/.
572. Associated Press, "Erhard Kicks Off '65 Vote Campaign," *Honolulu Advertiser*, August 9, 1965, 5, https://www.newspapers.com/article/the-honolulu-advertiser-germany-1965/20509103/.
573. "Campaign Whistle-Stopping Did Have Its Advantages," *The Gazette*, May 30, 1968, 7, https://www.newspapers.com/article/the-gazette-canada-history-and-analysi/20745453/.
574. Canadian Press, "Diefenbaker Plans 10 Speeches," 1; "Campaign Whistle-Stopping Did Have Its Advantages," 7.
575. Canadian Press, "May Revives Whistle Stop Campaign," *Sault Star*, September 22, 2008, 6, https://www.newspapers.com/article/the-sault-star-2008-canada-elizabeth-may/124103030/.
576. AFP, "Merkel Chugs Through Germany on Whistle-Stop Tour," *The Local*, September 16, 2009, https://www.thelocal.de/20090916/21949.
577. Saul Pett, "Khrushchev Acts Like Whistle-Stop Campaigner on Coast Train Ride," Associated Press, *La Crosse Tribune*, September 21, 1959, 6, https://www.newspapers.com/article/the-la-crosse-tribune-1959-khrushchev-ca/121961050/.
578. "Warm, Friendly Crowds Welcome Trudeau Express," *The Gazette*, May 30, 1974, https://www.newspapers.com/article/the-gazette-canada-trudeau-1974-f/20745192/.

579. United Press International, "Nixon Whistle-Stops in Egypt," *The Record*, June 13, 1974, 11, https://www.newspapers.com/article/the-record-1974-nixon-egypt/121179399/.
580. United Press International, "Banqueting Presidents' Peace Appraisals Differ," *Albuquerque Journal*, March 10, 1979, 3, https://www.newspapers.com/article/albuquerque-journal-egypt-sadat-and-ca/20691799/.
581. Nixon, *RN*, 1011.
582. United Press International, "Pact Near—Sadat," *Ottawa Journal*, March 9, 1979, 1, https://www.newspapers.com/article/the-ottawa-journal-egypt-sadat-and-car/20691777/.
583. Associated Press, "Whistle-Stop," AP photo, *Arizona Daily Sun*, November 25, 1992, 16, https://www.newspapers.com/article/arizona-daily-sun-1992-pakistan/122561557/.
584. Associated Press, "Whistle-Stop Tour," *Iowa City Press-Citizen*, April 22, 1993, 3, https://www.newspapers.com/article/iowa-city-press-citizen-1993-pakistan/121179890/.
585. Reuters, "Royal Train Delayed by Jammed Signal," *The Evening Sun*, January 7, 1954, 2, https://www.newspapers.com/clippings/?query=Hand-signal&user=4606739%3AEdwardsegal.
586. Maurice Weaver, "Whistle-Stop Crowds Greet the Queen," *Daily Telegraph*, June 28, 1973, 19, https://www.newspapers.com/article/the-daily-telegraph-1973-canada-queen-el/121182631/.
587. Graham Viney, *The Last Hurrah: The 1947 Royal Tour of Southern Africa and the End of Empire* (Jonathan Ball: Robinson, 2018), 69.
588. Viney, 82.
589. PA Media, "Prince Charles Starts Sustainable Living Rail Trip," *Times of Malta*, September 7, 2010, https://timesofmalta.com/articles/view/prince-charles-starts-sustainable-living-rail-trip.325820.

APPENDIX

590. "Riding the Rails with U.S. Presidents," *USA Today*, January 19, 2017, https://www.usatoday.com/story/travel/destinations/2017/01/19/amtrak-president-trains/96778962/.
591. Benjamin P. Thomas, *Abraham Lincoln: A Biography* (New York: Modern Library, 1952), 184.

592. Thomas, 185.
593. Garry Boulard, *The Swing Around the Circle: Andrew Johnson and the Train Ride That Destroyed a Presidency* (New York: iUniverse, 2008), 113.
594. "Arrival of the President-Elect," *Chicago Tribune*, November 9, 1868, 6, https://www.newspapers.com/article/chicago-tribune-1868-grant-after-ele/19105553/.
595. "Greeley's Movements," *Raleigh News*, September 20, 1972, 1, https://www.newspapers.com/article/the-raleigh-news-1872-greeley-1/19945021/.
596. "Gov. Dix at Utica," *New York Times*, October 11, 1874, 1, https://www.newspapers.com/image/20642315/?clipping_id=19987443&fcfToken=eyJhbGciOiJIUzI1NiIsInR5cCI6IkpXVCJ9.eyJmcmVlLXZpZXctaWQiOjIwNjQyMzE1LCJpYXQiOjE2ODk4ODI2NDgsImV4cCI6MTY4OTk2OTA0OH0.uyTmO15ivjUCjqj822-3LLNPj6OoZ5YIIWO_0W87RXs.
597. Bob Withers, *The President Travels by Train: Politics and Pullmans* (Lynchburg, VA: TLC, 1996), 40.
598. "Ovations to Garfield," *Summit County Beacon*, August 11, 1880, 3, https://www.newspapers.com/article/the-summit-county-beacon-1880-garfield/20013199/.
599. "Waiting at the Depot," *Detroit Free Press*, September 2, 1884, 8, https://www.newspapers.com/article/detroit-free-press-1884-butler-a/19579993/.
600. "Mr. Blaine's Train," *Evening Star*, September 25, 1884, 1, https://www.newspapers.com/article/evening-star-1884-blaine-1/19580544/.
601. "Grandly Greeted," *Summit County Beacon*, September 24, 1884, 7, https://www.newspapers.com/article/the-summit-county-beacon-1884-logan-z/19582005/.
602. "The Governor's Journey," *Democrat and Chronicle*, October 3, 1884, 1, https://www.newspapers.com/article/democrat-and-chronicle-1884-cleveland/20075663/.
603. "The Harrison Train," *Pittsburgh Dispatch*, April 21, 1891, 10, https://www.newspapers.com/article/pittsburgh-dispatch-1891-harrison-c/20074933/.
604. "A Triumphal Progress," *Asheville Weekly Citizen*, September 22,

1892, 7, https://www.newspapers.com/article/the-asheville-weekly-citizen-1892-stev/21118947/.

605. "Ovations for McKinley," *Akron Beacon Journal*, October 25, 1892, 3, https://www.newspapers.com/article/the-akron-beacon-journal-1892-mckinley/19587451/.
606. "Thro Two States," *Evening Star*, August 10, 1896, 1, https://www.newspapers.com/article/evening-star-1896-bryan-trip-to-new/19932432/.
607. "Strong Words from Goebel from the National Leader," *Twice-A-Week Messenger*, October 18, 1899, 5, https://www.newspapers.com/image/376126315/?match=1&clipping_id=128658422.
608. "The Greatest Record of Any Candidate," *Democrat and Chronicle*, November 3, 1900, 1, https://www.newspapers.com/article/democrat-and-chronicle-1900-roosevelt/20539767/.
609. "Busy Day for Depew," *Democrat and Chronicle*, November 3, 1900, 4, https://www.newspapers.com/article/democrat-and-chronicle-1900-depew-ne/20539888/.
610. "Prohibition Campaign Train," *Wichita Eagle*," September 19, 1900, 8, https://www.newspapers.com/article/the-wichita-eagle-1900-prohibition-par/20514295/.
611. "Parker Condemns 'Stand Pat' Idea," *Indianapolis News*, November 3, 1904, 1, https://www.newspapers.com/article/the-indianapolis-news-1904-alton-parke/18994014/.
612. "Makes Courageous Fight," *Nebraska State Journal*, October 12, 1904, 2, https://www.newspapers.com/article/the-nebraska-state-journal-1904-davis/19312444/.
613. "Five Speeches in a Day," *Washington Post*, October 5, 1904, 1, https://www.newspapers.com/article/the-washington-post-1904-fairbanks-c/19313424/.
614. "Debs, in 'Red Special' Will Criss-Cross Land for Socialists," *Evansville Press*, August 11, 1908, 2, https://www.newspapers.com/article/evansville-press-1908-deb-start-of-t/19251633/.
615. "Kern Speaks at Ten Towns on First Day," *Indianapolis Star*, October 27, 1908, 1, https://www.newspapers.com/article/the-indianapolis-star-1908-kern-xxx1/19475227/.
616. "Sherman in Indiana," *New York Tribune*, October 6, 1908, 4,

https://www.newspapers.com/article/new-york-tribune-1908-sherman-indian/19466509/.

617. "Gompers Rushing Through the State," *Indianapolis News*, October 16, 1908, 1, https://www.newspapers.com/image/37283521/?fcfToken=eyJhbGciOiJIUzI1NiIsInR5cCI6IkpXVCJ9.eyJmcmVlLXZpZXctaWQiOjM3MjgzNTIxLCJpYXQiOjE2ODk4ODYyNTcsImV4cCI6MTY4OTk3MjY1N30.o_cyUO9jiQtghsb80QViUeuCsMDgjPrPVUlzs47a5oE&clipping_id=19476435.

618. "Taft Has Talked to One Million," *Salt Lake Herald-Republican*, October 6, 1908, 1, https://www.newspapers.com/article/the-salt-lake-herald-republican-1908-t/20306331/.

619. "Train Speeds to Cattaraugus," *Buffalo News*, October 25, 1910, 1, https://www.newspapers.com/article/the-buffalo-news-1910-stimson-new-york-g/125441252/.

620. "Hiram Johnson to Speak in Illinois," *Oakland Tribune*, August 26, 1912, 16, https://www.newspapers.com/article/oakland-tribune-1912-johnson-do-more/21163280/.

621. "Candidates Push Campaigns by Train Tour of State," *Chicago Tribune*, May 18, 1912, 4, https://www.newspapers.com/article/chicago-tribune-1912-reid-illinois-u/21162606/.

622. "Candidates Push Campaigns," 4.

623. "An Exciting Trip Through Kansas," *Topeka Daily Capital*, October 9, 1912, 1, https://www.newspapers.com/image/64461859/?fcfToken=eyJhbGciOiJIUzI1NiIsInR5cCI6IkpXVCJ9.eyJmcmVlLXZpZXctaWQiOjY0NDYxODU5LCJpYXQiOjE2ODk5NDE3NTEsImV4cCI6MTY5MDAyODE1MX0.-L1fjKKjJp7YRnRlJIkeLSNfrNumgBDAXEWjlKWheZE&clipping_id=19281613.

624. "It's False!," *Cincinnati Enquirer*, October 28, 1915, 3, https://www.newspapers.com/image/33769126/?match=1&clipping_id=128769969.

625. Griffin Cochran, "Enthusiasm Everywhere for Republican Speakers," *Lexington Herald-Leader*, October 27, 1915, 1, https://www.newspapers.com/image/682744446/?match=1&clipping_id=128730783.

626. "Plans for President," *Manhattan Tribune*, August 31, 1916, 1, https://www.newspapers.com/image/487202445/?match=1&clipping_id=128730055.

627. "Golden Special Women Enjoy Exciting Time," *Oregon Daily Journal*, October 15, 1916, 1, https://www.newspapers.com/article/the-oregon-daily-journal-1916-golden-spe/126849544/.
628. "Enters Last Week of Long 'Western Swing,'" *Indianapolis News*, September 27, 1920, 15, https://www.newspapers.com/article/the-indianapolis-news-1920-cox-visit/19043527/.
629. Doris Kearns Goodwin, *Leadership in Turbulent Times* (New York: Simon & Schuster, 2018), 65.
630. "Leonard Wood to Speak Here Today," *Pantagraph*, April 7, 1920, 5, https://www.newspapers.com/article/the-pantagraph-1920-leonard-wood-ill/19347583/.
631. "Harding, on Speaking Trip, in Pennsylvania," *Indianapolis News*, September 27, 1920, 15, https://www.newspapers.com/article/the-indianapolis-news-1920-harding-s/19043500/.
632. "Dawes Closes Longest Tour," *Star Press*, October 15, 1924, 10, https://www.newspapers.com/article/the-star-press-1924-dawes-9/19023192/.
633. "Davis Tour of Indiana Resumed," *Indianapolis News*, October 13, 1924, 1, https://www.newspapers.com/image/39582558/?clipping_id=128628588.
634. "Republican Campaign to Be in Full Swing Tuesday When Roosevelt Will Speak Here," *Democrat and Chronicle*, October 12, 1924, 25, https://www.newspapers.com/article/democrat-and-chronicle-1924-tr-jr-ne/19724448/.
635. Ione Quinby, "Spontaneous Smith," *Journal Times*, September 21, 1928, 2, https://www.newspapers.com/article/the-journal-times-1928-smith-k/20478932/.
636. "Ottinger in Elmira Talk Opens Drive," *Democrat and Chronicle*, October 17, 1928, 1, https://www.newspapers.com/article/democrat-and-chronicle-1928-ottinger/20492386/.
637. Thomas L. Stokes, "Crowds Greet Hoover as He Nears Boston," United Press, *Pittsburgh Press*, October 15, 1928, 2, https://www.newspapers.com/article/the-pittsburgh-press-1928-hoover-8/19641815/.
638. "Curtis Will Be in Moline on Sept. 18," *The Dispatch*, September 6, 1928, 1, https://www.newspapers.com/article/the-dispatch-1928-curtis-illinois-p/20120520/.
639. "1000 Greet Garner and Wife as Train Stops Short Time," *Austin-*

American, July 19, 1932, 1, https://www.newspapers.com/article/the-austin-american-1932-garner-tex/20439283/.

640. Harriet Anderson, "Republican Candidate for President Stops Here Enroute East to Open His Campaign," *Carroll Daily Herald*, August 21, 1936, 1, https://www.newspapers.com/article/carroll-daily-herald-1936-landon-iowa/19935534/.
641. Associated Press, "Roosevelt Voice Goes Along on Knox Train," *Times Leader*, October 22, 1936, 26, https://www.newspapers.com/article/the-times-leader-1936-knox-use-of-re/19220773/.
642. Lewis C. Mills, "Benson Starts Campaign with Greatest Show," *Minneapolis Star*, September 22, 1936, 5, https://www.newspapers.com/article/the-minneapolis-star-1936-benson-min/18962877/.
643. "Willkie Train to Stop Here Sunday at 3:05," *Eugene Guard*, September 20, 1940, 1, https://www.newspapers.com/article/the-eugene-guard-1940-willkie-t/19958323/.
644. Victron McVicker, "Gov. Bricker's Tour—Here's What It's Like," *Akron Beacon Journal*, September 24, 1944, 39, https://www.newspapers.com/article/the-akron-beacon-journal-1944-bricker/18964099/.
645. Marian Lowry, "Sen. Truman Strives to Keep Spotlight on FDR on Oregon Tour," *Eugene Guard*, October 19, 1944, 1, https://www.newspapers.com/article/the-eugene-guard-1944-truman-oregon/20439641/.
646. Tarleton Collier, "Teamwork and Competency Stand Out in Dewey's Trip," *Courier-Journal*, October 17, 1948, 37, https://www.newspapers.com/image/108427288/?fcfToken=eyJhbGciOiJIUzI1NiIsInR5cCI6IkpXVCJ9.eyJmcmVlLXZpZXctaWQiOjEwODQyNzI4OCwiaWF0IjoxNjg5ODU2MDcyLCJleHAiOjE2ODk5NDI0NzJ9.w-peM2zgozGjoKbLA5bizjZRM4EdKGXe3fo9fwWkZeg.
647. Charles B. Degrees, "Warren Due Home from Vote Drive," *Oakland Tribune*, October 16, 1948, 1, https://www.newspapers.com/article/oakland-tribune-1948-warren-returns/19958611/.
648. Associated Press, "Dixiecrats Plan Train Tour of Fourteen States," *Florence Morning News*, August 29, 1948, 1, https://www.newspapers.com/image/67345166/?match=1&clipping_id=128729441.
649. George C. Baker, "Valley Gets Stevenson's Pledge for Farm Reclamation Programs," *Fresno Bee*, September 11, 1952, 1,

https://www.newspapers.com/image/25909007/?clipping_id=19905148&fcfToken=eyJhbGciOiJIUzI1NiIsInR5cCI6IkpXVCJ9.eyJmcmVlLXZpZXctaWQiOjI1OTA5MDA3LCJpYXQiOjE2ODk4NTExMzAsImV4cCI6MTY4OTkzNzUzMH0.b4iXMruVYk7JZrJOX-QQZx8p9JidZBCwuvIQ0J9HEBg.

650. "Stevenson Breaks Off WhistleStop Campaign; Sen. Fulbright to Be Stand-In," *Cumberland News*, October 31, 1952, 31, https://www.newspapers.com/article/the-cumberland-news-1952-fulbright-st/20393919/.

651. "Eisenhower Begins Whistle-Stop Series," *Noblesville Ledger*, September 15, 1952, 1, https://www.newspapers.com/image/353674661/?match=1&clipping_id=128490924.

652. "Record Nixon Welcome Here," *Times Herald*, October 15, 1952, 1, https://www.newspapers.com/article/the-times-herald-1952-nixon-michigan/21264951/.

653. United Press, "Weary Kefauver Launches 18-Speech Whistle-Stop Tour of Minnesota," *Evening Sun*, November 3, 1956, 8, https://www.newspapers.com/article/the-evening-times-1956-kefauver-minn/20409246/.

654. Irwin J. Miller, "Wickard Has 5-Car Train on C-I Line," Associated Press, *Kokomo Tribune*, September 27, 1956, 5, https://www.newspapers.com/article/the-kokomo-tribune-1956-wickard-indi/20605177/.

655. "Candidates Were There but Democrats Weren't," *Press Democrat*, October 5, 1958, 22, https://www.newspapers.com/article/the-press-democrat-1958-miller-congr/20632548/.

656. "County Demos Plan Whistle-Stop Tour," *Indianapolis Star*, October 16, 1958, 38, https://www.newspapers.com/article/the-indianapolis-star-1958-democrats/20606381/.

657. "County Demos," 38.

658. "County Demos," 38.

659. Associated Press, "Kennedy Whistle-Stops in Michigan; Pushes Progress," *Tampa Tribune*, October 15, 1960, 7, https://www.newspapers.com/article/the-tampa-tribune-1960-kennedy-michi/20390670/.

660. Dickson Preston, "Whistle-Stop Campaign Pays Off for Johnson," *El Paso Herald-Post*, October 13, 1960, 40, https://www.newspapers.com/article/el-paso-herald-post-1960-johnson-u/20721208/.

661. David Watt, "Rain Doesn't Depress Lodge," *Central New Jersey Home News*, November 1, 1960, 13, https://www.newspapers.com/article/the-central-new-jersey-home-news-1960/19554416/.
662. Associated Press, "Making a Whistle Stop," AP Wirephoto, *Los Angeles Times*, May 33, 1962, 3, https://www.newspapers.com/article/the-los-angeles-times-1962-connolly/18955117/.
663. Associated Press, "Lady Bird's Whistle Stop Tour Will Blanket Dixie," *Tampa Tribune*, September 17, 1964, 11, https://www.newspapers.com/article/the-tampa-tribune-1964-lady-bird-johns/20250813/.
664. John Mort, "Humphrey Whistle-Stops California," *Fort Worth Star-Telegram*, October 4, 1964, 26, https://www.newspapers.com/image/641299295/?match=1&clipping_id=128490570.
665. Associated Press, "Campaigns Gather Speed with Big 4 on the Go," *Fort Lauderdale News*, September 29, 1964, 10, https://www.newspapers.com/article/fort-lauderdale-news-1964-goldwater/18949596/.
666. "Miller Here Today on Upstate Swing," *Democrat and Chronicle*, October 24, 1964, 13, https://www.newspapers.com/article/democrat-and-chronicle-1964-miller2/18949982/.
667. "Salinger Train to Open Demo County Campaign," *Redlands Daily Facts*, August 25, 1964, 5, https://www.newspapers.com/article/redlands-daily-facts-1964-salinger12/18950090/.
668. Harold Liston, "Gov. Scranton Carries Fight to Heart of Central Illinois," *Pantagraph*, July 8, 1964, 3, https://www.newspapers.com/article/the-pantagraph-1964-scranton-illinoi/19691577/.
669. "Tydings Campaign Train to Stop in Hagerstown Oct. 17," *Daily Mail*, October 14, 1964, 1, https://www.newspapers.com/article/the-daily-mail-1964-tydings-maryland/128463643/.
670. "Tydings Campaign Train," 1.
671. "Tydings Campaign Train," 1.
672. United Press International, "Sooner GOP, Foes Confident," *Springfield News-Leader*, November 3, 1964, 23, https://www.newspapers.com/article/the-springfield-news-leader-1964-oklah/18933038/.
673. "Hartke, Branigin Train to 'Whistle Stop' Here," *Journal and Courier*, October 27, 1964, 23, https://www.newspapers.com/article/journal-and-courier-1964-hartkeraber/18934207/.

674. "Hoff Hitches Campaign to Whistle-Stop Tour," *Rutland Opinion*, October 6, 1966, 1, https://www.newspapers.com/image/658559367/?match=1&clipping_id=133724279.
675. "Whistlestops Follow Rally," *Lawton Constitution*, November 3, 1966, 1, https://www.newspapers.com/article/the-lawton-constitution-1966-democrats/21242752/.
676. United Press International, "Rolvaag Blasts Away at Polls," *Minneapolis Star*, November 3, 1966, 51, https://www.newspapers.com/article/the-minneapolis-star-1966-rolvaag-minnes/121179112/.
677. Taylor Pensoneau, "Percy Hammers at Local Issues in Train Tour," *St. Louis Post-Dispatch*, October 30, 1966, 3, https://www.newspapers.com/article/st-louis-post-dispatch-1966-percy-il/18980925/.
678. James Bacon, "Politico Tuck Now Hopes to Wipe Out Pratfall Image," Associated Press, *Independent*, August 14, 1966, 29, https://www.newspapers.com/article/independent-1966-dick-tuck/124509072/.
679. Paul Beck, "Brown Whistlestops in County, Vows Property Tax Cut in '67," *Los Angeles Times*, October 30, 1966, 3, https://www.newspapers.com/article/the-los-angeles-times-1966-brown-1966/18690092/.
680. "Whistlestops Follow Rally," *Lawton Constitution*, 1.
681. "Whistlestops Follow Rally," 1.
682. Associated Press, "Wilentz Campaigns by Train," *Atlantic City Press*, October 24, 1966, 10, https://www.newspapers.com/article/press-of-atlantic-city-1966-wilentz-new/137122439/.
683. Gordon G. Macnab, "Kennedy Valley Whistle Stop Crowds Small, Say Outsiders," Associated Press, *Statesman Journal*, May 19, 1968, 7, https://www.newspapers.com/article/statesman-journal-1968-kennedy-orego/19687331/.
684. "Rockefeller Train Makes Stop Here," *Hope Star*, August 14, 1968, 8, https://www.newspapers.com/article/hope-star-1968-rockefeller-2/19557101/.
685. Associated Press, "Democratic Train Stops in Wausau," *Journal Times*, September 29, 1968, 2, https://www.newspapers.com/article/the-journal-times-1968-nelson-and-lafo/19689711/.
686. "Republican Personalities Ride the 'Victory Special,'" *Argus-Leader*, August 20, 1968, 7, https://www.newspapers.com/image

/238976329/?clipping_id=124956295&fcfToken=eyJhbGciOiJIUzI1NiIsInR5cCI6IkpXVCJ9.eyJmcmVlLXZpZXctaWQiOjIzODk3NjMyOSwiaWF0IjoxNjg0NTAyOTIzLCJleHAiOjE2ODQ1ODkzMjN9.xyd0PWs6uGV5kx6jIOOBYKzNJL2tkFitVNsHiYpUEbg.

687. Associated Press, "Democratic Train," 2.
688. United Press International, "Cunningham 2-Day Train Tour Revealed," *Lincoln Journal Star*, September 24, 1968, 7, https://www.newspapers.com/article/lincoln-journal-star-1968-cunningham/18932060/.
689. "Toot! Clark Cannonball Echo of Old Days," *Pantagraph*, August 11, 1968, 3, https://www.newspapers.com/article/the-pantagraph-1968-clark-illinois-u/19147338/.
690. "McCarthy to 'Whistle-Stop' on Peninsula," *Peninsula Times Tribune*, May 30, 1968, 3, https://www.newspapers.com/image/839931257/?clipping_id=120632099&fcfToken=eyJhbGciOiJIUzI1NiIsInR5cCI6IkpXVCJ9.eyJmcmVlLXZpZXctaWQiOjgzOTkzMTI1NywiaWF0IjoxNjg0NTAzNDMwLCJleHAiOjE2ODQ1ODk4MzB9.rWtK4lKI8eyu1hzizzqwcrUcCO_w7ezGMG1WmeYZQsM.
691. Gary Hansen, "'Stop McGovern' Is GOP Train's Foremost Theme," Associated Press, *Rapid City Journal*, August 20, 1968, 1, https://www.newspapers.com/article/rapid-city-journal-1968-republicans/20475891/.
692. George Skelton, "Tunney Campaigns by Valley Whistle Stops," United Press International, *Redlands Daily Facts*, October 24, 1970, 2, https://www.newspapers.com/image/4994413/?clipping_id=18919143&fcfToken=eyJhbGciOiJIUzI1NiIsInR5cCI6IkpXVCJ9.eyJmcmVlLXZpZXctaWQiOjQ5OTQ0MTMsImlhdCI6MTY4NDUwMzUyNSwiZXhwIjoxNjg0NTg5OTI1fQ.ryOG56pcglt1E6R2z98IBvcMk12HLqWPB4jALqXlHqw.
693. United Press International, "Shapp Presents Agriculture Position in Old-Fashioned Whistle-Stop Tour," *Pocono Record*, September 22, 1970, 2, https://www.newspapers.com/image/44367314/?match=1&clipping_id=130927784.
694. Associated Press, "Candidates Map Separate Routes to California's Democratic Votes," *Arizona Daily Star*, June 4, 1972,

2, https://www.newspapers.com/article/arizona-daily-star-1972-mcgovern-cal/19614579/.

695. Walter Mears, "Muskie Carries Fight to Wallace in Florida," Associated Press, *Idaho State Journal*, February 20, 1972, 37, https://www.newspapers.com/image/16124418/?clipping_id=19931248&fcfToken=eyJhbGciOiJIUzI1NiIsInR5cCI6IkpXVCJ9.eyJmcmVlLXZpZXctaWQiOjE2MTI0NDE4LCJpYXQiOjE2ODQ1MDIzNTcsImV4cCI6MTY4NDU4ODc1N30.-Pab0pzgc76v8FVzysA5bZlcGz2OWFbbK8WV5J-clOs.
696. Associated Press, "Barnes Plans Three-Day Whistle Stop Train Trip," *Vernon Daily Record*, February 20, 1972, 17, https://www.newspapers.com/article/the-vernon-daily-record-1972-barnes/20562425/.
697. "Baker to Open Four-Day 'Whistle Stop' Train Trip," *Tennessean*, October 30, 1972, 9, https://www.newspapers.com/article/the-tennessean-1972-baker-tennessee/21162245/.
698. John Norberg, "Buckstopper Special Stops Short Here," *Journal and Courier*, October 5, 1974, 1, https://www.newspapers.com/article/journal-and-courier-1974-lugar-india/20251011/.
699. Tom Phillips, "Thousands Cheer McNulty's Railroad Caravan on County Whistle-Stop Tour," *Scrantonian Tribune*, May 18, 1975, 1, https://www.newspapers.com/article/scrantonian-tribune-1975-mcnulty-pen/128380512/.
700. Associated Press, "Ford 'Whistlestops' in Michigan," *Neosho News*, May 16, 1976, 1, https://www.newspapers.com/article/neosho-news-1976-ford-17/19608190/.
701. James H. Rubin, "Whistle-Stop Campaign Back," Associated Press, *The Reporter*, September 20, 1976, 1, https://www.newspapers.com/article/the-reporter-1976-carter/123938644/.
702. James Gerstenzang, "Mondale Tries Whistle Stops Aboard Train," Associated Press, *Lancaster Eagle-Gazette*, September 21, 1976, 3, https://www.newspapers.com/article/lancaster-eagle-gazette-1976-mondale-m/19609000/.
703. "Brock Train to Roll," *Jackson Sun*, October 17, 1976, 14, https://www.newspapers.com/article/the-jackson-sun-1976-brock-tennessee/20789853/.
704. "Heinz Whistlestop Tour to Start Here on Friday," *Scranton*

Tribune, October 10, 1976, 10, https://www.newspapers.com/article/scrantonian-tribune-1976-heinz-pennsylv/123871189/.

705. Associated Press, "Miller Takes Campaign on Train," *Danville Register*, June 12, 1977, 19, https://www.newspapers.com/article/the-danville-register-1977-andrew-mill/18954587/.
706. United Press International, "Maddy Moves Sagging Campaign to Tracks," *Press Democrat*, June 4, 1978, 4, https://www.newspapers.com/article/the-press-democrat-1978-ken-maddy-calif/18685219/.
707. "Carey Comes Out Fighting in Festive Elmira Visit," *Star-Gazette*, October 25, 1978, 14, https://www.newspapers.com/article/star-gazette-1978-carey-new-york-1/19556577/.
708. "Eckerd Proposed Homestead Increases," *Fort Lauderdale News*, October 15, 1978, 40, https://www.newspapers.com/image/233248381/?clipping_id=21213192&fcfToken=eyJhbGciOiJIUzI1NiIsInR5cCI6IkpXVCJ9.eyJmcmVlLXZpZXctaWQiOjIzMzI0ODM4MSwiaWF0IjoxNjg0NDIxNTk0LCJleHAiOjE2ODQ1MDc5OTR9.Th3OlN2SHqscsCnWA7WotPKOzifd0PlMIYLkw9zDmKk.
709. "Eckerd Proposed Homestead Increases," 40.
710. Associated Press, "Anderson Adopts Whistle-Stop Tactic," *Atlanta Constitution*, November 2, 1980, 6, https://www.newspapers.com/article/the-atlanta-constitution-1980-anderson/18983823/.
711. Associated Press, "Whistle-Stop," AP photo, *Austin American-Statesman*, July 6, 1982, 12, https://www.newspapers.com/article/austin-american-statesman-1982-clement/20328517/.
712. Associated Press, "Proposals Pitched to Robb," *Daily Press*, February 1, 1982, 3, https://www.newspapers.com/article/daily-press-1982-robb-baliles-do-m/20328239/.
713. Associated Press, "Proposals Pitched to Robb," 3.
714. Jon Margolis, "Askew's 'A-Train' Is Off Track," *Chicago Tribune*, November 1, 1983, 5, https://www.newspapers.com/article/chicago-tribune-1983-askew-snafus-u/20686248/.
715. "Campaign Kickoff," *Sunday Oklahoman*, July 29, 1984, 16.
716. Chris Reidy, "Hart Stumps from Train in Pennsylvania," *Orlando Sentinel*, April 8, 1984, 7, https://www.newspapers.com/article/the-orlando-sentinel-1984-hart-penns/20509842/.

717. Charles F. J. Morse, "Belaga Starts on the Track for Governor," *Hartford Courant*, December 15, 1985, 7, https://www.newspapers.com/article/hartford-courant-1984-belaga-connect/128345033.
718. Bill Boyarsky, "Bradley's Camp Ending Campaign with Mixture of Hope, Pessimism," *Los Angeles Times*, November 2, 1986, https://www.newspapers.com/article/the-los-angeles-times-1986-bradley-g/31238989/.
719. Pat Murphy, "Give 'em Hell, John? McCain Whistles While He Works," *Arizona Republic*, February 2, 1986, 2, https://www.newspapers.com/article/arizona-republic-1986-mccain-arizona/21266144/.
720. Robert McCarson, "Along the Campaign Rail," *Asheville Citizen-Times*, October 14, 1986, 9, https://www.newspapers.com/article/asheville-citizen-times-1986-broyhill/20288249/.
721. Douglas Birch, "Obscenities Halt Schaefer Tour in Its Tracks," *Evening Sun*, June 24, 1986, 33, https://www.newspapers.com/article/the-evening-sun-linthicum-1986-schaefer/63678321/.
722. Amy Herring, "James 'Whistle Stops' Across State," *Montgomery Advertiser*, June 1, 1986, 2, https://www.newspapers.com/article/the-montgomery-advertiser-1986-fob-jam/20313989/.
723. "Sloane Plans Whistle Stops on His Inauguration Day," *Courier-Journal*, January 3, 1986, 10, https://www.newspapers.com/article/the-courier-journal-1986-harvey-sloane/20314663/.
724. Sidney Williams, "Campaign Train Rolls into Town," *Alexandria Daily Town Talk*, June 24, 1987, 1, https://www.newspapers.com/article/the-town-talk-1987-tauzin-first-page/20677972/.
725. "Coleman to Seek Post," *Daily News Leader*, November 22, 1988, 1, https://www.newspapers.com/article/the-daily-news-leader-1988-coleman-v/21067302/.
726. Andrew Rosenthal, "High-Tech Whistle-Stops for Dukakis," *New York Times*, August 20, 1988, 7, https://www.nytimes.com/1988/08/20/us/high-tech-whistle-stops-for-dukakis.html.
727. Associated Press, "Jackson's 'Rainbow Express' Does Tour in New Hampshire," *Greenville News*, February 15, 1988, 7, https://www.newspapers.com/article/the-greenville-news-1988-jackson-new/20275600/.
728. William E. Gibson, "Simon," *Fort Lauderdale News*, February 7,

1988, 18, https://www.newspapers.com/article/fort-lauderdale-news-1988-paul-simon-1/20275497/.

729. John Hughes, "Tracking Central Minnesota Voters: Durenberger Rides Campaign Rails," *St. Cloud Times*, October 30, 1988, 13, https://www.newspapers.com/article/st-cloud-times-1988-durenberger-fir/20389882/.
730. Mark Barrett, "Martin Keeps Re-Election Bid on Trade," *Asheville Citizen-Times*, October 25, 1988, 11, https://www.newspapers.com/article/asheville-citizen-times-1988-martin/18953880/.
731. Jeff Copeskey, "Dowdy Rides the Rails down His Campaign Trail," *Clarion-Ledger*, September 8, 1988, 11, https://www.newspapers.com/article/clarion-ledger-1988-dowdy-mississipp/20763264/.
732. Samuel Goldreich, "Schaefer Toots Jimeno's Horn on Whistle-Stop Tour," *Baltimore Sun*, October 11, 1990, 60, https://www.newspapers.com/article/the-baltimore-sun-1990-schaefer-mary/20289233/.
733. Kim Vosicky, "Campaign Express Stops at North Fond de Lac," *The Reporter*, November 4, 1990, 1, https://www.newspapers.com/article/the-reporter-1990-thompson-wisconsin/20754266/.
734. "Candidate Plans Campaign on Rails," *Iowa City Press-Citizen*, October 4, 1990, 7, https://www.newspapers.com/article/iowa-city-press-citizen-1990-lloyd-jon/21213356/.
735. Bob Thaxton, "Williams' Train to Make Seguin Stop," *Seguin Gazette-Enterprise*, November 1, 1990, 1, https://www.newspapers.com/article/the-seguin-gazette-enterprise-1990-cla/27346921/.
736. Jay Miller, "King's Whistle-Stop Tour Was a Show of Humility," *Santa Fe New Mexican*, November 9, 1990, 9, https://www.newspapers.com/article/the-santa-fe-new-mexican-1990-king-n/20781917/.
737. Peter Eichstaedt, "Rain, Small Crowds Don't Daunt Democrats on Whistle-Stop Tour," *Santa Fe New Mexican*, November 3, 1990, 1, https://www.newspapers.com/article/the-santa-fe-new-mexican-1990-richards/27346983/.
738. Eichstaedt, 1.
739. Eichstaedt, 1.
740. Cathleen Decker, "Feinstein Sounds Populist Call in Whistle-Stop Tour," *Los Angeles Times*, November 4, 1990, 343, https://

www.newspapers.com/article/the-los-angeles-times-1990-feisntein/21119278/.

741. Marc Duvoisin and Doreen Carvajal, “Mayoral Hopefuls Hit the Road, and the Rails,” *Philadelphia Inquirer*, November 4, 1991, 11, https://www.newspapers.com/article/the-philadelphia-inquirer-1991-randell/20676086/.
742. Julia Malone, “Bush Blasts Clinton on Ohio Train Stop,” *Dayton Daily News*, September 27, 1992, 16, https://www.newspapers.com/image/409079525/?clipping_id=128273709.
743. “Quayle’s Tour Draws Supporters, Detractors,” *Rocky Mount Telegram*, August 26, 1992, 2, https://www.newspapers.com/article/rocky-mount-telegram-1992-quayle-nor/19659672/.
744. Susan Allen, “Governor Dean Indulges His Love for Vermont’s Railroads,” *Brattleboro Reformer*, May 21, 1992, 3, https://www.newspapers.com/article/the-brattleboro-reformer-1992-howard-dea/130788277/.
745. Bob Gibson, “Democrats Stump at Whistle-Stop,” *Daily Progress*, October 23, 1993, 1, https://www.newspapers.com/image/966395754/?match=1&clipping_id=128264095.
746. Gibson, 1.
747. Gibson, 1.
748. Jim Clardy, “Allen Runs Like It’s 4th Down and He’s Behind,” *Washington Times*, October 16, 1993, C4.
749. Carla Silva, “Underdog Roosevelt Runs Hard Against Weld,” *Berkshire Eagle*, November 6, 1994, 1, https://www.newspapers.com/image/532325588/?match=1&clipping_id=128263155.
750. Silva, 1.
751. “Tracking Votes,” *Boston Globe*, November 6, 1994, 41, https://www.newspapers.com/image/440629787/?match=1&clipping_id=128262896.
752. “Tracking Votes,” 41.
753. Robert Whereatt, “Whistle-Stops Give Carlson Chance to Rail Against Marty,” *Star Tribune*, September 28, 1994, 24, https://www.newspapers.com/image/193854323/?clipping_id=27036023&fcfToken=eyJhbGciOiJIUzI1NiIsInR5cCI6IkpXVCJ9.eyJmcmVlLXZpZXctaWQiOjE5Mzg1NDMyMywiaWF0IjoxNjg0NDE0ODY1LCJleHAiOjE2ODQ1MDEyNjV9.R2pskrY95TMinjzpoGUWXZ1RuRedneF0fH1HN28UCSk.

754. Jim Parsons, "IR Whistle-Stop Not Derailed, but Must Switch Tracks," *Star Tribune*, September 22, 1994, 106, https://www.newspapers.com/image/193784588/?clipping_id=27035927&fcfToken=eyJhbGciOiJIUzI1NiIsInR5cCI6IkpXVCJ9.eyJmcmVlLXZpZXctaWQiOjE5Mzc4NDU4OCwiaWF0IjoxNjg0NDE0OTc5LCJleHAiOjE2ODQ1MDEzNzl9.dImb6vsBTBPKR_Yu-Kz4YfBO3Av4lu66Pnpw3wZDUxI.
755. Associated Press, "Dole Joins Primary, Vows to Win This Time," *Sioux City Journal*, December 9, 1995, 22, https://www.newspapers.com/article/sioux-city-journal-1995-dole-balanced/18686315/.
756. Claudia Van Ness, "Whistle-Stop Tour Sends Democratic Candidates on the Campaign Rails," *Hartford Courant*, September 9, 1995, 42, https://www.newspapers.com/article/hartford-courant-1995-connecticut-debo/128735543/.
757. Mark Mayes, "Clinton's Train Keeps Rolling," *Lansing State Journal*, August 29, 1996, 1, https://www.newspapers.com/article/lansing-state-journal-1996-clinton-m/20249974/.
758. "Huckabee to Make Whistle-Stop Tour," *Baxter Bulletin*, October 21, 1998, 1, https://www.newspapers.com/article/baxter-bulletin-1998-huckabee-arkans/20602071/.
759. Tom Raum, "Bush, Cheney Engage in Whistle-Stop Tour," Associated Press, *Daily Spectrum*, August 5, 2000, 23, https://www.newspapers.com/article/the-daily-spectrum-2000-bush-and-chene/19660493/.
760. Raum, 23.
761. Associated Press, "Carnahan Begins 22-City Train Tour of Missouri," *Springfield News-Leader*, July 20, 2000, 16, https://www.newspapers.com/article/the-springfield-news-leader-2000-carna/19499494/.
762. Associated Press, "Candidate Bailey Rides the Rails Across State," *Springfield News-Leader*, June 9, 2000, 15, https://www.newspapers.com/image/207823787/?clipping_id=20663365&fcfToken=eyJhbGciOiJIUzI1NiIsInR5cCI6IkpXVCJ9.eyJmcmVlLXZpZXctaWQiOjIwNzgyMzc4NywiaWF0IjoxNjg0MzU3Mzk2LCJleHAiOjE2ODQ0NDM3OTZ9.2V_1a6VP6tl7LdLMKqUe4Tnpj0kROjLBGTp2VbB9Kuw.
763. David Hendee, "From Coach to Candidate: A Smooth Transition for Osborne," *Omaha World-Herald*, September 6, 2000, 15, https://

www.newspapers.com/image/892961010/?match=1&clipping_id=128257272.

764. Associated Press, "Underdogs Debate Pataki's Faults," *Poughkeepsie Journal*, October 28, 2002, https://www.newspapers.com/article/poughkeepsie-journal-2002-pataki-new/19658304/.
765. Associated Press, "Blagojevich's Inaugural Whistle-Stop Tour Begins," *Quad-City Times*, January 12, 2003, 4, https://www.newspapers.com/article/quad-city-times-2003-blagojevich-ill/20249445/.
766. Bill Bartleman, "Fletcher Upbeat in Train Tour of Area," *Paducah Sun*, October 25, 2003, 1, https://www.newspapers.com/article/the-paducah-sun-2003-fletcher-kentuc/21059032/Ernie.
767. Jill Zuckman, "Heckled in the Heartland," *Chicago Tribune*, August 7, 2004, 1–9, https://www.newspapers.com/image/231483379/?match=1&clipping_id=130929288.
768. Zuckman, 1–9.
769. Howard Greninger, "Congressional Hopeful Greg Goode Rides the Rails for Campaign Tour," *Tribune-Star*, October 24, 2008, https://www.tribstar.com/news/local_news/congressional-hopeful-greg-goode-rides-the-rails-for-campaign-tour/article_90ff4b7a-d62a-51a6-bfdf-60ce9b5ec3c8.html.
770. Liz Sidoti, "Obama Takes Whistle-Stop Tour Through Pennsylvania," Associated Press, *The Ledger*, April 19, 2008, https://www.theledger.com/story/news/2008/04/20/obama-takes-whistle-stop-tour-through-pennsylvania/25814732007/.
771. Rod Boshart and Charlotte Eby, "Culver Promotes Rail Line Project with Statewide Train Ride," *Quad-City Times*, June 24, 2009, https://qctimes.com/news/state-and-regional/iowa/culver-promotes-rail-line-project-with-statewide-train-ride/article_40869a58-60dd-11de-bfee-001cc4c03286.html.
772. Sean Murphy, "Fallin Traveling by Train Through Western Oklahoma," Associated Press, *McAlester News-Capital*, September 12, 2014, https://www.mcalesternews.com/news/local_news/fallin-traveling-by-train-through-western-oklahoma/article_f1c07277-d2a4-5893-8f81-15eee9bebd1a.html.
773. "Daily Post: Campaign Train, Aug 2010," BrianSolomon.com, accessed August 21, 2023, http://briansolomon.com/trackingthelight/daily-post-campaign-train-aug-2010/.

774. William Petroski, "David Young to Campaign on Iowa Passenger Train Saturday," *Des Moines Register*, October 22, 2014, https://www.desmoinesregister.com/story/news/elections/2014/10/22/young-train-iowa-campaign/17739557/.
775. Petroski.
776. Annie Linskey, "Inside Joe Biden's Whistle-Stop Tour of Ohio and Pennsylvania," *Washington Post*, September 29, 2020, https://www.washingtonpost.com/politics/inside-joe-bidens-whistle-stop-tour-of-ohio-and-pennsylvania/2020/09/28/d2868f30-01f3-11eb-897d-3a6201d6643f_story.html.
777. WCAX News Team, "Candidates Out Stumping the Weekend Before Election Day," November 6, 2022, WCAX-TV, https://www.wcax.com/2022/11/07/candidates-out-stomping-weekend-before-election/.

INDEX

Page numbers in *italics* indicate illustrations.

K

L

Y

ACKNOWLEDGMENTS

I'm grateful to the family members, friends, colleagues, journalists, and politicians who were generous with their time and advice, which helped make this book possible.

At the top of the list is my wife, Pamela Kervin Segal. Her observations and recommendations about every aspect of the book—from cover to cover—improved and led to a better finished product.

Special thanks to Nancy Kervin, David Nellis, Bob James, Mary Anne Heffernan, and Arnold Sanow for their feedback concerning the first drafts of several chapters; John Vargo, a fellow member of the American Political Items Collectors, for sharing photographs, newspaper articles, and other items from his collection of whistle-stop-related materials; and John Willig, my literary agent, whose advice strengthened the original book proposal.

I owe a big debt of gratitude to the journalists and authors who, over the years, shared their experiences covering campaign trains. The list includes Mary McGrory of the *Washington Post*; George Herman of CBS News; Robert J. Donovan, a journalist, author, and former bureau chief of the *Los Angeles Times*; Jim Wooten of ABC News; David Hoffman of the *Washington Post*; Gardner Bridge of the Associated Press; Sarah McClendon of the McClendon News Service; Morrie Landsberg, former Sacramento bureau chief for the Associated Press; Joseph Latin of the *Washington Post*; Mel Elfin, former senior editor of

Newsweek; British journalist Alistair Cooke; Richard L. Strout of the *Christian Science Monitor*; Walter Mears, a Pulitzer Prize winner and former Washington bureau chief for the Associated Press; and Walter M. Brasch, a syndicated newspaper columnist.

I want to acknowledge Leo Orso of Orsonic Recording Services for sending a copy of what he said was the original and only recording of "Operation Whistle-Stop," the October 1964 panel discussion at the Women's National Press Club in Washington, DC. The panel of political reporters shared their recollections, anecdotes, and stories about campaign trains ranging from Al Smith to Barry Goldwater and from Eleanor Roosevelt to Lady Bird Johnson—a span of thirty-six years and nine presidential elections. The panelists included Elizabeth Carpenter, press secretary to Lady Bird Johnson (President Lyndon Johnson's wife); Associated Press reporters Frances Lewine, Arthur Edson, and Bess Furman; Bonnie Angelo of Newhouse News Service; Loye Miller Jr. of *Time* magazine; and Isabelle Shelton of the *Washington Star*.

I'm grateful to Robert Devaney, publisher of the *Georgetowner* newspaper, for connecting me with Jules Witcover, the prize-winning former Washington, DC, journalist who wrote the foreword to this book, and to photographer and former colleague Benedict Bacon, for taking my book jacket photo.

I was fortunate to hear from former presidential candidates Barry Goldwater and George McGovern, and to interview Edmund Muskie about his recollections on the campaign train trail.

Robert Warren, son of Republican vice-presidential candidate Earl Warren, generously provided information and materials from his father's 1948 campaign train tour. Jay Tunney shared behind-the-scenes details about the successful 1970 whistle-stop tour of his brother John V. Tunney, the former Democratic senator from California, and thanks to Cooby Greenway for connecting me with Jay Tunney, who is her second cousin.

Among the many members of Congress who responded to my requests for their campaign train stories were former senators Alan Simpson, Republican from Wyoming; Paul Simon, Democrat from Illinois; William L. Armstrong, Republican from Colorado; and James Abdnor, Republican from South Dakota; Nancy Kassebaum, the daughter of Alf Landon, who was the Republican Party's presidential nominee in 1936; former House Speaker Carl Albert, Democrat from Oklahoma; and two former Democratic congressmen from California: Lionel Van Deerlin and James Roosevelt, the last surviving child of Franklin and Eleanor Roosevelt, who accompanied his father on several train trips.

And my thanks to former congressman Mickey Edwards, Republican from Oklahoma, who gave me the green light to organize his successful 1984 whistle-stop campaign train tour in the Sooner State.

The stories and perspectives of the staff who helped organize the trips, or rode on the trains with the candidates, were greatly appreciated. My thanks to Mike McCurry, former White House spokesperson for President Bill Clinton, and Warren J. Sawall, a staff member for Senator Gaylord Nelson, Democrat from Wisconsin, for sending me their anecdotes. I also heard from comedian Bob Newhart, who went with California Governor Edmund G. "Pat" Brown on his 1966 campaign train tour and introduced him at some of the trackside rallies.

In addition to *telling* the story of campaign trains, I wanted to *show* it. In this regard, the Library of Congress provided assistance finding a treasure trove of whistle-stop-related images.

The staff at the library's Prints & Photographs Division were instrumental in helping me locate in its extensive collection many of the political cartoons and photographs included in these pages. Special thanks to reference librarian Jon Eaker; reference specialists Ryan Brubacher, Kristi Finefield, Jan Grenci, Melissa Lindberg, and Hanna Soltys; and library technician Georgia Joseph for their guidance. Courtney Matthews, customer service representative at the Library of Congress's duplication services, was helpful in obtaining copies of images from the library's *Look* magazine collection.

My thanks to the National Press Club and the National Press Club Journalism Institute for their assistance in tracking down documents about some of the reporters who covered whistle-stopping politicians.

In my search for train-related newsreels, television shows, and movies, I consulted with the Library of Congress's Moving Image Research Center National Audio-Visual Conservation Center. Reference specialist Zoran Sinobad, viewing technician Dorian Hartmann, and reference librarian Josie Walter-Johnston were particularly helpful.

To read original copies of whistle-stop-related materials and recollections, I have the staff at the Library of Congress's Manuscript Division to thank. They included Kerrie Cotten Williams, head of Research and Reference Services; Michelle A. Krowl, PhD, a Civil War and Reconstruction specialist; Ryan Reft, a historian who focuses on modern-day domestic policy and politics in the United States; and Patrick Kerwin, manuscript reference librarian.

I was fortunate to visit or take advantage of the resources of several presidential libraries, including those of John F. Kennedy, Richard M. Nixon, Lyndon B. Johnson, Franklin D. Roosevelt, Harry S. Truman, George H. W. Bush, George W. Bush, and Ronald Reagan.

My thanks to Laurie Austin in the audiovisual archives of the Harry S. Truman Presidential Library & Museum and the staff at the Franklin D. Roosevelt Presidential Library & Museum, including Chris Belena and archivist Matthew C. Hanson.

As a great admirer and collector of political cartoons, I'm grateful to the Herb Block Foundation for allowing me to use many of the famous cartoonist's drawings. My thanks to Sarah Alex, copresident of the foundation, and intern Daysi Romero.

The National Archives was another resource for newsreel stories of whistle-stopping politicians. My thanks to Michael Taylor, an archivist at the Moving Image and Sound Branch, Special Media Archives Services Division, at the National Archives at College Park, Maryland.

For help in completing my search for whistle-stop-related images, I want to thank Matthew Lutts of the Associated Press for his assistance in finding decades-old photographs to illustrate some of the stories in *Whistle-Stop Politics*; and Kim Reis, senior director of sales and licensing at Imagn, part of the USA Today Network. For an international perspective on campaign trains, I'm grateful to Yolanda Meyer, an information specialist at Transnet, who shared photos from the 1947 royal train tour of South Africa.

The experienced and talented staff and consultants at Girl Friday Productions were responsible for turning my manuscript into a book. Their team included COO Dave Valencia, developmental editor Dan Crissman, publishing manager Kristin Duran, art director Paul Barrett, production editor Laura Dailey, senior designer Rachel Marek, and marketing strategist Adria Batt.

My thanks to Eric von Vorys, an intellectual property and entertainment law attorney at Shulman Rogers, for his guidance in navigating the legal issues associated with publishing a book.

And to help with my hands-on research about copyright-related questions, I want to thank Raphael Tali, a copyright records specialist at the US Copyright Office, for his unwavering patience, and his colleague, Terra Johnson, a copyright specialist.

Because you *can* tell a book by its cover, I am indebted to the Lawrence Public Library in Lawrence, Massachusetts, for the image that appears on the front of *Whistle-Stop Politics*, and to Lindsey Gazla, the library's reference librarian and special collections archivist.

The image is of President Theodore Roosevelt standing at the back of a railroad car at the South Lawrence Train Station. There is a large crowd, and the spires of St. Patrick Roman Catholic Church are visible in the background. Roosevelt stopped in Lawrence twice: in 1902 and 1912, according to the library, and the image is thought to be from his visit in 1902.

I was especially pleased to find and use the photo because it is one of the few images of a whistle-stopping politician I discovered that shows the interaction between the politician and the crowd at a trackside rally. Roosevelt is waving his top hat—and several members of the crowd are waving back.

The negative is part of the Gilbert Aspeslagh Negatives Collection, which was donated to the Special Collections of the Lawrence Public Library on July 5, 2011, by Glen Aspeslagh, grandson of Gilbert Aspeslagh. The library noted that "family legend declares that photo was part of a collection that was payment for a bar tab to the brother of Gilbert's mother. There is no sign of the name of the photographer."

And I want to thank my lifelong friend and photographer Bob Sachs for working his magic on the image and bringing out the best in the photograph, and for his feedback on various versions of the book cover. Bob, along with Ed Barks, Nancy Kervin,

David Nellis, Bob James, and Arnold Sanow, provided helpful comments about the drafts for the cover design and other aspects of the book.

Finally, a nod to our dog, Tootsie Roll, who, like Charlie before her, never tires in reminding me when to take a break—or take her for a walk.

ABOUT THE AUTHOR

Photo © Benedict Bacon

Edward Segal is one of the few people to organize a modern-day whistle-stop campaign-train tour. He served as a campaign manager, press secretary, and aide to Democratic and Republican presidential and congressional candidates. Segal has written about the history of the trains for the *Washington Post, Roll Call, Washington Journalism Review,* and the American Political Items Collectors.

He is the bestselling author of the award-winning book *Crisis Ahead: 101 Ways to Prepare for and Bounce Back from Disasters, Scandals, and Other Emergencies*; a Leadership Strategy Senior Contributor for Forbes.com; and a freelance journalist whose articles have appeared in the *Washington Post, Wall Street Journal, New York Times, Los Angeles Times,* and other major publications.

Printed in the USA
CPSIA information can be obtained
at www.ICGtesting.com
LVHW090102240224
772642LV00005B/132/J